Metropolitan Circles Development and the Future of Urbanization

Metropolitan Circles Development and the Future of Urbanization

Editors

Wei Shan

National University of Singapore, Singapore

Lijun Yang

South China University of Technology, China

華南理工大學 公共政策研究院

Institute of Public Policy
South China University of Technology

World Scientific

Published by

World Scientific Publishing Co. Pte. Ltd.

5 Toh Tuck Link, Singapore 596224

USA office: 27 Warren Street, Suite 401-402, Hackensack, NJ 07601

UK office: 57 Shelton Street, Covent Garden, London WC2H 9HE

Library of Congress Cataloging-in-Publication Data
Names: Shan, Wei, editor. | Yang, Lijun, 1963– editor.
Title: Metropolitan circles development and the future of urbanization /
editors, Wei Shan, National University of Singapore, Singapore,
Lijun Yang, South China University of Technology, China.
Description: Singapore ; Hackensack, NJ : World Scientific, [2020] |
Includes bibliographical references and index.
Identifiers: LCCN 2019052150 | ISBN 9789811207075 (hardcover)
Subjects: LCSH: City planning--Economic aspects. | City planning--Social aspects. |
City planning--Environmental aspects.
Classification: LCC HT166 .M4465 2020 | DDC 307.1/216--dc23
LC record available at https://lccn.loc.gov/2019052150

British Library Cataloguing-in-Publication Data
A catalogue record for this book is available from the British Library.

For any available supplementary material, please visit
https://www.worldscientific.com/worldscibooks/10.1142/11468#t=suppl

Desk Editors: Herbert Moses/Sylvia Koh

Typeset by Stallion Press
Email: enquiries@stallionpress.com

About the Editors

Dr. Wei Shan received his BA and MA in International Studies from Peking University and PhD in Political Science from Texas A&M University. His research focuses on the political behavior of citizens and the elite in the context of political and economic development. His research topics include Chinese citizens' political participation, changes in political culture, and ethnic politics. His research papers have appeared in *China Quarterly* and other academic journals. He is the author of two monographs, *Political Leadership and Political Change in Rural China* and *Political Stability in China's Changing Social Landscape* (forthcoming).

Dr. Lijun Yang is Professor of Sociology at the Institute of Public Policy at South China University of Technology (SCUT). She has studied social changes and social movements in contemporary China, particularly the Cultural Revolution and nationalism. Her research papers have appeared in academic journals such as *The China Quarterly, Journal of Contemporary China, The Review of History, Asian Studies, and Chinese Affairs*. Her book *Social Structure and the Cultural Revolution in China: Citizenship*

and Collective Violence was selected as one of the five best books in all social science subjects in the Asian Pacific region, and for this, she received the Ohira Memorial Foundation Award in 2005. She has also edited and co-edited many volumes on contemporary China. Professor Yang received her BA in media studies from Beijing Broadcasting College, now The Communication University of China; her MA in politics from Yokohama City University, Japan; and her PhD in sociology from Hitotsubashi University, Japan. Before join SCUT, she held various research and teaching positions in the State Language Work Committee of the State Council China, Hitotsubashi University, Aochi Prefectural University, Aoyama Gakuin University, Waseda University (Japan), and National University of Singapore.

Contents

Introduction

Hans d'Orville

Former Deputy Director-General/Assistant Director-General,
Strategic Planning of UNESCO
Hansdorville@yahoo.com

1. An Era of New Metropolises

Some 100 years ago only 10% of humanity lived in urban areas. In recent years, the migration from rural areas to urban centers has rapidly increased and it is expected that by the year 2030 close to 75% of the world population will live in cities. The urban population of the developing world alone will triple over the next two generations.

The urban industrial centers built between the 19th and early 20th centuries were products of great technological innovations in transport, trade and communications, and a new social division of labor. The legacy of that era can still be experienced in the preserved districts of central cities, which feature period buildings, that is, markers of architectural styles, along with urban parks and cultural institutions. Developing country cities experienced a later but intense process of industrialization and urbanization. There, population growth rates have surpassed the abilities of their societies to equip cities with adequate infrastructure and provide the population with basic social services. In the centrally located old neighborhoods of cities in many countries, irreplaceable baroque and neoclassical architecture coexists with later industrial structures — warehouses, sheds, train stations, and terminals — juxtaposed with skyscrapers and office buildings of the modern city.

The latest global economic outlook points to an ongoing restructuring of the global urban system. An era of new metropolises is taking off. In relation to sustainable development, the key concern is how best to unlock the transformative power of cities. Thanks to the economies of scale in metropolises, many cities in the developing world today — including even the mega-cities in the developed world — remain densely populated. According to the World Cities Report 2016 released by United Nations-Habitat, the top 600 cities, which are home to almost one-fifth of the world's population, make up 60% of global gross domestic product (GDP). Mega-cities with a population of over 10 million people have risen from 14 in 1995 to 28 in 2015, 22 of which were in Latin America, Asia, and Africa. The world's largest metropolitan circle, namely the Tokyo metropolitan area, continues to boom while remaining economically dense as the full-fledged mega-cities of London and Paris are successful in turning the tide on population decline. Hence, a new round of global urban expansion offers tremendous potential for economic development. However, if left unmanaged, issues ranging from market failure, climate change, social inequality, and the security dilemma of the migration crisis could undermine the long-term sustainable development of global metropolises and their stability.

Be it domestic or cross-border migration into metropolises, it reflects a desire for higher income and better quality of life — essentially an inevitable outcome of market-based resource allocation. As a response to challenges associated with urbanization, the developmental concept that highlights metropolitan circles development is receiving widespread attention globally. It encourages metropolitan core cities to shape and promote the coordinated development between small and medium-sized cities in peripheral areas. The metropolitan circles formed around global mega-cities such as New York, Chicago, Tokyo, London, Paris, Shanghai, or Guangzhou are the world's most densely populated and the economically most dynamic regions as well as major sources of innovation and new technologies.

The success of these metropolitan circles has propelled many more countries to build their own metropolitan circles as economic hubs in pursuit of the commanding heights of global competition. This is then often accompanied by a liberalization of city settlement permits, such as the Chinese *hukous*, for rural migrants.

Whether metropolitan circles can overcome the bottlenecks encountered in urbanization depends on finding practical solutions to urban diseases caused by over-concentration of population and resources while integrating various populations, industries, and administrative functions with social life. This requires not only in-depth theoretical research but also cooperation among countries.

2. China's Endeavor

Today, city cluster development has been set as a priority goal on the Chinese government's agenda. The Guangdong–Hong Kong–Macau Greater Bay Area (GHKMGBA) is yet another focus of China's regional development strategy, after the Beijing–Tianjin–Hebei Integration and the Yangtze River Economic Belt. This aims to break through inter regional geographical, cultural, and political barriers as part of the development of a world-class bay area-based metropolitan circle.

China's proactive engagement with metropolitan circles development necessitates dialogue with countries and cities experienced in the field, in China and elsewhere. The chapters in this book strive to enhance the theoretical understanding of metropolitan circles development and contribute wisdom to the enhancement of human welfare through knowledge sharing and mutual learning as well as infrastructural provision.

One great example of China's endeavor in developing metropolitan circles is the Greater Bay Area, which pools Hong Kong and Macau together with nine mainland cities to form an economic powerhouse aimed at rivaling Silicon Valley. Cross-border infrastructure projects such as the Hong Kong–Zhuhai–Macau bridge have been built to international standards. HK has already spent HKD 10.7 billion on the project.

The Chinese Pavilion at the 2018 Venice Architecture Biennale will explore the future of rural development highlighting the country's focus on "Building a Future Countryside." The exhibition will present the development of countryside through six episodes: poetic dwellings, local production, cultural practices, agricultural tourism, community reconstruction, and future exploration. According to Li Xiangning, Curator of the Chinese Pavilion: "The motivation for this exhibition is more than just *xiangchou*, a Chinese term that refers to nostalgia for rural lands. We return to the countryside where Chinese culture originated to recover forgotten values and overlooked possibilities; from there, we will build a future countryside."

Forty years after China's reform and economic opening up, the fundamental drivers for the creation of new growth engines, poles, and opportunities — or indeed new metropolitan circles — for the world economy will be the Industrial Revolution 4.0 driven by digitalization, artificial intelligence, and robotics.

3. United Nations' New Urban Agenda

The United Nations' New Urban Agenda shall be guided by the following interlinked principles, relevant in particular for the new metropolitan circles:

(a) Leave no one behind, by ending poverty in all its forms and dimensions, including the eradication of extreme poverty, by ensuring equal rights and opportunities, socio-economic and cultural diversity, integration in the urban space, enhancing livability, education, food security and nutrition, health and well-being; including promoting safety and eliminating discrimination and all forms of violence; ensuring public participation providing safe and equal access for all; and providing equal access for all to physical and social infrastructure and basic services as well as adequate and affordable housing.

(b) Sustainable and inclusive urban economies, by leveraging the agglomeration benefits of well-planned urbanization, high productivity, competitiveness, and innovation; promoting full and productive employment and decent work for all, ensuring decent and green job creation and equal access for all to economic and productive resources and opportunities; preventing land speculation; and promoting secure land tenure and managing urban shrinking where appropriate.

(c) Environmental sustainability, by promoting clean energy, sustainable use of land and resources in urban development as well as protecting ecosystems and biodiversity, including adopting healthy lifestyles in harmony with nature; promoting sustainable consumption and production patterns; building urban resilience; reducing disaster risks; and mitigating and adapting to climate change.

Based on these principles, the new metropolitan circles will work toward an urban paradigm shift that will:

(a) readdress the way we plan, finance, develop, govern, and manage cities and human settlements, recognizing sustainable urban and territorial development as essential to the achievement of sustainable development and prosperity for all;
(b) recognize the leading role of national governments, as appropriate, in the definition and implementation of inclusive and effective urban policies and legislation for sustainable urban development, and the equally important contributions of subnational and local governments, as well as civil society and other relevant stakeholders, in a transparent and accountable manner;
(c) adopt sustainable, people-centered, age- and gender-responsive and integrated approaches to urban and territorial development by implementing policies, strategies, capacity development, and actions at all levels, based on fundamental drivers of change including:
    (i) developing and implementing urban policies at the appropriate level including within local–national and multi-stakeholder partnerships, building integrated systems of cities and human settlements, promoting cooperation among all levels of government to enable them to achieve sustainable integrated urban development;
    (ii) strengthening urban governance, with sound institutions and mechanisms that empower and include urban stakeholders, as well as appropriate checks and balances, providing predictability and coherence in the urban development plans to enable social inclusion, sustained, inclusive, and sustainable economic growth and environmental protection;
    (iii) reinvigorating long-term and integrated urban and territorial planning and design in order to optimize the spatial dimension

of the urban form and to deliver the positive outcomes of urbanization;

(iv) supporting effective, innovative, and sustainable financing frameworks and instruments, enabling strengthened municipal finance and local fiscal systems in order to create, sustain, and share the value generated by sustainable urban development in an inclusive manner.

While the specific circumstances of cities of all sizes, towns, and villages vary, the New Urban Agenda is universal in scope, participatory, and people-centered, protects the planet, and has a long-term vision, setting out priorities and actions at the global, regional, national, subnational, and local levels that governments and other relevant stakeholders in every country can adopt based on their needs.

4. Toward a Sustainable Development

How can we bring about a sustainable design of future mega-cities, which shall be cities for growth, creativity, diversity, and habitable living? The key issue will be whether it will be possible to bring about a transformation toward sustainable and resilient societies in metropolitan circles. All national, subnational, and local governments, as well as all relevant stakeholders, in line with national policies and legislation, shall engage to revitalize, strengthen, and create partnerships, enhance coordination and cooperation to effectively implement the New Urban Agenda.

Today, cities are assembling a concentration of material, spiritual, and cultural resources which attract people to urban areas in the hope and indeed quest for a better life and creative and inspiring living. For its part, China is currently undergoing a historically unprecedented urbanization process across the country. Within a few decades, a rural exodus on a scale matching the country's speedy economic development has brought about the influx of hundreds of millions of people to the cities. By 2035, nearly 70% of the Chinese population will live in urban areas, which means over a billion city dwellers most of them in metropolises.

However, urbanization at such a scale does not only generate positive outcomes but also patterns of unsustainable development, overburdening and lack of infrastructure, emergence of slums, pollution and other environmental damage, disintegration of the social fabric — the list of undesired side-effects is long. They pose enormous challenges for policy-makers and all stakeholders, as well as architects. Indeed, they call for new innovative solutions to make metropolitan circles sustainable and attractive.

This trend will give rise to a unique global network whose potential power and impact is enormous. The world must be able to cope with and overcome through new cooperative models the congested and unhealthy urban living patterns of today and provide avenues for a new sustainable future. Cities are cradles of cultural, social, and economic activity, where the very diversity of interactions breeds and creates new initiatives, new ideas and new synergies. Cities — especially mega-cities — are unimaginable without culture and their innate creative forces. What is impressive is the ability of cities to retain tradition and blend it alongside advanced technology and innovation.

Hence, we need to define parameters for the future evolution of cities with technological dimensions on the one hand and strong culture and heritage dimensions on the other hand. Human and economic diversity represents the central factor for urban life and provides a launchpad for diverse architecture, innovation, and design.

Cities are struggling to provide agreeable living and decent jobs for an ever-increasing population, which drives continuously urban development and innovation and *vice versa*. How can we reconcile the need for urban development with the imperative of preserving our cultural heritage and keep it attractive and not monotonous? We need to achieve a balance between preservation and regeneration, between memory and perspective, between productivity and sustainability.

Culture is an essential component of human and sustainable development and represents a source of identity, innovation, and creativity for individuals and communities as well as a tool for reconciliation and social cohesion and, ultimately peace. Culture is pervasive in all our lives. We live in and with our culture; our thoughts and behavior are conditioned by our culture, we eat according to our culture, our dresses reflect our culture, our musical and artistic preferences are conditioned by our culture and our living environment reflects many dimensions of our culture. Our consumption patterns are conditioned by our culture and artistic expressions around us are generated by cultural traits and perceptions.

Only in human and culturally rich environments can intellectuals, artists, creators, and innovators of all kinds realize their creative potential. This then is at the heart of the notion of creative cities and creative economies. Today's focus must shift toward a recognition of the pivotal role of culture in all its facets — which is embodied not only in arts, buildings, monuments and landscapes but also in museums, music, the performing arts, festivals, customs, films, poetry, publishing, design, the crafts. Culture has proved to be a lubricant for city development besides political and social efforts. Culture is an essential component of human and sustainable development and represents a source of identity, innovation, and creativity for individuals and communities. Cities breed and create new initiatives, new ideas, and new collaborations.

A city without culture is a city without soul. The preservation and promotion of urban cultural heritage has thus become of particular challenge in the management of the development of metropolises and urban villages. Cultural heritage is not only an irreplaceable treasure of a city but it is also a responsibility for all — a responsibility to preserve, to regenerate, and to revitalize this heritage. Regeneration is a natural process of cities. As with development in general, no single urban model of reference fits all. Any city's future must be rooted in its individual identity. Its urban heritage is always a meaningful starting point for the elaboration of urban policies.

Culture is increasingly recognized as "soft power," nationally and on a world scale. Culture and intercultural engagement have the capacity to bring nations and peoples closer together and to foster their mutual understanding and cooperation. Complementing the economic, political, and military dimensions, culture — together with education and the media — has become part of a holistic grand design for the world. The soft power approach denotes the dynamics, synergies, and creative force of bringing together people from diverse cultural, linguistic, and ethnic backgrounds and making them understand, respect, and cooperate with each other for the attainment of higher goods: peace, harmony, sustainable development, and prosperity.

Over and over again, cities have to be recreated as attractive and productive places where people will want to live and work and where they will enjoy leisure, cultural pursuits, and entertainment. The emergence of the eco-city concept and of the notion of sustainable cities adds an entirely new dimension to the challenge of urban regeneration.

With the acceleration of urbanization, much of the cultural heritage is frequently lost or diluted. We are living in a world where urbanization becomes inextricably linked with mounting environmental challenges and the daunting impact of climate change. The degradation of the urban environment limits the abilities of a growing, shifting population to establish communities with adequate and decent housing. The predicted increase in global mean surface temperature will give rise to manifold challenges, including public health problems, food supplies, carbon-free mass transportation, water shortages, resort to renewable energies, and housing. Hence, the trend toward eco-cities, green economies, and eco-civilization.

In the process, we may have to focus on other metaphors, such as ecological responsibility, eco-values, heritage protection, innovation, and creativity. City planners must be able to handle density, to uphold the value of public spaces, to promote sustainability and brownfield regeneration, and to provide a new attraction for public transport.

Green architecture must become an overriding philosophy and movement where design approaches to modernity and modern living are not merely an aesthetic exercise. They are henceforth an integral element of the soft power of a country and they will have to compete globally. Today, the role of designers (town planners, architects, transportation planning professionals, engineers) is not just limited to designing towns and cities to build housing and direct traffic, they must also focus on inducing and supporting positive changes in lifestyles of people which must continue to be in sync with cultural traditions, habits, and practices. Green architecture needs to be concerned with long-term environmental, economic, and human consequences and costs.

Sustainability will become a unique challenge for the practice of architecture, city construction, and expansion. How can modern designs fit the multiple and diverse expectations of people undergoing migration, new education models, and an individual desire for innovation and creativity? Sustainable construction is understood as "the creation and responsible management of a healthy built environment based on resource efficient and ecological principles." Sustainably designed buildings aim to lessen their impact on our environment through energy and resource efficiency.

The quest for building green economies and societies as well as sustainable eco-cities adds an entirely new dimension. It is only through innovation, education, and knowledge that new — and green — jobs can be created and new technologies developed that will be critical to solving real-life problems. Scientific and intellectual leadership is the key to creating the low-carbon, "green" economy of the 21st century. We must avoid borrowing from the future to live well today.

5. The Précis of the Book

This volume reflects our latest efforts in understanding the new tendencies, opportunities, and challenges in metropolitan circle development all over the world. The Institute of Public Policy (IPP) at the South China University of Technology has a long tradition to study political, economic, and social development of the world and contemporary China. Cooperating with the United Nations Educational, Scientific and Cultural Organization, IPP has hosted a series of international conferences to discuss the major challenges to China and the world. The chapters in this volume are selected from papers presented at the Conference on Metropolitan Circles Development and Urbanization held in 2018.

The chapters consist of three thematic clusters. The first cluster discusses governance issues. Our authors review the effects of local governance systems, central–local relations, and administrative borders on metropolitan area development. The second cluster surveys economic, social, and environmental issues. Emphases are given to how interconnectivity, circular economy, and climate change issues should be integrated into mega-region development planning. The final cluster focuses on experience of metropolitan circle development and urbanization in Asia, Latin America, and Africa, discussing their lessons and challenges.

The first thematic cluster begins with "A Tale of Two Cities" in Japan. Economically, Tokyo and Osaka are the two largest cities in Japan. Before Meiji Restoration, Osaka was far more developed than Tokyo. But today, Tokyo continues to thrive while Osaka's economy has been on the decline. What's behind the fate of the two cities? Professor Godo, in his chapter, argues that the difference of the local governance systems in the two cities could help to explain their distinct economic trajectories. In Osaka, there is always tension between the city government and the prefectural government. They often fail to coordinate with each other in many of their administrative activities. In contrast, Tokyo metropolitan government has strong administrative power and hence has been efficient in stimulating economic growth. This government is also powerful in promoting a comprehensive urban planning in the metropolitan area. The negative side of Tokyo's governance system, however, is that it may be too centralized in view of democracy. The chapter points out that the way to reform Japan's local governance system is one of the most debated issues in the country today.

Political boundaries exist between different countries and different regions. What are the effects of those boundaries on development of metropolitan circles? In Chapter 2, Professor O'Flaherty finds that the boundary between the states of New York and New Jersey has in fact a negative impact on their economic developments. Hudson River became the boundary between the two states due to a series historical events, which can be traced back to as early as 17th century. Because of path dependence, the cost of changing state borders today is very high. This chapter argues that the border between the two states negatively affects both interstate trade and urban development. For instance, the border leads the state governments to invest less in improving transportation and infrastructure, which would allow more people to live and work in the area. The author also points out that bi-state agencies were created once in a while to address the barrier between the two states, but they did not work well in organizing development of the metropolitan area. In this sense, the New York–New Jersey metropolitan circle could have been more prosperous without the border line. The bordering effects also have implications for development of metropolitan area in other parts of the world such as the Canton–Hong Kong–Macau region, in which its success of development may depend on how this mega-region can improve coordination and reduce barriers.

Chapter 3 examines the development of metropolitan circles in the United Kingdom through case studies on three regions, namely London and the Southeast of England, Great Manchester, and Central Scotland.

Professor Hague first proposes an analytic framework composing three interrelated factors — evidence, values and ideologies, and constraints — which jointly shape public policy decision-making. The initiatives to develop the three metropolitan areas are based on the logic of agglomeration economy and the purpose to enhance national and international competitiveness. In comparison, Great Manchester has successfully established a combined authority to coordinate development, whereas the Central Scotland region failed to do so because of its smaller population size. This study demonstrates the significance and the interaction of different spatial scales in public policy decision-making, and how past policies and institutional practices could become constraints on policy-making. Base on the three cases, the author finds that ideologies have filtered evidence and also shaped perceptions of constraints.

What is the role of state intervention in development of mega-region? In Chapter 4, Professor Ren conducts a comparative study on mega-region planning and governance in China and India. This chapter attempts to reveal that in both countries, the central governments have played a primary role in the planning of regional development, although they have different policy goals. In India, the current attempt in mega-region development is to promote manufacturing and to attract global investment, as part of the Make-in-India Campaign launched by the Modi administration. In China, mega-region planning has multiple goals, including boosting regional competitiveness, upgrading industries from low-end to hi-tech manufacturing, and environmental sustainability. In the two countries, different sub-national governments play as key enforcers of the mega-region development initiatives. In India, state authorities take full control and set up special agencies to supervise project implementation, often bypassing municipal governments. In China, by contrast, provincial governments only provide funding and policy guidance, while municipal governments are crucial promoters of mega-region development. In both countries, the idea behind the regional development is to coordinate rich cities with less developed cities. But economically more powerful cities and states are more likely to benefit from infrastructure investment brought by mega-region development. Hence, metropolitan circle planning is likely to bring about more uneven development both within the mega-region and across the country. The author also believes it is questionable how ordinary citizens could benefit from those ambitious metropolitan circle planning initiatives.

If governance structures could result in different trajectories of metropolitan area development, policy considerations of transport, culture, and environment protection could further shape the development of those mega-city regions. The second thematic cluster of this book deals with these issues. In Chapter 5, Professor Scott addresses the economic logic of the current waves of urbanization from theoretical perspectives. Based on the analysis of urban redevelopment and rebuilt environment in both commercial and residential properties, this chapter points out that the economic logic of urbanization is intertwined with global finance, urban policy, and the role of local governments. The general tendency is deregulation and allowing the market to play a more important role in urban development. But the state is still crucial in the process, especially the local governments. Local governments guide the process of urbanization through partnership with the real estate industry, introducing large development projects and redeveloping industrial and residential land. The author recasts the overall argument in three important trends, namely, the economic and architectural revival of central business districts, the gentrification of inner-city neighborhoods, and the emergence of a new post-suburban urban expansion.

In Chapter 6, Professor Madarshahi gives more emphasis on the sustainability of metropolitan regions with advocacy on circular economy. The author argues that the principle of the circular economy must be embedded in the designing of metropolitan circles. The new thinking of urban planning should focus on design for circular reuse based on renewable resources. To build an urban design based on circular economy means less building and more efficient form of infrastructural constructions. To achieve sustainable metropolitan development based on circular principles, the administration should be able to coordinate cultural, industrial, environmental policies, and urban planning with the help of new technologies and research. For this purpose, administrative reform may be necessary to make bureaucracy more horizontal, to cut off red types, and to recreate organizational culture within the government.

Professor Blanco provides an overview of recent developments of the Los Angeles mega-city region in Chapter 7. The region is characterized by low residential density and has been suffering from one of the worst traffic congestions in the world. The chapter discusses how metropolitan form and transportation are related to motor vehicle, air pollution, and climate change mitigation efforts. The author argues that California's climate change mitigation program is actually a state-wide urban growth management program which is focused on internal urban form features. Then the chapter goes ahead to examine two major future drivers of metropolitan region development, technological advancement and climate change. The rise of e-commerce and automation technology have considerable impact on the land use for shopping malls, the industrial land demand, and urban traffic congestion, thus fundamentally changing large patches of the urban fabric. Climate change issues call for future urban planners to focus on how to avoid extreme events such as wildfires and flooding when they choose urban development locations.

One of the major issues of sustainable metropolitan circle development is how to efficiently connect urban cores and nearby cities. Many western urban developments are based on low residential density and private car transportation, which leads to serious traffic congestion and less efficient public transport network. In Europe, the most recent initiative to address this issue is the Sustainable Urban Mobility Plan, a multi-step process involving relationship between urban densities, public transport, and metropolitan development. Base on case studies of two French cities, Paris and Strasbourg, Professor Mazzoni and Professor Grigorovschi in their chapter introduce correlated top-down and bottom-up approaches to organize sustainable metropolitan development with balanced interconnection between urban cores and the circles. These approaches pay attention to the specifics of each location, including landscape features, local settlement patterns, ways of life, and historical legacies.

How did those metropolitan circles come into formation and what was the experience during urbanization process? The third thematic cluster in this book shows that there are different lessons to be drawn from various countries. Base on the study of metropolitan development in Seoul and its vicinity, Professor Joo in Chapter 9 reveals the two faces of mega-region formation. On the one hand, considering factors of environmental sustainability and balanced regional growth, the South Korean government has imposed stringent policies to constrain the over-expansion of the city of Seoul. On the other hand, a number of new towns have been built up on the outskirts of Seoul to support and boost the growth of Seoul. These new towns are closely connected to Seoul and they together form a huge metropolitan urban network. The efforts to restrict the growth of a metropolitan city have in turn facilitated the development of a greater metropolitan region. The region now accounts for about half of the country's population and GDP. The author argues that if well-planned and -governed, a mega-region could be effective in resolving urban problems of overcrowding while enhancing competitiveness in the global arena. However, the rise of those mega-region produces more difficulties for other regions in the country, which may imply that it is futile to fight against the rising trend of unbalanced development.

Since the democratic transition in 1998 in Indonesia, the capital city of Jakarta and its neighboring cities have been experiencing rapid urbanization process. Different from Seoul of South Korea, there are no restrictions on the expansion of the city of Jakarta. The capital city has expanded to consume the spaces between it and the nearby cities, and connect itself to the satellite cities with modern highways and mass rapid transit systems. Now, Jakarta and its neighboring cities are socially and economically integrated. Citizens in Jakarta and the peripheral towns are not different in terms of lifestyle, language variety, and cultural orientations. This integration has led to the formation of a mega-city. In Chapter 10, Professor Gumilar Rusliwa Somantri believes that the future development of this mega-city may require a single administrative authority to better coordinate Jakarta and about 10 nearby cities. A number of governmental functions should be moved out of the capital city to reduce the burden of this metropolitan area. The author also calls for the participation of universities and civil society in the development of this mega-city area to address social and cultural issues as well as environmental sustainability.

Mexico will become one of the largest urbanized countries in the world by 2050. Chapter 11 shows that drivers of urbanization in this country include manufacturing restructuring and export-oriented economy on the basis of the North American Free Trade Agreement. Many metropolitan areas are on the rise because of the concentration of various clusters of industries. One major problem of the development of those metropolitan cities is the lack of planning and coordination. A single governmental administration may be required to coordinate different counties or even different states and ministries in each metropolitan area. The lack of planning has led to uneven development across the country. Regional inequality has resulted in socio-economic inequalities among general population. Professor Durán argues that metropolitan development should be able to increase its connectivity and integration with economically disadvantaged areas.

Africa today is one of the most rapidly urbanizing regions in the world, only second to Asia. Chapter 12 discusses challenges faced by African countries in the urbanization process. First, urbanization in this continent has failed to reduce poverty and bring about economic growth. This is related to the second problem, urbanization without industrialization. As manufacturing has been on the decline since 1960s, the urbanization process goes side by side with the movement of labor from high productivity sectors to lower ones, or even informal sectors. The majority of the working population in African cities are concentrated in informal jobs. The third problem is most of Africa's economies are dependent on export of natural resources and therefore it is difficult for the cities to generate job-rich industries. In addition, in many African countries, industries are predominantly located in the capital city or larger cities. This unbalanced development can have a negative impact on the quality of life, healthcare, education, and economic growth in smaller cities and towns. Looking to future, the author, Professor Moshi, calls for better planning and management of national and regional development agenda in the continent.

Trying to summarize current trends and new challenges in metropolitan circle development in one volume is too ambitious for us. Yet with this book, we do hope to make a preliminary contribution to the understanding of this unprecedented and global wave of urbanization. The intellectual journey calls for continuous involvement of broader scholarship from different disciplines. We thank the IPP for organizing this conference and the speakers who contributed to this book. Special thanks to the World Scientific for its effort in publishing the book, especially to Ms. Lixi Dong who was actively involved in its publication. Our colleagues in IPP, particularly Ms. Zou Ying and Ms. Sun Xiao, were also involved the publishing process.

I. Governance Structure

Chapter 1

Thriving Tokyo and Declining Osaka: The Role of the Local Governance System

Yoshihisa Godo

Department of Economics
Meijigakuin University, Japan
godo@eco.meijigakuin.ac.jp

1. Introduction

Tokyo leads today's Japan. The central government offices, leading research institutes, popular theaters and museums, headquarters of famous companies, and major entertainment facilities cluster in Tokyo — the mecca of cultural and economic activities.

However, this is not a time-honored situation. Japanese society used to be more diversified. In particular, Osaka had been a formidable rival for Tokyo. Osaka is placed near the sea and developed as a commercial city. Osaka's nickname is *Tenka No Daidokoro*, which means "the Nonpareil Kitchen of the Nation." Throughout the Tokugana Shogunate period (1608–1868), Osaka was more advanced than Edo — which was renamed Tokyo during the Meiji Restoration of 1868 — in economic and cultural activities. Japan's top-level merchants lived in Osaka and fostered its own culture.

For years, Osaka and Tokyo formed the "Big Two" of the Japanese economy. During the postwar high-growth era, many big manufacturing companies such as Daihatsu, Daikin, Matsushita (renamed Panasonic in 2008), Yamaha, and Yanmar emerged in Osaka. Its GDP grew faster than any other area in Japan throughout the 1950s and 1960s. However, since the Oil Price Crisis of 1973, Osaka's economic performance has been poor. As a result, today's Osaka suffers from low per capita income, a high unemployment rate, and large numbers of per capita welfare recipients and homeless people (Sakaiya *et al.*, 2012). Osaka has lost its leading position in the Japanese economy. In contrast, Tokyo continues to thrive, and the so-called "Tokyo Centralization" is in progress. What made the difference between Osaka and Tokyo? There are various discussions on this question. One of the key points is the difference in the local governance systems of Osaka and Tokyo. Indeed, Tokyo has a unique local governance system, which is not seen in any other city within or outside Japan. Recently, there have been fierce debates about whether Osaka's local governance system should be reformed into a system similar to Tokyo's.

This chapter conducts a comparative study on the local governance systems of Osaka and Tokyo. Section 2 reviews the contrast in economic performance between Osaka and Tokyo, based on statistics. Section 3 sketches general information on the relationship between Japan's central and local governments, and Section 4 describes details of Tokyo's local governance system. Sections 5 and 6 discuss the necessity of local governance system reform in Osaka and Tokyo, respectively, and Section 7 concludes.

2. Comparison of Osaka and Tokyo's Economic Performance

Japan consists of 46 prefectures (including the Osaka Prefecture) and one metropolis (the Tokyo Metropolis). The Osaka Prefecture is the largest in GDP and population among the 46 prefectures. Figure 1 shows Tokyo and Osaka's population as percentages of Japan's total population. As can be seen, these two percentages increased in the early postwar period, and have been almost constant since the early 1960s. This means that the migration from rural to urban areas was almost complete around 1960.

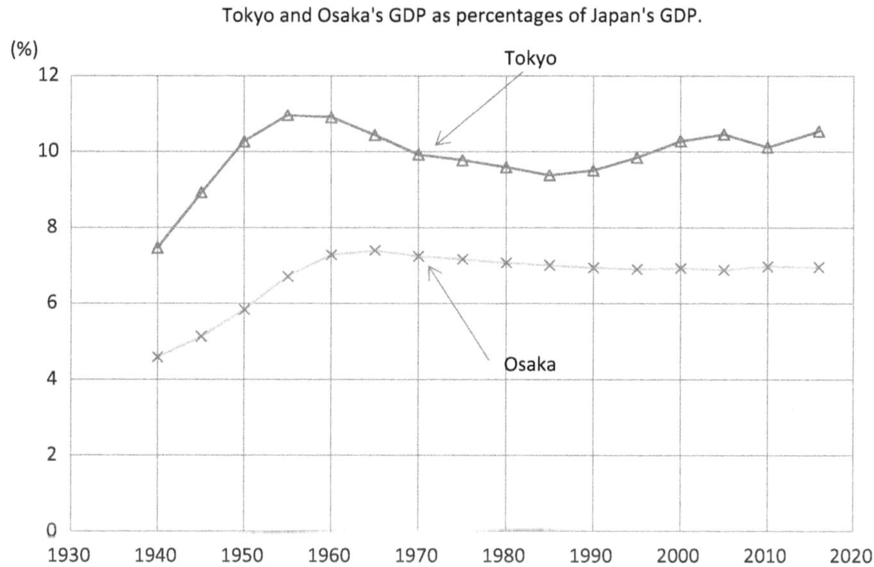

Figure 1. Tokyo and Osaka's population as percentages of Japan's total population
Source: Report on prefectural accounts produced by the Cabinet Office.

Table 1. Tokyo and Osaka's GDP as percentages of Japan's GDP.

	Tokyo				Osaka			
Year	2015 standard	2005 standard	1990 standard	1980 standard	2015 standard	2005 standard	1990 standard	1980 standard
2014	18.5				7.4			
2001	18.2	16.9			7.8	7.7		
1990		17.0	16.9			8.5	8.0	
1975			16.8				9.0	
1970				17.1				10.2
1955				16.9				7.4

Source: Report on prefectural accounts produced by the Cabinet Office.

Table 1 shows Tokyo and Osaka's GDP as percentages of Japan's GDP. As can be seen, Tokyo's percentage remained almost constant during these 50 years. In contrast, Osaka's percentage increased until 1970, but declined since then.

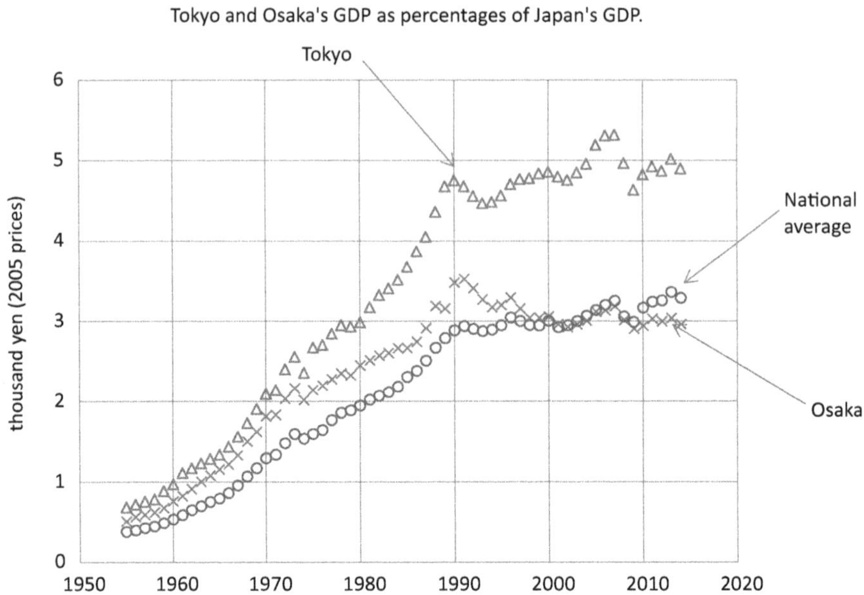

Figure 2. Comparison of per capita income.

Source: Report on prefectural accounts produced by the Cabinet Office.

Figure 2 compares the per capita GDP of Tokyo, Osaka, and the national average, and clearly depicts Osaka's unfavorable economic performance over a 50-year period. Osaka's per capita income had been the highest among the 46 prefectures up until 1983. However, it is now less than the national average level.

"Tokyo Centralization" became a popular political buzzword in the late 1980s. For example, Noboru Takeshita formed the cabinet in 1987 under the slogan of "Overcoming Tokyo Centralization and Vitalizing the Local Economy." However, Figures 1 and 2 as well as Table 1 imply that, instead of "Tokyo Centralization," "Osaka's Decline" is a more appropriate description of what happened during this period.

3. Japan's Local Governance System

The Local Governance Act (LGA) stipulates the legal framework of Japan's local governance system. Tokyo's local governance system is unique and different from other areas. It is useful to review Japan's local governance system for non-Tokyo areas first.

There are two layers of local government. The administrative system of the first layer of governance is known as "municipality," and is the basic unit of local governance. Japanese citizens living within the boundaries of these administrative units must register as residents of that area with the municipal government, and must provide details of their residence to their registry. Municipal governments are responsible for providing basic public services, such as operating public elementary schools and granting pension payouts/allowances to the elderly.

The administrative unit of the second administrative layer is called a "prefecture." The prefectural government supports the municipal governmental units within its jurisdiction by providing public services that require special knowledge, additional resources, and/or that cover a broader scope than a municipality. For example, the prefectural government is responsible for constructing the main roads, granting approval for and providing guidance to public nursing-care organizations, and constructing and operating wide-area sewerage facilities.

A municipality can be classified into three categories (village, town, and city) according to its population size. If the population of a municipality is less than a certain number (usually designated in most municipal units as approximately 8,000) stipulated by the prefectural order, the municipality will be termed a "village." In excess of this figure, the municipality qualifies as a "town." When the excess surpasses 50,000, the municipality is considered a "city."

If the population of a city exceeds 500,000 and the Prime Minister's office recognizes the city office as having a high level of administrative ability, the city qualifies to become an "ordinance-designated city."[1]

---

[1] The system of ordinance-designated cities started in 1956. Five cities, namely, Yokohama, Nagoya, Kyoto, Osaka, and Kobe became ordinance-designated cities. At that time, the minimum population size for an ordinance-designated city was 1,000,000 instead of 500,000. It should be noted that Kyoto is only 40 km northeast from Osaka, while Kobe is only 30 km west from Osaka. The area comprising Kyoto, Kobe, Osaka, and their neighboring cities is popularly called the Keihanshin Metropolitan area, which is the second biggest metropolitan area next to the Tokyo Metropolitan area. Osaka is the center of the Keihanshin Metropolitan area.

By this definition, there were 181 villages, 739 towns, and 768 cities (20 ordinance-designated cities and 748 ordinary cities) in the 46 prefectures of Japan as of June 2018.

Traditionally, an overwhelming majority of municipalities were villages. For example, when the LGA was established in 1952, more than 80% of the municipalities were villages.[2] However, many villages have become towns and cities since then due to population growth and merging of municipalities, leading to a sharp decline in the number of villages.

Administratively, towns and villages are treated equally by the LGA. As the word "village" suggests, villages comprise agriculture-oriented, traditional societies. A "village" becomes a "town" after it has undergone modernization symbolically and in real terms, though there is no actual change in the role of the municipal government when the former becomes the latter's unit.

However, when a "town" becomes a "city," it implies greater autonomy for the municipality unit. For example, in providing social benefits, the municipality governments, which exist in units defined as "cities," can decide on the groups in their jurisdiction that are needy individuals; in towns and villages, this decision rests with the prefectural governments instead of the municipal governments.

An ordinance-designated city government has far greater autonomy than an ordinary city government. For example, while an ordinary city government needs the approval of the prefectural government to design a city development plan, an ordinance-designated city government can make its own decisions.

With an increase in population, effective communication between the municipal government and citizens becomes more difficult. To overcome this, ordinance-designated cities have a unique administrative system called the "ward" system. The area of an ordinance-designated city is divided into wards, each with its own office, which provides the basic services to the residents in the ward.

Every citizen of an ordinance-designated city comes under the purview of the ward, for example, in terms of paperwork, residential registration,

---

[2] For details, see the Ministry of Internal Affairs and Communications' website at http://www.soumu.go.jp/gapei/gapei2.html.

marriage registration, and a seal certification service are provided at the ward office of the applicant's residential area for resident applicants.

Each municipal or prefectural government has its own head and assembly. The heads of a municipal government and a prefectural government are called the "mayor" and "governor," respectively. Residents older than 18 years have voting rights in the elections of the municipal mayor, the prefectural governor, and members of the municipal assembly and prefectural assembly.

In the municipal assembly elections of villages, towns, and ordinary cities, the boundaries of a single constituency (i.e., for the whole area of a municipality) are drawn up and an elector votes for a single entry, even though the number of assembly members is more than one.

For the prefectural assembly election, the prefecture is divided into plural constituencies. The total number of assembly members varies according to the constituencies: some are single while others are plural. Whichever the case, an elector may only vote for a single entry.

As in the case of an ordinary city, an ordinance-designated city has a single mayor and a single assembly. However, unlike the case of an ordinary city, the assembly member's election in ordinance-designated cities takes place in plural constituencies that use each ward as a constituency. The number of assembly members for a ward is determined by the city ordinance.

The basic unit of local governance is not a ward but an ordinance-designated city. The head of each ward is appointed by the mayor of the ordinance-designated city (not by election). This is because the head of a ward is responsible for administrative matters alone, and not for making political decisions.

4. Tokyo's Unique Local Governance System

Similar to the 46 prefectures, Tokyo's local governance system also comprises two layers of administration. However, the upper layer is called a "metropolis" instead of a "prefecture." There are 8 villages, 5 towns, and 26 cities (all of which are ordinary cities) in the Tokyo Metropolis, which also has another type of municipality unit (i.e., in the lower layer of administration) called the "special ward."

Unlike the wards in ordinance-designated cities, a special ward is recognized as the basic unit of local governance. The head of each special ward is elected by residents who are above 18 years old, and each special ward has its own assembly, with members who are elected by the voting procedure in a single constituency system.

There are 23 special wards in Tokyo. The administrative activities/powers of a special ward government are limited compared to the other municipality types (i.e., village, town, and city). The Tokyo Metropolitan Government oversees some of the activities often conducted by ward-level municipal governments in other municipality types.

For example, while the public bus system is usually operated by the municipal government, it is operated by the Tokyo Metropolitan Government in the 23 special wards of Tokyo. The taxation powers of special ward governments are also limited. The imposing and collection of asset taxes in the 23 special wards is within the purview of the Tokyo Metropolitan Government, but is usually done by the municipal governments.

A portion of the asset taxes imposed on special wards that is collected by the Tokyo Metropolitan Government is transferred to the 23 special ward governments. Every year, the Tokyo Metropolitan Government and the 23 special ward governments negotiate on the allocation of duties to provide basic services to residents and to divide the tax revenues.

As for prefectures, the Tokyo Metropolitan Government has its own assembly, with a head that is denoted by "governor." Residents older than 18 years have voting rights in the elections for the Tokyo Metropolitan Governor and the Tokyo Metropolitan Assembly. The election for the Tokyo Metropolitan Assembly takes place within the 42 constituencies.

In 12 of the relatively large cities and in 23 special wards, the municipality forms a constituency for election to the Tokyo Metropolitan Assembly. The other 14 cities, 5 towns, and 8 villages are grouped into seven constituencies. The total number of assembly members from a constituency varies among constituencies: some are single and others are plural. In either case, an elector votes for a single entry alone.

Figures 3 and 4 depict the two types of local governance systems. In Figure 3, the area of the ordinance-designated city government overlaps with that of the prefectural government, indicating that the

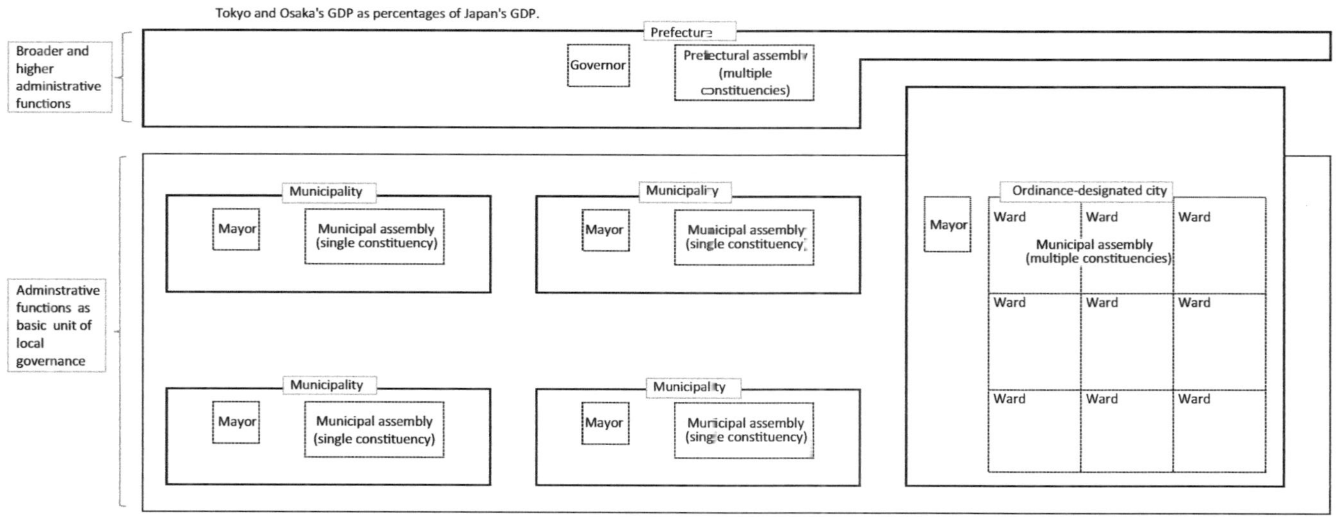

Figure 3. Local governence in 46 prefectures.

Source: Report on prefectural accounts produced by the Cabinet Office.

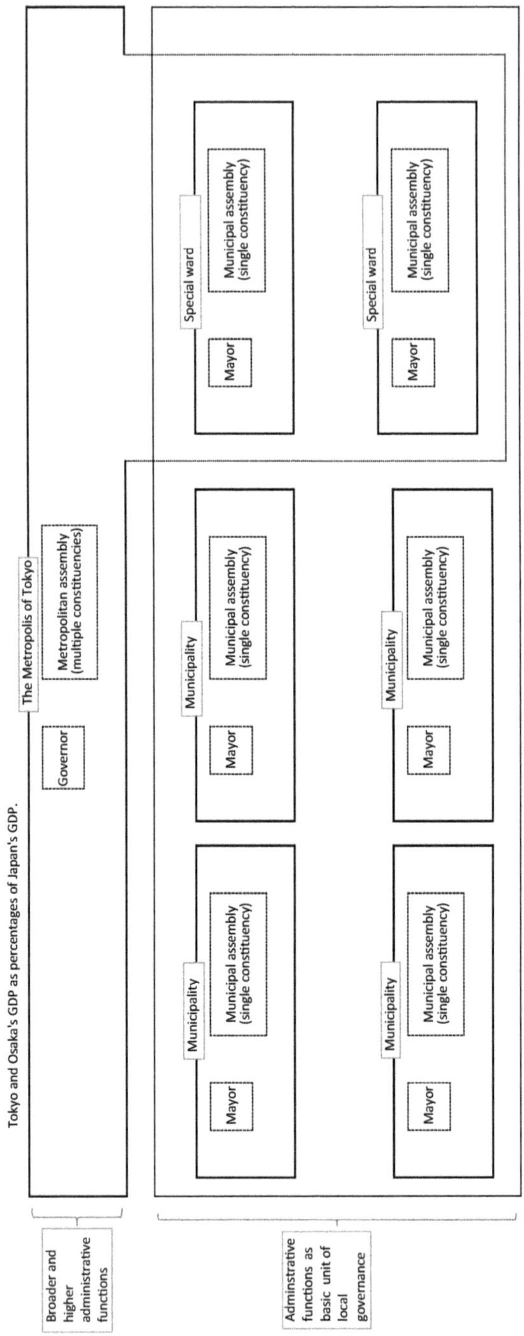

Figure 4. Local governance in Tokyo.

Source: Report on prefectural accounts produced by the Cabinet Office.

ordinance-designated city government is qualified to perform more functions than other types of municipal governments.

In Figure 4, the Tokyo Metropolitan Government enters the administrative purview of special ward governments. This reflects the fact that budgets and activities of special wards are dependent on the Tokyo Metropolitan Government.

5. Local Governance Problems in Osaka

The Osaka Prefecture has 1 village, 9 towns, and 33 cities. Osaka City and Sakai City are ordinance-designated cities and have 24 and seven wards, respectively. Osaka City contributes 70% of the GDP of the Osaka Prefecture.

In the prewar period, Osaka City constituted 70% of the Osaka Prefecture's total population.[3] However, based on the development of the public transportation system in the postwar period, the population of individuals who live outside Osaka City and commute to Osaka City for work has increased; in particular, an increasing number of high-income families moved to luxurious residential areas that sprouted during the postwar period.

This has led to various problems. A typical example is the Osaka Municipal Subway (OMS), operated by the Osaka City Government, which is the biggest subway system operated by a local government in Japan.

A limitation of the OMS is that it only operates within the jurisdiction of Osaka City, while 60% of passengers of the OMS live outside Osaka City (Ueyama and Kida, 2015). The Osaka City Government has constructed new subway lines based on its own city development plan. However, the plan may not be suitable for the neighboring municipalities. As a result, the overall layout of the railway network in Osaka Prefecture turned out to be inefficient.[4]

[3] Historical data on the population in Osaka are available at http://osaka-salon2.seesaa.net/article/371363001.html.

[4] OMS was privatized on April 1, 2018. However, there has not been any significant change in the railway operation system to date. It may be too early to judge the economic effects of this privatization.

In addition, an increase in the size of the commuting zone has had negative effects on the fiscal condition of the Osaka City Government. The aged and/or the jobless, who need social benefits from the municipal governments, tended to stay in the traditional residential areas in Osaka City.

Further, the Osaka City Government faces a problem with its water utility service. The Osaka City Water Works Bureau (OCWWB), a bureau of the Osaka City Government, manages the water utility services for citizens in Osaka City. In the other 42 municipalities in the Osaka Prefecture, water utility services are provided by a special local public entity called the Osaka Water Supply Authority (OWSA), jointly founded by the Osaka Prefectural Government and all 42 municipal governments.

The OCWWB and the OWSA constructed independent water pipelines. A lack of coordination led to complicated and inefficient pipeline layouts. For example, some areas in Osaka City were better served when the water supply was supplied via the OWSA instead of the OCWWB. There is potential room for improvement in the water utility service system of the Osaka Prefecture.

Local governance experts assert that Osaka's water utility service will be more efficient if the OCWWB is merged with the OWSA (Ueyama, 2012). However, for fear of losing their jobs after the merger, public servants of the OCWWB — who form a powerful section of the labor union of public servants of the Osaka City Government — raised their opposition.

Duplicate investments by the Osaka City Government and the Osaka Prefectural Government also present a significant problem. Each invests in its own libraries, sport facilities, and schools without coordination.

In sum, the Osaka City Government and the Osaka Prefectural Government are so unsystematic that they often fail to coordinate with each other in many administrative activities. This is unfavorable for promoting the private sector's economic and social activities.

In such a situation, Toru Hashimoto, one of the most popular opinion leaders, launched the "Osaka Metropolis Plan" in January 2010 to change the framework of local governance. This plan aims to convert the Osaka Prefecture to the Osaka Metropolis, and to convert Osaka City and its neighboring nine cities to 20 special wards; it modeled the Osaka

Metropolitan Government and the governments of the 20 special wards on the Tokyo Metropolitan Government and the governments of the 23 special wards in Tokyo.

Hashimoto believed that planning would be made more consistent and innovative by concentrating decision-making procedures of the entire area that makes up today's Osaka Prefecture in the hands of the Osaka Metropolitan Government. Hashimoto also believed that the relationship between citizens and the local government would become closer and more accountable by rezoning today's Osaka City and its neighboring cities into a more reasonable layout for resource allocation, and by introducing elections for the heads of special wards.

Arguments exist both for and against the Osaka Metropolis Plan. One of the most compelling counterarguments to Hashimoto's assertion is that the Osaka Metropolis Plan may invite serious conflicts between special ward governments and the Osaka Metropolitan Government.

Hashimoto and his followers have been conducting a campaign to implement the Osaka Metropolis Plan. However, facing fierce counterarguments, the plan has not yet gone into effect.

6. Local Governance Problems in Tokyo

The evaluation of Tokyo's local governance system differs among people. The current system is efficient in stimulating economic activities, because it enables the Tokyo Metropolitan Government to conduct comprehensive urban planning. However, the current system also has problems, for example, the Tokyo Metropolitan Government and the 23 special ward governments often cannot agree on the allocation of budgets and administrative power/tasks, making discussions fruitless and time-consuming. As such, special ward governments in Tokyo occasionally advance the idea of converting special wards to cities.

It should be noted that the basic structure of today's special ward system was established in 1943 for military reasons. Until then, Tokyo City existed as the basic unit of local governance for the central part of the Tokyo Metropolis. However, the central government found that the mayor of Tokyo City did not respond fast enough in developing the air defense infrastructure that was necessary for the Pacific War. Thus, the central government dissolved Tokyo City into special wards and implemented direct control. The Governor of the Tokyo Metropolis became responsible for appointing heads of special wards.

Following defeat in the Pacific War, Japan was democratized under the sovereignty of the General Headquarters of the Supreme Commander for the Allied Power. Accordingly, a system of free election for the head of a special ward was implemented in 1947. However, the Tokyo Metropolitan Government retained a major part of the administrative power at special wards. Reflecting such actual circumstances, the free election system for the head of a special ward was abolished in 1952. By this abolishment, a special ward assembly and the governor of the Tokyo Metropolitan Government became responsible for appointing the head of a special ward. However, such a system was severely criticized as being undemocratic. In response to civic groups' request for democratization, the election system for the head of a special ward was re-instituted in 1975. In 2000, the central government presented a new agenda for transferring some portion of administrative power from the Tokyo Metropolitan Government to the special ward governments. However, important aspects of administrative power still remain in the hand of the Tokyo Metropolitan Government.

7. Conclusion

This chapter finds that "Osaka's Decline" instead of "Tokyo Centralization" represents a more accurate description of the current situation of the Japanese economy. The inefficiency of Osaka's local governance system is one of the major reasons for "Osaka's Decline." While reform-minded politicians raised a reform plan called the "Osaka Metropolis Plan," it is unsure whether this plan provides a proper prescription.

This chapter also finds that Tokyo's unique local governance system is effective in stimulating economic growth in Tokyo. However, it is not favorable from the viewpoint of democracy.

It is the time for Japan to review its entire local governance system (not only for Osaka and Tokyo). In fact, the Japan Federation of Economic Organization — one of the most influential business groups in Japan — is active in promoting a local governance reform plan called "A 'state and county' system," whereby the present regional administrative structures of prefectures, cities, towns, and villages are combined into larger administrative units. As such, Japan's local governance system is now at a crossroads.

References

Sakaiya, T., S.-I. Ueyama and E. Hara (2012). *Osaka Ishin towa Nanika* (Initiatives from Osaka), Tokyo: Togensha.

Ueyama, S.-I. (2012). *Kokyo Keiei no Saikouchiku* (Public Management Reform), Tokyo: Nikkei BP.

Ueyama, S.-I. and K.-R. Kida (2015). *Kensho Osaka Ishin Kaikaku* (A Review on Osaka Reform), Tokyo: Gyosei.

Chapter 2

How Wide is the Hudson River? The Effect of the State Border on the New York–New Jersey Metropolitan Region

Brendan O'Flaherty

Department of Economics,
Columbia University, New York, USA
bo2@columbia.edu

1. Introduction

New York rose to prominence in the early 19th century as the primary port through which trade between the United States and Europe was conducted; it was the main connection between the United States and Europe. Since then the New York–New Jersey metropolitan region has grown to acquire worldwide stature as one of the most productive regions. Throughout this process, and even today, the region has been fragmented by a political boundary, the border between the states of New York and New Jersey. This border emerged from a grant in 1664 by James, Duke of York, the younger brother of King Charles II, and was confirmed after the United States was founded as a confederation of states in 1776 and became a federal nation in 1787. States are not subsidiaries of the federal government; they are the federal government's shareholders. In the 241 years since the Constitution was written, state borders have been added — some states have split off from other states (the most recent being West Virginia in 1863) — but no state border has ever disappeared.

The main question for this chapter is what difference has this seemingly indelible line made to the development of the New York–New Jersey metropolitan area. How would things be different today if the Duke of York had rewarded his courtiers in some other fashion in 1664? The parallels with the Guangzhou–Dongguan–Shenzhen–Macao–Hong Kong region are obvious.

I begin with a brief political history of the border. The main point is that the border is an anachronism that solves no modern problem. Then I look at how trade economists have measured border effects. The third section is about border effects in urban economics, and it includes an estimate of the size of the effect of the border between New York and New Jersey.

Throughout the chapter 1 refer to the Hudson River as the border between New York and New Jersey. I use this expression for brevity; the border is actually more complicated. The east–west border begins in the north in the Hudson River where the borough of Tappan in New York is adjacent to the town of Alpine in New Jersey. The border then continues south in the Hudson until the river (it is actually a tidal estuary) runs into Upper New York Bay. In Upper New York Bay, 90% of Ellis Island and all of the waters surrounding the Statue of Liberty are in New Jersey (Liberty Island is an exclave of Manhattan). At Staten Island, the border turns west and runs through the Kill Van Kull, turning south again, through the Arthur Kill to Tottenville (in Staten Island) and Perth Amboy (in New Jersey). It then continues through Raritan Bay, between Staten Island and the New Jersey Bayshore, to Sandy Hook and the Atlantic Ocean. The Hudson River section between Manhattan and Bronx on the east, and Bergen and Hudson Counties in New Jersey on the west, is the best-known and most heavily populated section.

2. Why is there a Border in the Hudson River?

In this section, I will argue that the border between New York and New Jersey is a historical artifact that does not correspond to any underlying fundamentals. It was not present before English rule, and was put in place by the Duke of York for reasons unconnected with the development of what later became the metropolitan region.

The Lenni Lenape were the first inhabitants of the New York–New Jersey region about whom we have some information. The area that they lived in, which they called Lenapehoking, extended from Delaware Bay north through much of the Hudson Valley (see Figure 1). They were

Figure 1. Map of Lenapehoking.

Source: https://upload.wikimedia.org/wikipedia/commons/0/08/Delaware01.png.

divided by dialect, with Munsee predominant north of the Raritan River in New Jersey and Unami predominant south of Trenton. The Munsee region is a decent approximation of today's metropolitan region.

The first Europeans to settle in Lenapehoking were Dutch and Swedish. In 1626, the Dutch West India Company, having obtained a patent from the Dutch government, sent settlers to Manhattan, and "purchased" it from the local Munsee-speaking clans. They called the island New Amsterdam, and called the surrounding region New Netherlands. Soon there were Dutch settlements on both sides of the Hudson.

The Swedes settled in Unami territory on both sides of the Delaware River in 1638, and established New Sweden. The Dutch Republic conquered New Sweden in 1655, during the Second Northern War, and incorporated it into New Netherlands. Thus, by 1655 New Netherlands approximated Lenapehoking.

New Netherlands came to an end in 1664. In England, after the restoration of a high church monarch in 1660, the new king, Charles II, planned to assert his power in North America. He made his younger brother James, the Duke of York, head of the Royal Navy, and gave him a patent for New Netherlands. As part of the Second Anglo-Dutch War in August 1664, four English warships sailed into New Amsterdam harbor, and the Dutch there surrendered. (The Dutch briefly re-conquered New Netherlands in the Third Anglo-Dutch in 1673, but they did not hold it long.)

On June 24, 1664, before the warships sailed into New Amsterdam harbor, the Duke of York granted the part of New Netherlands east of the Delaware River and west of the Hudson River to his friends, Sir George Carteret and John, Lord Berkeley, in recognition of their service to the monarchy during the Civil War. Carteret had served as governor of the isle of Jersey at the outbreak of the Civil War, and had made it the last monarchist holdout. So the Duke of York named the land he gave to Carteret and Berkeley New Jersey. Carteret and Berkeley were "the Proprietors": they owned the land and they were the government. Neither ever set foot in North America.

Not everyone approved of the Duke's beneficence. The royal governor of New York strongly objected almost immediately and, in 1697, 65 inhabitants of Elizabeth-Town in East Jersey also petitioned the crown to unite East Jersey with New York. But nothing came of these protests. In 1680 and 1682, the Duke of York reaffirmed the separateness of New Jersey, and in 1702 Queen Anne made New Jersey a royal colony (Klett, 2014).

New Jersey continued as a separate colony for the rest of the colonial period. The Declaration of Independence in 1776 was issued by "United Colonies" which thereupon called themselves "United States." After the revolution, representatives of the new states met to establish some form of central government, first under the Articles of Confederation and then through the Constitution of 1787. Article IV, Section 3 of the Constitution states the following: "New states may be admitted by the Congress into this Union, but no new State shall be formed or erected within the jurisdiction of any other State; nor any State be formed by the junction of two or more States, or parts of States, without consent of the Legislatures of the States concerned as well as of the Congress." And so the border established by James, Duke of York, to reward his friends, none of whom ever set foot on the North American continent, remains to this day. It is not a border that anyone on the ground — either the Lenape or the Dutch or the Swedes — ever used.

If this border in the Hudson River is such a bad idea (as I seem to be implying), why couldn't people have gotten rid of it before now? Doesn't its survival indicate that it was never to everyone's advantage, once compensation was paid, to get rid of the division and create a colony or state like Lenapehoking, or the Munsee-land?

I have two answers about why "unfit" borders can survive. The first is that in colonial times, the border probably caused so little harm, if any, that revising it was probably not worth the trouble. Given the technology of the time, the Hudson was a formidable barrier, especially in poor weather; New York was a village that did not generate huge agglomeration economies, and commerce was slow and halting, even without borders. Taking over New Jersey would have been gratifying to Governor Andros, who governed New York before the Glorious Revolution of 1688, but whatever Andros would have gained, Carteret and Berkeley, or their successors, would have lost; and the potential losers had good connections in court (James succeeded his brother to the throne). There was no great surplus that Andros could have used to compensate them if a deal had gone through.

After independence, the situation was different. Redrawing borders might well have generated surplus that winners could have used to compensate losers. But as Coase (1960) has famously argued, mutually advantageous deals cannot happen without a legal system that permits them. Many people who would need to be compensated probably could not receive any credible promise of compensation.

For instance, begin with Congress, which would have to approve. Adding or rearranging states changes the partisan balance in the Senate because, for instance, the voters in the new state of Munsee could not credibly commit to do something like elect a Republican senator every 18 years. In the 19th century, the balance was sometimes maintained (with great difficulty) by pairing the admission of a slave state with the admission of a free state (in the Missouri compromise of 1820, for instance). Ultimately, this structure fell apart with the Kansas–Nebraska Act of 1850 and the *Dred Scott* decision of 1857. Even then, this strategy for maintaining balance could work only for Senate votes where a simple majority was required, but for many important Senate votes, three-fifths or two-thirds is required. It is impossible to maintain a balance at majority, three-fifths, and two-thirds simultaneously.

Each existing state legislature would also have to approve. In the US system, states retain a considerable degree of sovereignty, and legislatures find it hard to bind future legislatures and judges, especially those of different states. For instance, the reason why the *Dred Scott* decision ended the 19th century system of horse-trading on new states is that it ruled (in part) that Congress could not prescribe the laws on slavery that a state could establish. So the agreements needed to revise the New York–New Jersey state border and set up a new state of Munsee would be in great danger of not being enforceable.

The transaction costs of changing state borders today would also be huge, and borne by many people. Many of the rules that people live by — lawyers, teachers, police officers, barbers, plumbers, boiler operators, architects, and lead abatement technicians, to name just a few — are set by states, and are not standardized. Drivers' licenses are issued by states, and states write the laws governing driving, accident liability, and insurance. States govern marriage, too, and the issuance of birth and death certificates. Each individual's cost of switching may not be great, but the aggregate is, and finding a way to pay compensation is hard.

State borders are thus an example of what David (1985) has called path dependence. The QWERTY keyboard is David's main example of path dependence. QWERTY refers to the letters in the upper left row of almost all Western keyboards. This keyboard was designed in the 1870s by Christopher Sholes and Remington, Inc. engineers to reduce the problems of jamming with the original mechanical keyboards. The keys would jam if two letters close to each other were struck in quick succession, and so the keyboard was designed to separate the letters that commonly follow each other in American English. Today, QWERTY is still almost the only keyboard that any Westerner uses, even on computers, which do not have keys and cannot jam. Other keyboards have been designed that are about 10% more efficient, but almost nobody uses them (Norman, 1990). In David's story, Remington produced some of the first commercial typewriters, and people learned eight-finger touch typing on the QWERTY keyboard. Firms therefore purchased QWERTY typewriters so they could hire QWERTY typists, and aspiring typists learned QWERTY because firms had QWERTY typewriters.

If we were to start fresh today, we would probably not use QWERTY. But we are not starting fresh today, and the costs of switching to another keyboard would be very large, possibly larger than the gains to people living today, and there is no feasible way for people not yet born to compensate people living today. That is the meaning of path dependence.

QWERTY, railroad gauges, and seven-day weeks are some of the world's most stable practices, and they are all examples of path dependence. So are American state borders. They are extremely stable, too, with no serious changes since the Civil War over 150 years ago. But as with all path-dependent practices, stability is not evidence of *ex ante* optimality today. The Duke of York had no idea of what the New York–New Jersey metropolitan area would look like when he decided how to reward his friends in 1664. And his actions have shaped the metropolitan area ever since.

3. Do Borders Matter? The View from Trade Economics

What difference does it make today that a border runs down the middle of the Hudson River? Trade economists were the first to explore this question. Clearly borders with walls to prevent the passage of people or goods are going to have real effects, as will those that are fortified with high tariffs and tight quotas. The interesting question is what difference relatively open borders like those between Canada and the US, Mainland China and Hong Kong, or New York and New Jersey make.[1]

Engel and Rogers (1996) is the seminal paper in this literature. They look at the prices of tradable goods in different cities on both sides of the border between the US and Canada. Their chief concern is the volatility of the relative prices of these tradable goods, which they take as a measure of market integration. For many reasons, a tradable good should not be expected to have the same price in two different cities with perfectly integrated markets, but price changes should be fairly well correlated: when the price of toothpaste goes up 10% in Guangzhou, it should also go up close to 10% in Nanjing so that the relative price of toothpaste between Guangzhou and Nanjing would not move very much. So Engel and Rogers compute the standard deviation of two-month changes in the log relative price of toothpaste between Guangzhou and Nanjing over a period of time. They do this for many goods, and many pairs of North American cities. These relative price volatilities are their main dependent variables.

Then they ask what determines how well integrated the markets of two cities are. They use two variables to explain market integration: distance and the US–Canada border. Within a country, they expect only distance to matter: the further apart two cities are, the greater the cost of transporting goods, the harder it is to move, and the less price information is likely to be available. So as the price of toothpaste in Harbin is buffeted by different shocks, the arbitrage mechanisms to bring it into line with the price of toothpaste in Fujian are very weak, and so the relative price should be very volatile. But the relative price between Guangzhou and Dongguan should be fairly constant, because, for instance, if the Guangzhou price of toothpaste rose sharply against the Dongguan price,

[1]Article I, Section X, of the US Constitution prohibits states from imposing tariffs on imports from other states without Congressional approval, and Article 1, Section VIII, Clause 3 reserves to Congress the power to "regulate commerce with foreign nations, and among the several States, and with the Indian tribes."

consumers would flock to Dongguan and wholesalers would steer clear of Dongguan, and so the relative price would quickly move toward its former position. A border may also make relative prices more volatile. Some movements may be impeded, different currencies may be used, and information may diffuse more slowly.

Engel and Rogers regress price volatility between pairs of cities on the log distance between them, a dummy indicating whether they are on opposite sides of the border, and commodity and city fixed effects. Cities that are further apart have markets that are less integrated, and of pairs of cities that are the same distance apart, those separated by a border, are less well integrated. They summarize their result by estimating the "distance" that a border adds to the physical distance between two cities: 121,000 km. Seattle seems to be very far from Vancouver.

Gorodnichenko and Tesar (2009), however, argued that Engel and Rogers had not specified their equation correctly and so had mistaken differences in intra-national relative price volatility (Canadian relative prices are less volatile than US relative prices, holding the distance between two cities constant) for the border effect.

To see this, follow Gorodnichenko and Tesar and assume that the effect of distance is known and the same over any interval. Then our observations are distance-corrected relative price volatilities σ_{ij} between city i and city j. There are three kinds of pairs: both cities are in the US (and so we say $UU_{ij} = 1$); both cities are in Canada (and so we say $CC_{ij} = 1$); and one city is in each country and a border is between them (and so we say $UC_{ij} = 1$). Then the true model is as follows:

$$\sigma_{ij} = \beta UC_{ij} + \gamma_u UU_{ij} + \gamma_c CC_{ij} + \sum_{s=1}^{N} \alpha_S D_S. \tag{1}$$

In Equation (1), β is the border effect, γ_u is the within-US effect, γ_c is the within-Canada effect, and α_s is the fixed effect for city s. There are N cities and D_s is a dummy variable for city s. The first k cities are in Canada and the remainder are in the US.

This equation cannot be estimated because of collinearity. Specifically two identities hold

$$CC_{ij} = -\frac{1}{2} UC_{ij} + \frac{1}{2} \sum_{s=1}^{k} D_S.$$

$$UU_{ij} = -\frac{1}{2}UC_{ij} + \frac{1}{2}\sum_{s=k+1}^{N} D_s.$$

For the Canadian identity, if both cities are in Canada, $CC_{ij} = 1$, $UC_{ij} = 0$, and $\frac{1}{2}\sum_{s=1}^{k} D_s = 2$. If one city is in Canada, $CC_{ij} = 0$, $UC_{ij} = 1$, and $\frac{1}{2}\sum_{s=1}^{k} D_s = 1$. If no cities are in Canada, $CC_{ij} = 0$, $UC_{ij} = 0$, and $\frac{1}{2}\sum_{s=1}^{k} D_s = 0$. So for all possibilities the Canadian identity holds. Similar reasoning works for the US identity.

In contrast to the true model (1), Engel and Rogers estimate the following:

$$\sigma_{ij} = \beta UC_{ij} + \sum_{s=1}^{N} \alpha_s D_s.$$

Substituting the two identities into (1), Gorodnichenko and Tesar obtain

$$\sigma_{ij} = \left[\beta - \frac{1}{2}(\gamma_u + \gamma_c)\right] UC_{ij} + \sum_{s=1}^{N} \alpha_s D_s.$$

Thus, the Engel–Rogers estimate is not the cross-border effect β, but the difference between the cross-border effect and the unweighted average of the two within-country effects, which are the omitted variables.

Gorodnichenko and Tesar point out that adding either a UU_{ij} term or a CC_{ij} term to the Engel–Rogers equation, but not both, changes the coefficient on the UC_{ij} term in an interesting way. If a UU_{ij} term is added, then CC_{ij} becomes the omitted variable, and the coefficient on UC_{ij} becomes $[\beta - \gamma_c]$: the difference between the cross-border effect and the within-Canada effect. Adding a CC_{ij} term instead makes the coefficient on UC_{ij} the difference between the cross-border effect and the within-US effect.

Which term should be added? It makes a difference: the border is 47 km wide from the US perspective, and 108 million km wide from the Canadian perspective. Gorodnichenko and Tesar solve a structural model that suggests that adding the term for country where the within-country effect is smaller (Canada in this case), and making the larger within-country effect the omitted variable, will usually get closer to the true effect. The Engel–Rogers effect is too big.

Notice that if Canada has only one city, there is no CC_{ij} effect, and the Engel–Rogers equation (with city fixed effects) is the only alternative (with UU_{ij} the implicit omitted term). This is relevant to estimating a cross-border effect for Hong Kong.

Of the many papers that have been written following Engel and Rogers, the most relevant three are Wolf (2000), Yilmazkuday (2012), and Fan *et al.* (2016). Wolf and Yilmazkuday both try to estimate the border effect between the US states, but they use the Engel–Rogers methods (Yilmazkuday cites Gorodnichenko and Tesar, but does not apply their conclusions). Wolf uses commodity flows and finds considerable home bias. Yilmazkuday uses methods very similar to Engel and Rogers, but has a sample of primarily Midwestern and southwestern states; he estimates a state border effect of 3,300 km, which is probably far too big.

Fan *et al.* is the only paper of these three that takes Gorodnichenko and Tesar seriously, and since the main comparisons involve a border with only one city on one side, the estimates should be taken seriously. They estimate the width of the border between Hong Kong and Mainland China at 266 km. Their price data, however, come from a single supermarket chain, and so may underestimate the width of the border.[2]

Thus, the international trade literature involving prices and commodity flows of tradable goods indicates noticeable border effects on many fairly open borders, but a credible study of the New York–New Jersey border for tradable goods has not yet been done. There is credible evidence of a border effect between Hong Kong and Mainland China.

4. Do Borders Matter? The View from Urban Economics

While the trade literature concentrates on market integration for tradable goods, borders within metropolitan areas can also affect how non-tradable goods are produced and distributed. In this section, I look first at goods that have markets, and then goods that do not have markets.

[2]I am grateful to Professor Ming Lu for pointing out this weakness.

4.1. *Market goods*

Many non-traded goods are regulated by states, and these state regulations often differ. A person in one state often cannot purchase a good or service from another state, or purchase it on the same terms as others. The law of one price does not hold across state borders.

Licensed occupations are one source of these trade barriers. About a quarter of full-time prime-age US workers are licensed — that is, they must have a document issued by a state board saying that they meet the state's requirements for training, knowledge, and good character for the occupation in which they work (Nunn, 2016). Licensing is most prevalent in healthcare, legal, and educational occupations, but is not confined to these: beauticians and barbers, for instance, are licensed in many states, including New York and New Jersey. Some states recognize licenses issued by other states, but for barbers and beauticians neither New York nor New Jersey recognizes the other state's licenses. State-specific licensing is a barrier to the law of one price: beauticians are earning higher wages in Staten Island in New York than they are in Avenel in New Jersey; if Avenel beauticians cannot simply cross the Arthur Kill to move Staten Island wages down and Avenel wages up. They would have to do additional training, meet the New York requirements, and pay fees to New York. (Staten Island consumers could go to Avenel instead, but it is less expensive for one beautician to cross the Arthur Kill than dozens of customers. Round-trip tolls on the bridges across the Arthur Kill are at least $10.50.)

Some institutions are likewise authorized to operate in particular states. Certain banking and insurance companies are chartered and regulated in particular states, and cannot extend their operations into other states without special permission. Healthcare facilities like hospitals, nursing homes, and ambulatory surgery centers are also licensed by states, and so movements across state lines are impeded. Although hospital mergers within each state have been frequent in the last decade, no cross-state mergers have occurred yet, and the presence of New York hospital systems in New Jersey is meager. Universities are also regulated by states. Neither Columbia nor New York University operates any facility in New Jersey, and Princeton and Rutgers have none in New York.

The burden of learning codes and regulations themselves, even when they do not explicitly prohibit someone from working in another state, is also an impediment to inter-state commerce. The legal requirements for French drains and toilets, for instance, differ between the two states, and contractors who are proficient in one state are likely to make mistakes working in the other unless they make significant investments in learning new codes.

Some commodities are legal in one state but not in the other. New Jersey prohibits sale of raw milk, but New York allows it on farms under certain conditions (ProCon, 2016). New York allows self-service gasoline and alcohol in supermarkets, but New Jersey does not. New Jersey is likely to legalize recreational marijuana before New York does, but New York legalized needle exchange before New Jersey. In the world of consumer fireworks, New York permits cylindrical fountains but New Jersey does not. The opposite is the case for metal wire sparklers (American Pyrotechnics Association, 2018).

Finally, differing tax rates and tax systems also introduce wedges between prices in the two states, for both tradables and non-tradables. Suppose barbers are charging $30 for a haircut in Staten Island in New York, and Joe in Staten Island is willing to pay only $25 for a haircut at this time. Suppose further that barbers in Avenel across the Arthur Kill in New Jersey now get $20 for a haircut but that Joan in Avenel, who is licensed in New Jersey, works only a few hours a week because her reservation wage is $23 per haircut. Then Joan will never cut Joe's hair if she has to go through licensing in New York and Joe will never pay the toll to go to Avenel to get a haircut. But both Joe and Joan would be better off if Joan's New Jersey license were recognized in New York and she could go to Staten Island and cut Joe's hair and the hair of many people like him. Since these wedges affect areas like housing, healthcare, and education that account for a large proportion of consumer spending in a large and rich metropolitan area, the deadweight losses are probably not trivial.

But there is a further problem that urban economists pay attention to. Cities exist because of agglomeration economies, either within industries (localization economies) or among many industries (urbanization economies). Agglomeration economies arise from many different sources, and state trade barriers can interfere with several of these sources.

For instance, specialization is a major source of agglomeration economies, and state trade barriers can reduce specialization. As Adam Smith wrote, specialization is limited by the extent of the market, and so the larger markets that larger cities offer allow more people to specialize in ever-narrower areas, and become even more proficient in them. A small city can support only a few lawyers, all of whom are generalists (jacks of all trades but masters of none), but a large city can support family lawyers, patent lawyers, entertainment lawyers, tax lawyers, divorce lawyers, estate lawyers, and so on. The border in the Hudson River, however, with its differing bar associations and legal systems, makes specialization hard, and so deprives the metropolitan area of some of the agglomeration economies it could bring.

Consider a legal area like judicial misconduct, defendant-side. Only large cities can support lawyers who specialize in this area, but to become a defendant-side judicial misconduct specialist for the entire New York–New Jersey metropolitan area would require qualifying for two separate bar associations and learning two separate bodies of statutes and precedents. Nobody does it. Instead, the relevant markets are either New York by itself or New Jersey by itself, and both of them are smaller than the combined metropolitan area. As a result, fewer lawyers specialize and they specialize less deeply than they would if there were no border in the Hudson River.

Demand smoothing is another agglomeration economy that barriers to trade can impede. Suppose there is no border and the New York–New Jersey metropolitan area can support two craftspeople who repair a particular type of Victorian stained glass window. Demand for their services varies stochastically and so sometimes neither is working, and sometimes both are working and a homeowner with a broken window is waiting, at some cost, until one of the craftspeople is free. Both have informative websites, however, and so it is never the case (in a world without borders) that a homeowner is waiting to get a window fixed at the same time that a craftsperson is idle.

Now install a border and suppose that one craftsperson works in New York and one works in New Jersey, and that licensing rules make it hard for either to cross over to the other's state. Then it will be possible for a homeowner to be waiting for repairs while a craftsperson is idle, something that was impossible with open borders: if the waiting homeowner is in New Jersey, for instance, and the idle craftsperson is in New York, or *vice versa*. Thus, the border reduces the timeliness of service for homeowners and the remuneration for craftspeople — and so discourages specialization. The metropolitan area would be more productive, given its size, without the border.

Avoiding monopolies is a final agglomeration economy. Continuing with the Victorian stained glass window example, without a border, the two craftspeople compete, and consumers benefit from low prices and good service. With the border, each craftsperson is a monopolist in her own state, and will charge a higher price. This is good for the craftspeople, but bad for the consumers, and, as is well known, the loss to consumers is greater than the gain to craftspeople (some windows that would have been repaired at competitive prices will be replaced or boarded up at monopolistic prices, even though everyone would have been better off if they had been repaired).

For all these reasons, then, the border makes the New York–New Jersey metropolitan area less productive. Were we to revert to the borders of the Munsee-speakers or Lenapehoking or New Netherlands, its productivity would increase. That would also make it bigger.

4.2. *Publicly produced goods*

The effect of borders on publicly produced goods may be greater than that on privately produced goods. A metropolitan area divided is unlikely to build the type of infrastructure that will serve an optimally sized area. Population and infrastructure in one part of the metropolitan area produce external benefits for other parts of the metropolitan area, but governments that represent only pieces of the metropolitan area have inadequate incentives to recognize the external benefits. This is especially true with agglomeration economies: a government that increases population in its small area increases the population of the metropolitan area, which makes everyone in the metropolitan area more productive, and so raises wages and land prices everywhere.

We can see how this works in a simple urban model where we use transportation investment as an example of infrastructure investment.

Consider a long, narrow metropolitan area. All production takes place (on land of measure zero) in the central business district (CBD) and workers live along a line from the CBD. Each worker lives on one unit of (one-dimensional) land. The line segment between 0 and $c > 0$ is the responsibility of one government (call it New York) and the half-line between c and infinity is the responsibility of another government (call it New Jersey).

The job of each government is to install transportation in its territory. Various kinds of transportation are available. Some kinds are rudimentary, like an unpaved footpath, and some are more proficient, like bullet trains that run every minute. No one can live in a place without transportation to the CBD. So government j chooses a cost per unit distance d_j that a worker traveling through its territory will bear. The cost includes time. The cost to the government per unit distance is $S(d_j)$, where $S'>0$, $S''>0$. Unpaved footpaths (large d_j) are cheap; bullet trains are expensive to build.

Output produced in the CBD is sold in the world market at price one. Workers earn their marginal value product w, which in general depends on the size of the city:

$$w = \alpha + \beta L, \alpha > 0, \beta \geq 0. \tag{2}$$

In Equation (2), L is the labor force (population) of the metropolitan area. If $\beta > 0$, we say that there are agglomeration economies. (The discussion about privately produced goods indicated that borders may reduce both α and β) For exposition purposes, we will solve without agglomeration economies first.

All workers are identical. We assume an open city with reservation utility u. Worker utility is wage minus rent minus travel cost. Each worker rents land from competitive landlords, whose rents are completely taxed away by local governments. In New York, rent at distance t is

$$w - u - d_y t$$

and in New Jersey rent at distance t is

$$w - u - d_y c - d_j(t - c).$$

The two governments maximize land rent (their revenue) minus the cost of transportation. Assume that the metropolitan area is sufficiently productive (α is large enough) and that New York will always build some transportation for the entire length of the city. Then the New York government maximizes

$$V_y(d_y, d_j) = \int_0^c (w - u - td_y)dt - S(d_y)c = c(w - u - \frac{c}{2}d_y) - S(d_y)c.$$

The populated land in New Jersey, and hence the population of the metropolitan area, depends on both how much transportation New Jersey builds and what its quality is. Since L is the population of the metropolitan area, it is also the distance from the furthest worker's residence to the CBD. Hence,

$$L - c = \frac{1}{d_j}(w - u - cd_y). \tag{3}$$

Hence, the New Jersey government maximizes

$$V_j(d_y, d_j) = \int_c^L (w - u - cd_y) - (t - c)d_j)dt - S(d_j)(L - c)$$
$$= \frac{1}{2d_j}(w - u - cd_y)^2 - S(d_j)(L - c).$$

First, I assume no agglomeration economies. Then $w = \alpha$ and transportation investments have no effect on productivity or wages. Suppose that governments choose their transportation investments independently. Since New York's objective function depends only on d_y, its first-order optimization is

$$-S'(d_y) = \frac{c}{2}.$$

Given New York's transportation investment, New Jersey's first-order condition is

$$-S'(d_j) = \frac{1}{2d_j}.$$

These are not the investments a planner who controlled the entire metropolitan area and maximized total surplus would make. Such a planner would maximize $V_y(d_y, d_j) + V_j(d_y, d_j)$, and take account of the effect that New York's transit investment has on New Jersey's population. For the efficient case, New Jersey's first-order condition is the same, but New York's is

$$-S'(d_y) = \frac{c}{2} + \frac{w - u - cd_y}{2d_j}.$$

The second term of the right-hand side of this equation is positive by assumption, and so the efficient investment for New York is larger than the investment an independent New York would make. Better New York infrastructure increases the value of New Jersey land, but an independent New York government does not take this external benefit into account.

The inefficiencies are even greater when agglomeration economies are present. Because better infrastructure creates more population and more population creates higher wages and rents, to be efficient both governments have to invest more than they would independently (especially if they consider wages parametrically), and more than a planner would invest in the case without agglomeration economies.

To see this, we need to solve Equations (2) (think of this as an inverse demand curve for labor) and (3) (think of this as a supply of labor condition) simultaneously to see how transportation investments affect population and hence wages. The resulting equilibrium relationship is

$$L = \frac{1}{d_j - \beta}\left\{\alpha - u - c\left(d_y - d_j\right)\right\}.$$

Stability of this equilibrium requires $d_j > \beta$ and $\alpha > u$, which we assume. Hence,

$$\frac{\partial L}{\partial d_y} = \frac{-c}{d_j - \beta} < 0$$

and

$$\frac{\partial L}{\partial d_j} = \frac{-1}{(d_j - \beta)^2}\left\{-\beta c - \left(\alpha - u - cd_y\right)\right\} < 0.$$

From (1), for any variable x, $\partial w/\partial x = \beta \partial L/\partial x$. Hence, the derivatives of wages with respect to both transportation investments are also negative. Moreover, since $\partial V_i/\partial w < 0$, for $i = y, j$, it follows that

$$\frac{\partial w}{\partial d_i}\left(\frac{\partial}{\partial w}\left(V_y\left(d_y,d_j\right)+V_j\left(d_y,d_j\right)\right)\right)<0 \ \textit{for}\ i=y,j.$$

Thus, the first-order conditions for efficient transit investments are

$$-S'(d_y)=\frac{c}{2}+\frac{w-u-cd_y}{2d_j}-\frac{1}{c}\frac{\partial w}{\partial d_y}\left(\frac{\partial}{\partial w}\left(V_y\left(d_y,d_j\right)+V_j\left(d_y,d_j\right)\right)\right)$$

$$-S'(d_j)=\frac{1}{2d_j}-\frac{1}{2-c}\frac{\partial w}{\partial d_j}\left(\frac{\partial}{\partial w}\left(V_y\left(d_y,d_j\right)+V_j\left(d_y,d_j\right)\right)\right).$$

So for both governments, optimal investment with agglomeration is greater than optimal investment without agglomeration and, *a fortiori*, greater than the investment independent governments would make.

Thus, the border makes the metropolitan area too small. This result would be even stronger if I had somewhat complicated the model by allowing density to vary as well as the distance from the CBD. Density depends on land rent because fundamentally it reflects a trade-off between using land and using capital. Better transportation raises land rents, and so raises density. So the border reduces density below the optimum, also.

4.3. *Empirical*

Lee (2005) tests the proposition that the border in the New York–New Jersey metropolitan area matters in the way that I have described previously, and finds support for this interpretation. Population density, the density of worker residences, and the density of the residences of Manhattan workers all fall discontinuously at the state border. They also fall discontinuously at the city border within New York State: city borders act like "the border" in the model because deals between municipal governments are difficult, but for municipalities within the same state, the state budget and state authority may internalize some of the external benefits.

Specifically, Lee looks at the densities of populations, workers, and Manhattan workers, and how they vary with distance from Manhattan and political borders. She regresses the log of these densities on distance from Times Square, distance squared, and dummies for whether the area observed is outside New York City but within New York State — the city border effect — and whether it is outside New York State — the state border effect. For all three categories she finds large border effects, with the largest being for Manhattan workers (for whom the density gradient is also steepest). To translate these effects the way that trade economists did, the Hudson River is about 15–20 km wide (physically, the river is about 1.4 km wide around Midtown Manhattan, and the Kill Van Kull and Arthur Kill are about 300 m wide). The city border effect is also significant, but only about half the size of the state border effect.

What causes these border effects? The obvious candidate explanation is transportation. The city has better transportation, especially to Manhattan, than the suburbs, and the New York suburbs have better transportation than the New Jersey suburbs. The model in the previous subsection is a story about why this should be so.

The subway operates only within New York City, and together with Staten Island Rapid Transit covers the entire city. For automobiles, there are two tunnels under both the Hudson River (from New Jersey) and the East River (from Long Island in New York State and Queens and Brooklyn in New York City), but there are four bridges over the East River (possibly five, if you count the Triborough) and only one over the Hudson (the East River is between 0.2 and 1.2 km wide, 0.5 km at the Brooklyn Bridge).

Railroads are perhaps where the difference that the state border makes is most stark. Under the Hudson there is one railroad tunnel and two subway tunnels, but one railroad tunnel and 15 subway passages (tunnels or bridges) span the East River. New Jersey Transit carries about 308,000 passengers on an average workday (including those coming and going from Philadelphia and workplaces in New Jersey), while the New York commuter railroads (Long Island Rail Road and Metro North) carry a combined 655,000 (Wikipedia, 2018). New Jersey Transit has 164 stations (including those in South Jersey), while the New York commuter railroads have a combined total of 246. Since New Jersey covers almost everything west of Manhattan and the two New York railroads cover almost everything east of Manhattan, you would naively expect New Jersey Transit to be the same size as the Long Island Railroad and Metro North combined. But it is not.

4.4. *Bi-state agencies*

One alternative to uniting the states or writing contracts would be for New York and New Jersey to set up a bi-state agency to act in the best interests of the metropolitan area rather than any particular state. In fact, three bi-state agencies have been established: the Palisades Interstate Park Commission (1900), the Port Authority of New York and New Jersey (1921), and the Waterfront Commission of the Port of New York (1953). Each has a circumscribed domain of influence, and none has made progress in reducing any of the large inefficiencies we identified in this chapter.

The Waterfront Commission was set up to reduce corruption in the port, and whether it has done so is unclear, but it does not address a major concern of this chapter. Since almost all port activities are now concentrated in New Jersey while a large share of the costs of port corruption would be (or are) borne by New York businesses and residents, the commission may help make New Jersey regulate the waterfront to serve the interests of both states. Recently, New Jersey has moved to abolish this commission.

The Palisade Interstate Park Commission's goal is to run a park on the rock formations on the Hudson's west bank, roughly north of the George Washington Bridge. Thus, it provides a public good that both states benefit from, and successfully internalizes some of the recreational and scenic externalities. The primary impetus to establish it came from New Yorkers who wanted to halt quarrying operations in New Jersey, and much of the park's growth was financed by John D. Rockefeller. So like the Waterfront Commission, the Palisades Park Commission is primarily a way to constrain New Jersey from letting its businesses harm New Yorkers.

The Port Authority was established when escalating congestion in the harbor and a series of legal disputes led both states to believe that they needed some way to bring order to the chaos. At that time, most freight railroads terminated in New Jersey, and huge numbers of barges crisscrossed the Hudson and the harbor at the same time that ocean-going vessels had to come and go from piers on the Hudson, the East River, and Brooklyn.

In keeping with this mission, the Port Authority built the Union Inland Terminal on Eighth Avenue in Chelsea, a massive 15-story warehouse and exhibition building that was until 1963 the largest building in New York City by floor area. As shipping moved away from Manhattan to New Jersey, the Port Authority first concentrated its offices in the building, and then sold it. Google now owns the building and makes it its New York headquarters.

Soon after its establishment, the Port Authority became involved in constructing automobile crossings between New York and New Jersey, and by the early 1930s had two tunnels (Holland and Lincoln) and four bridges (George Washington, Bayonne, Goethals, and Outerbridge). These crossings are its main revenue source. In the 1960s, the Hudson Tubes, a small subway system linking New Jersey and Manhattan, went bankrupt, and the Port Authority took it over, renaming it Port Authority Trans Hudson (PATH). Starting in the late 1930s, the Port Authority started operating airports. It now operates three major airports (Newark, LaGuardia, and Kennedy) as well as several smaller ones. It also operates major seaports at Port Newark–Elizabeth and Port Jersey in New Jersey, and the Howland Hook container terminal in Staten Island. New York's major bus terminals, the Port Authority Bus Terminal in midtown, and the George Washington Bridge terminal uptown are also operated by the Port Authority.

Finally, it operates real estate projects in several cities, most famously the World Trade Center.

Like the other bi-state agencies, the Port Authority is governed by a board on which half of the members are appointed by each governor. Each governor also has explicit veto power over the board's minutes. The Port Authority does not have tax or police power; its revenue comes from tolls, fees, and rents — which for some projects are abundant.

The Port Authority operates as a vehicle by which the two governors can come to agreement on specific projects. For the past half century, at least, the agreements have not been long term, apparently because governors have no power, beyond specific bond issues, to bind their successors.

So, for instance, when the governor of New York wanted to build the World Trade Center, no long-term deal was possible and the only way New Jersey would go along was for the Port Authority to acquire the PATH, too, simultaneously. By unwritten law, the executive director is selected by the governor of New York and the governor of New Jersey selects the chair of the board.

Thus, the bi-state agencies have resolved some of the problems that the border has created. They have provided important infrastructure and public goods that benefit the entire metropolitan population. But they have not resolved all of the border problems.[3] Because these agencies — the Port Authority especially — are accountable solely to the two sitting governors, they are both too powerful and not powerful enough. They are too powerful in the sense that they can easily indulge activities of personal benefit to the governors or to their staffs — witness, most recently, the Bridgegate incident. They are not powerful enough in that they have no way of addressing border problems that do not require revenue-producing construction or that require ongoing monitoring by involved voters.

5. Conclusion

Although the Hudson River is about 1.4 km wide around midtown Manhattan, the state border makes it act like a barrier at least 15–20 km wide. Credible national border width estimates (after Gorodnichenko and Tesar) are probably an order of magnitude larger, usually several hundred kilometers, and so this may seem small. But land in the New York–New Jersey metropolitan area is worth about a thousand times as much as land near the Canadian border in the western US.[4] Land value measures the value of access, and so the cost of the state border may be considerably greater than the cost of the national border.

Does this mean that New Jersey should be abolished? Of course not. Even when Engel and Rogers estimated the width of the US–Canada

[3]For instance, before Uber, New York taxis could take passengers from Manhattan to Newark airport, but they could not pick passengers up there and so had to return empty.
[4]Suburban New Jersey land is now about \$40–\$50 per square foot, or \$1.7–\$2.2 million per acre. Undeveloped land in Montana appears to be about \$1,000–\$2,000 per acre.

border at 121,000 km, they did not call for the abolition of either country. But state borders may have to be re-thought soon in the US for other reasons: by 2040, current projections are that 70% of Americans will live in only 15 states, and so have only 30% of the votes in the US Senate (Bump, 2017). In the meanwhile, it is good to remember that now, over 350 years later, colonialism still has costs.

References

American Pyrotechnics Association (2018). *2018 State Fireworks Control Laws*. Retrieved on July 27, 2018 from: http://www.americanpyro.com/state-law-directory.

Bump, P. (2017). By 2040, Two-thirds of Americans Will Be Represented by 30 Percent of the Senate. *Washington Post*, November 28. Retrieved on July 27, 2018 from: https://www.washingtonpost.com/news/politics/wp/2017/11/28/by-2040-two-thirds-of-americans-will-be-represented-by-30-percent-of-the-senate/?noredirect=on&utm_term=.6778f4e18894.

Coase, R. (1960). "The Problem of Social Cost." *Journal of Law and Economics* 3(October): 1–44.

David, P. A. (1985). "Clio and the Economics of QWERTY." *American Economic Review* 75(2): 332–337.

Engel, C. and J. Rogers (1996). "How Wide is the Border?" *American Economic Review* 86(5): 1112–1125.

Fan, S. C., W. Xiangdong and W. Jia (2016). "Border Effect between Hong Kong and Mainland China." *Pacific Economic Review* 21(1): 3–12.

Gorodnichenko, Y. and L. L. Tesar (2009). "Border Effect or Country Effect? Seattle May Not Be So Far from Vancouver after All." *American Economic Journal: Macroeconomics* 1(1): 219–241.

Klett, J. R. (2014). *Using the Records of the East and West Jersey Proprietors*. New Jersey: New Jersey State Archives.

Lee, C. W. A. (2005). Essays on Public Procurement. PhD dissertation, Columbia University Department of Economics.

Norman, D. (1990). *The Design of Everyday Things*. New York: Doubleday.

Nunn, B. (2016). *Occupational Licensing and American Workers*. Washington, DC: The Brookings Institution.

ProCon (2016). Raw Milk Laws State-by-State. Retrieved on July 27, 2018 from: https://milk.procon.org/view.resource.php?resourceID=005192.

Wolf, H. C. (2000). "Intranational Home Bias in Trade." *Review of Economics and Statistics* 82(4): 555–563.
Yilmazkuday, H. (2012). "How Wide is the Border across US States?" *Letters in Spatial and Resource Sciences* 5(1): 25–31.
Wikipedia (2018). List of US Commuter Rail Systems by Ridership.

Chapter 3

Metropolitan Circles: Experience from the UK

Cliff Hague

Planning and Spatial Development,
Heriot-Watt University, Edinburgh, United Kingdom
thehagues@blueyonder.co.uk

1. Introduction

The term "metropolitan circles" is not familiar in the UK, and there is no practice that demonstrates and develops the concept. However, it is possible to look at metropolitan region planning and development in the UK from the perspective of the Chinese experience. Debates about urbanization and appropriate policy responses have now become global, in a way that they were not even a decade ago. The New Urban Agenda, adopted at the United Nations summit meeting in Quito in 2016, is intended to be a catalytic document for urban policymakers everywhere. Therefore, this is a good time to look at urban development in one country through the lens of practices and policies in other countries.

In seeking to understand recent patterns of metropolitan development in any situation, we must incorporate not only the insights provided by the New Economic Geography but also the way that policymakers respond those findings. The emergent form of urban and regional development is the outcome of that interaction: policy shapes geography, but geography, and other factors, also constrain policy. The proposition then is that this interface, between the institutional form of public policy-making (agencies, legal and administrative structures, ideologies and practices, including relationships between different spatial scales from international to urban) and the specific dynamics of urbanization in any place (e.g., clustering, key sectors, the property industry, etc.) is a critical area for research, and that a comparative methodology can be a fruitful way to conduct such analysis.

The chapter begins by proposing a way to analyze the process of making public policy. Metropolitan development is fundamentally a concern for spatial planning, though spatial planning policy is not necessarily the major determinant of metropolitan development. The analytical framework proposed is used to discuss briefly the re-evaluation of urbanization that has taken place over the past two decades, including China's metropolitan circles, and the wider context of the UN and European Union (EU) thinking about management of urban growth. Comparisons are then made of policy and development in three highly urbanized UK regions: London and the Southeast of England, Greater Manchester, and then the Central Belt of Scotland (Glasgow–Edinburgh). Finally, conclusions are drawn.

2. A Way to Analyze Spatial Planning as Public Policy-Making

While scientists may advocate an evidence-based approach to policy-making, *evidence* can be interpreted in different ways, and is only one of the factors that shape decisions. Policymakers may draw on a range of evidence and not all findings will be accorded equal weight. Decisions are likely to be influenced by the *values and ideologies* that have inspired politicians or other decision-makers, and these may even cohere into institutional cultures which frame thinking and prioritize performance criteria, explicitly or implicitly. Furthermore, decisions are taken within constrained contexts. *Constraints* can take several forms. For spatial planning, the inherited urban system is one of them, as is the unique topography of any particular urban situation. Another obvious constraint is economic: urban development and provision of infrastructure are expensive, and what is desired may be unaffordable and beyond reach. There can also be institutional constraints, notably in terms of having an agency with powers to act at metropolitan scale. Furthermore, as discussed in the subsequent sections, there appears to be a strong economic dynamic toward agglomeration that impacts on any spatial policy decision from national to metropolitan scale.

As Figure 1 shows, evidence, values, and constraints are relational, not sequential or hierarchical. In other words, they exist in relation to each other and shape each other. Thus, values and ideology not only filter the collection and interpretation of evidence and constraints but are also influenced by those factors. Collection and presentation of evidence is subject to constraints, such as the availability or cost of collection. In turn, evidence may reveal the extent to which constraints are real, or are constructs of ideology. Furthermore, policy-making takes place in a dynamic context. New evidence appears; the facts can change, as can values among policymakers or the wider society. Similarly, inherited policies may become a constraint on new policy-making.

The framework advanced here can be criticized as loose, overly descriptive, and lacking explanatory power. However, its strength is that it

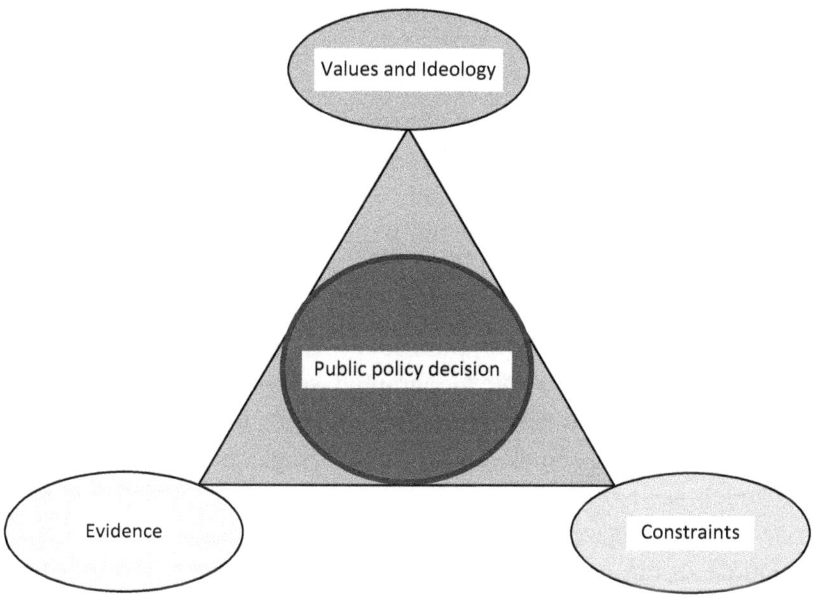

Figure 1. The inter-related factors shaping public policy decision-making.

can accommodate the complexities and particularities that characterize the making of spatial planning policy in any situation. In an international context, it can guard against reductionist and uncritical transfers of ideas and practices.

The framework prompts exploration of the fundamental questions about public policy-making, in particular who has power to decide, why is there often a disconnect between policy aims and outcomes, and how rational is policy-making in any specific situation. It will now be used to guide discussion of the emergence of new ideas about spatial policy-making internationally, and then to review policy in the EU and the UK.

3. New Urban Agendas: Agglomeration, Metropolitan Circles, and Polycentric Development

Between the Habitat II summit in 1996 and Habitat III in 2016, the issue of managing urban development gained traction with governments internationally. This can be demonstrated by the inclusion of the "urban goal," Goal 11, in the 2016–2030 United Nations Sustainable Development Goals, and by the adoption in 2016 of the New Urban Agenda (Habitat III, 2016). Evidence has been the key factor shaping this policy shift. This may be because, by their nature, non-binding declarations of good intentions at an international scale are inherently less susceptible to constraints or ideology than urban development issues at more local and immediate levels. However, the facts about the scale and pace of urban growth, its slum-led nature in many rapidly urbanizing countries, and its significance for countering climate change and poverty certainly played a part.

The World Bank (2009) published its 31st World Development Report. "Reshaping Economic Geography" sought to reframe "the policy debates on urbanization, territorial development and regional integration," with a particular focus on the rapidly urbanizing countries, and to "stimulate a much-needed discussion on 'balanced growth' which has proved elusive" (p. xiii). It explained why economic activity and people tend to concentrate in big cities, and how this can be a route to prosperity and innovation. The simple, but telling, statistic given was that half of the world's production takes place on just 1.5% of the land (p. xiii).

In explaining the nature of agglomeration economies, the leading example cited was Dongguan, midway between Guangzhou and Shenzhen: once occupied by 400,000 people mainly involved in fishing and farming, it had become "the factory of the world," home to 7 million people and achieving annual economic growth rates of 20%. Economies of scale and agglomeration effects enabled knowledge spillovers and reduced logistics costs, with the telecommunications, electronics, and computer components cluster a notable beacon.

While jettisoning the idea of "perfect competition," one of the strong messages of the report was that policymakers tend to underestimate the power of market forces. Cities "deliver agglomeration economies to producers and workers. So city administrators (should) … help it do this well" (p. 128). Thus, a key message was that agglomeration is a self-reinforcing process that spatial planners and policymakers should facilitate. However, diseconomies of agglomeration were also noted and attributed largely to land shortage or frictions on conversion of land to higher value uses. These blockages could be resolved by better transport networks and more permissive spatial planning policies, the report argued.

These evidence-based policy prescriptions, and in particular the idea of embracing urban growth, have been pursued in (and influenced by) China. The World Bank has been systematically studying China's urbanization since 1999. Shanghai now vies with Tokyo as the world's leading metropolitan circle, and is particularly notable for the very high densities in its central districts (*China Daily*, 2016). Similarly, densities in central Beijing are greater than in Tokyo or New York, though on the fringes of the cities they are lower (Zhou Xian, 2017). The Yangtze River Delta, the Pearl River Delta, and the Beijing–Tianjin–Hebei region are China's three metropolitan circles, in each case building on geographic advantages. They house some 100 million people. There are also 10 smaller circles. Together these are the drivers of China's national economy, and a central feature of spatial planning.

Zhang Laiming (2015) has explained the concept: "In a metropolitan circle, congregation and systematization have gone beyond the scope of a single city related to population, industry, social activities and governance, but are the result of in-depth integration of cities of different sizes with different features and functions in a larger space. Similar to cities that inject vigour to economic and social development of a country, metropolitan circles can integrate and optimize various national resources and promote national vigour and competitive edge to a higher level." Zhang Laiming continues, "people hope that while creating material prosperity, metropolitan circles can also keep sustainable environment and resources, with a fair and social order and a well-managed city governance, so as to improve the living standard and quality of residents and enhance their sense of happiness. More importantly, there are objective rules to follow for the formation and growth of cities, the optimization of urban spatial structure and the development and application of advanced technologies in cities."

While this chapter does not attempt to discuss in depth China's urbanization strategies, or its metropolitan circles, some aspects should be noted as a preface to the discussion of the UK experience. Gu *et al.* (2012) in a very wide-ranging overview of research on China's urbanization make a number of important points. They note how, after the Asian financial crisis of 1997, China used state investment in urbanization and infrastructure to restore domestic demand and economic growth. This meant that "the role of urbanization in promoting national economic and social growth was recognized by government leaders and policymakers" (p. 108). Urbanization featured as part of the 10th Five Year Plan in 1999 and again in the 11th Plan (2005). Even during the reforms of the 1980s, as Gu *et al.* (2012) show, research demonstrated that government policies, rather than economic growth itself, were the prime factor in moving people into the cities (p. 115). While many factors have driven the growth of China's metropolitan circles, from macro forces such as globalization and technological change to specific local geographies, it is clear that public policy interventions, at different scales, have been crucial, and that those policies have been informed by evidence and supported by state investment in infrastructure.

In summary, a body of research has provided evidence for policymakers highlighting the significance of agglomeration and metropolitan growth. This theme has then been taken up in the New Urban Agenda (Habitat III, 2016), and is both inspired by and reflected in the promotion of metropolitan circles within China.

4. European Union Policy on Metropolitan Development

The EU does not have legal powers over spatial planning, which remains a matter for the member states. However, the EU has a regional policy function, and from the mid-1990s began to work with spatial planning ministries in the member states to influence policy (Faludi and Waterhout, 2002). The idea of polycentric urban development, which had its origins in Germany and in France (Nordregio *et al.*, 2005, p. 35), gained ground, as Europe moved toward creating a single market, and sought to enhance its global competitiveness. Development of "a polycentric and balanced urban system, and strengthening the partnership between urban and rural communities" was promoted in the European Spatial Development Perspective (ESDP) (Commission of the European Communities, 1999, p. 19). This aspiration required "Strengthening of several larger zones of global economic integration in the EU, equipped with high quality global functions and services, including the peripheral areas, through transnational spatial development strategies" (Commission of the European Communities, 1999, p. 21). Europe was perceived as having only one such zone. It was called "the Pentagon," because it was defined as the area between five major cities — London, Paris, Milan, Munich, and Hamburg — shown in Figure 2. The Pentagon produced roughly 50% of the then EU's GDP, and housed 40% of its citizens in 20% of its land area: it was agglomeration at a continental scale.

While this formulation recognized the importance of cities as economic nodes and service providers even in the peripheral and rural parts of Europe, and argued that polycentric development would boost competitiveness, it stopped short of endorsing agglomerations as the preferred development path for Europe. Thus, there was ambiguity about just what polycentricity meant (Kloosterman and Musterd, 2001; Davoudi, 1999). This ambiguity probably helped to forge political acceptance: the Pentagon could continue to grow, while growth of other regions would create "balance"; an agglomeration could claim to be (internally) polycentric. At the heart of the polycentric idea was the notion that cities could cooperate as well as compete, and have complementary roles, linked to

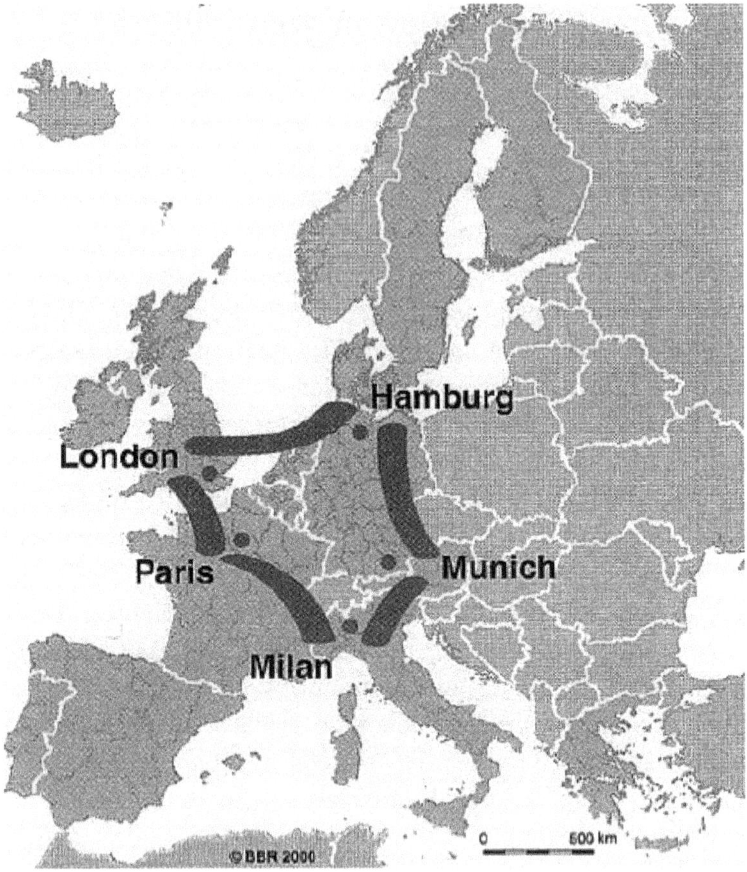

Figure 2: The European "Pentagon."
Source: Faludi (2002, p. 28).

specializations. The French Presidency (2000) further elaborated the potential development of Global Economic Integration Zones in Europe, as shown in Figure 3.

Though zones of global economic integration have a basis in reality, and the idea of growth poles has a long history in spatial policy and practice, advocacy of polycentric development came before a sound evidence base to support it. As Faludi and Waterhout (2002) showed, the intention had been to set up a European research observatory to inform the preparation of the ESDP, but technical and legal obstacles resulted in the

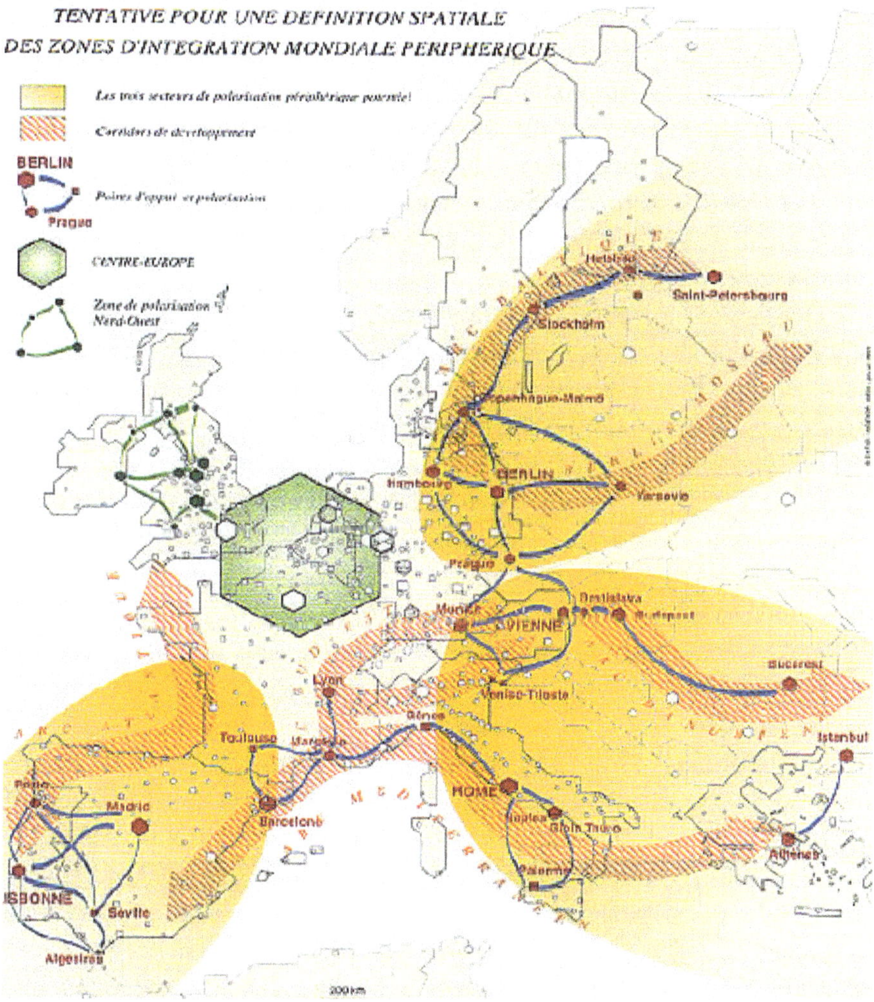

Figure 3. Possible new global economic integration zones in Europe.

Source: French Presidency (2000) in Faludi (2002).

observatory, the European Spatial Planning Observation Network (ESPON), being delayed until after the ESDP had been published. Once ESPON began to produce research findings, two things became clear about polycentric development. Firstly, the morphological dimension was easier to define than the functional integration which the concept implied.

Secondly, there were contradictions between spatial scales: to increase polycentricity and balance at pan-European scale, the capitals and other major urban areas of the countries joining the EU in 2004 and later needed to grow, thereby narrowing the gap between them and the big cities of the previous 15 EU member states. However, such growth made those newer member states less polycentric internally, because capital cities boomed while small towns and rural regions suffered significant out-migration (Nordregio *et al.*, 2005).

During the long period of growth from 1993 to 2007 (the Asian crisis of 1997 had relatively little impact in the EU) this ideology was not seriously tested. The 10 states that joined EU in 2004 were able to enjoy strong growth immediately, albeit driven mainly by their capital cities. As late as 2008, the ambiguity at the heart of the polycentric policy could be sustained. The Green Paper of that year argued that the way to territorial cohesion lay in "avoiding excessive concentrations of growth and facilitating the access to the increasing returns of agglomeration in all territories" (Commission of the European Communities, 2008, p. 6). However, the 2007–2008 crisis triggered a change of direction. This was first evident in the Barca Report (2009) which presented polycentricity as a descriptive tool rather than a prescription for policy.

Furthermore, despite the enthusiasm to promote Global Economic Integration Zones, as Pain and Vinciguerra (2012, p. 1) noted "the role of agglomeration and the specialized functions associated with their city-based business services clusters have largely been overlooked in EU spatial development initiatives." In other words, there was a gap in the evidence base. The European Commission produced a State of the Cities report in 2016. Consistent with the New Urban Agenda, it stated that one aim was "to change the perception of cities from being a source of problems to places with potential" (European Commission/UN-Habitat, 2016, p. 9). A further objective was to promote more evidence-based policy-making (p. 11). The report set European cities in a global context. It recited the advantages that cities offer, while also noting some of the challenges they face. It was produced along with the Urban Agenda for the EU (Informal Meeting of EU Ministers Responsible for Urban Matters, 2016), in which the idea of polycentric development received only passing reference.

In summary, the advocacy of polycentric development in the ESDP drew somewhat on evidence, but constraints were a more significant factor. These included the legacy of uneven development across the European space, and in particular the development gap between the Pentagon and the countries in central and eastern Europe that in the late 1990s were on their way to accession to the EU. A further and related constraint was the move toward the single market within EU, which was recognized as pointing toward more intensive competition. In these circumstances, the advocacy for polycentric development (and the ambiguous nature of the concept) can be seen as being strongly influenced by ideology. However, the ideology was not of the traditional "Left" or "Right" kind, rather it was an ideology of building a cohesive EU after the collapse of the USSR and the consequent intensified stage of globalization.

5. The UK Geography and Institutions: Constraints and Path Dependency

In relation to China, the UK is small, in terms of population (65 million) and land area (242,000 km^2). Its level of urbanization is high (around 83%), and the urban system is long established. Even London, with a population of around 10 million, only ranks at 28 in the list of global urban agglomerations (Eurostat, 2016, p. 10).

Nordregio *et al.* (2005, p. 5) put the UK in a middle ranking on an index of polycentricity. Despite there being plenty of cities and adequate connectivity, by EU norms, the concentration in London and the south-east of England reduced the UK's polycentricity score. Looking in more detail, the ESPON study led by Nordregio devised a category which they called "MEGAs" — Metropolitan European Growth Areas. These were the 76 Functional Urban Areas (FUAs) that scored best on a combination of indicators: population, transport connectivity, tourism, manufacturing, knowledge, and decision-making in the private sector (business headquarters) and decision-making in the public sector. A further sift compared the MEGAs with each other in terms of mass (population size and size of the economy), connectivity (number of airport passengers and multi-modal accessibility), competitiveness (GDP per capita and the headquarters of Europe's 500 largest companies), and knowledge base (percentage of the population with higher education and the share of the workforce working in research and development). This led to a further division of the 76 into four categories of relative significance. On this basis, London and Paris were identified as Europe's largest, best connected, and most competitive cities. This analysis put 17 other cities in category 1, none of them from the UK. Manchester was placed in the second category, along with seven other cities — Athens, Dublin, Geneva, Gothenburg, Helsinki, Oslo, and Torino. These were described as "relatively large, competitive and often with a strong knowledge basis," but as having "one or two qualities that are notably weaker than the others, usually relating to either mass or accessibility." Three other UK cities — Edinburgh, Glasgow, and Birmingham — made category 3, and Southampton was placed in category 4.

The dominance of London as a metropolitan region is thus a significant feature of the geography of the UK. Eurostat (2016, p. 92) reveals that the next largest metropolitan region, that based on Manchester, has less than 20% of London's population, while the third region in UK, the West Midlands, based on Birmingham has only 17.5%. The only European similarity to these wide differences is in France: elsewhere the population of the next largest metropolitan region usually exceeds 40% of that of the capital city region.

Thus, it can be argued that the challenge facing UK policymakers is to sustain the leading global role of London, while also seeking to grow the other metropolitan regions so that they can achieve the mass and connectivity to compete globally. In the context of the ESDP, and more especially the French Presidency (2000), the "*Zone de polarisation Nord-Ouest*" required a promotional approach to connecting and developing around the growth poles of Birmingham, Cardiff, Dublin, Belfast, Glasgow, Edinburgh, Liverpool, Manchester, and Leeds, as shown schematically in Figure 3.

So, what constituted the institutional context to address the potential creation of something approximating to "metropolitan circles" in the UK? The UK is a unitary, not a federal state, though in 1999 a separate tier of government was created in each of Scotland, Wales, and Northern Ireland with (differing) powers over fields important to spatial planning and regional development. These include transport, environment, housing, and spatial planning itself. In England, the UK government retained overall power on all matters. A metropolitan scale of local government had been established in London and six areas of England in the 1970s, but these authorities were abolished in the 1980s. However, the election of a New Labour government in 1997 not only brought the devolution of powers to Scotland, Wales, and Northern Ireland but also the creation of regional development agencies in England, only for these to be abolished when a change of government came in 2010.

These shifts in institutional arrangements and practices have constrained the capacity for decisive public policy engagement at the metropolitan scale, at least outside London (where a more powerful city-wide scale of administration has survived from the 1990s). In addition, the financing of UK local government has been exceptionally centralized, with city-level councils only raising about 15% of their incomes from local taxes. Central government sets the budgets for more local levels of government to a large degree. In these circumstances, how has the development of three contrasting metropolitan regions been undertaken over the past 20 years? The chapter now addresses this question, focusing first on London, then on Greater Manchester and its relations to other cities in the north of England, and finally the relationship between Glasgow and Edinburgh in Scotland.

6. London and the Southeast of England

As noted previously, London's global role and capital city status makes it preeminent within the UK. Hall and Pain (2006) analyzed the growth of the Southeast of England as a mega-city region.

As Figure 4 shows, the influence of London extends beyond its administrative boundaries, leading Hall and Pain to describe the region as functionally polycentric. While the city itself lost population between 1981 and 1991, there was a sharp increase from 1991 to 2001. In addition, a number of the "outlying" cities — e.g., Milton Keynes, Swindon, Oxford, and Cambridge — which have functional connections to London in the key field of financial services, experienced strong population growth from 1999 to 2009 (Centre for Cities, 2011).

Hall and Pain (2006) and Pain and Vinciguerra (2012) undertook a network analysis of the advanced producer services that connected

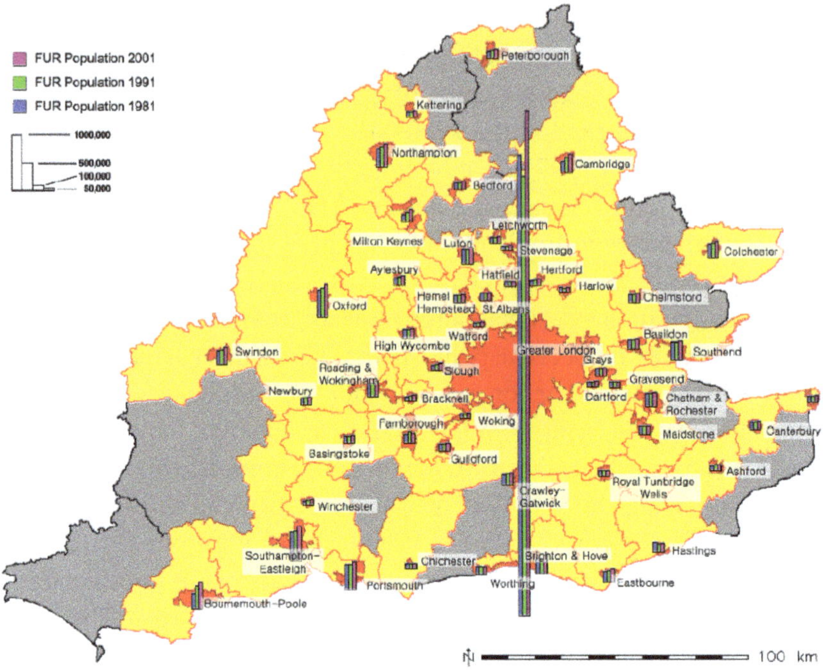

Figure 4. The growth of the Southeast of England as a mega-city region 1981–2002.
Source: Hall and Pain (2006, p. 24).

London globally, and which were so significant to its growth. This revealed the particular importance of banking and financial services within advanced producer services in general, and that London's strongest links in this sector were with New York and the financial hubs of East Asia — Hong Kong, Singapore, Tokyo, and Shanghai. Within Europe, London's strongest linkages were with Milan, Madrid, Brussels, Frankfurt, Warsaw, Amsterdam, and Zurich. In addition, the research explored the nature of clustering within London's advanced producer services. This demonstrated a strong degree of clustering for banks, auxiliary financial services, and insurance. Pain and Vinciguerra (2012, p. 3) summarized their findings: "The international and multi-sector constitution of the City of London cluster means that transnational interactions and transactions are taking place within the space of the City which is a node for flows of labour, information, business, capital etc. …. This means that this dense space has developed a critical mass of commercial office real estate for international corporate businesses and an international investment asset." Thus, London's mega-region demonstrates in practice many of the propositions advanced by the new economic geography. The benefits of agglomeration and connectivity, along with the dynamics of clustering fuel a growth economy of international significance.

The scale and spontaneity of the metropolitan growth is notable, but it is important to understand the contribution of public policy. In 1979, the newly elected UK government under Prime Minister Thatcher abolished exchange controls, thereby hugely enhancing the mobility of capital into and out of the UK. Then in 1986, the government of Mrs. Thatcher further de-regulated the financial industry through what was called the "big bang." This was ahead of similar moves elsewhere in Europe and resulted in London becoming a magnet for international banks and other financial traders. Within London, the UK government established the London Docklands Development Corporation, with powers to acquire land and subsidize and promote major property development. While Development Corporations were established in other cities, nowhere else were they combined with the kind of market pressure generated by the "big bang," and nowhere else did they generate such spectacular outcomes.

By the late 1990s, average incomes in London were 15% above the UK national average (Townroe, 1999). Meanwhile, for the 2000–2006 funding period the UK was the only EU country, apart from Finland, where there was an increase in the number of people living in regions eligible for Objective 1 funds, i.e., living in regions where average GDP per capita was less than 75% of the EU average. Merseyside and South Yorkshire (traditional urbanized industrial regions) and West Wales and the Valleys along with Cornwall and the Scilly Isles were these regions. In other words, the economic success of the metropolitan region centered on London failed to benefit some other urban regions, which experienced a decline.

The metropolitan growth in London and the Southeast was also supported by major UK government investment in transport infrastructure. The Channel Tunnel opened in 1994, providing a fast rail connection from central London to Paris and Brussels. Airports serving London at Stansted and Luton were expanded, and a new airport was created in London

Docklands. Combined with the leading role already played by the other London airports, Gatwick and Heathrow, these investments further increased the dominance within UK of London's infrastructure for air travel and global transport connectivity.

To boost the development of the then relatively isolated London Docklands, the Docklands Light Railway was constructed in the 1980s, connecting the area to the London underground network. The Piccadilly line tube train had been extended in 1986 to connect to Heathrow, and in 1993 work began on extending the Jubilee line (opened in 1979) to connect east and west London. The idea for mainline rail connections to join up the routes entering London from west and east had long been promoted. This scheme, called Crossrail, was supported by the Conservative government in the early 1990s who hoped that it could be financed by private investors. However, a financial crisis in 1993 put the scheme on hold, and it soon became clear that the private sector would not pick up all the costs. Eventually in 2000, the New Labour government included Crossrail in its 10-year national transport plan. After protracted consultation and evaluation, work began in 2009 on a scheme that is jointly funded by the UK government, Transport for London, and the private sector. The 2012 Olympic Games further channeled large amounts of government investment into the development of the capital city. Provision of infrastructure for metropolitan growth of the London region has continued with plans for a high-speed rail connection to Birmingham, and a decision to allow further expansion at Heathrow through development of a third runway.

None of these huge investments, with all their implications for where economic growth is being fostered, have been part of any formal national spatial strategy, whether for the UK as a whole or for England. No such strategy has ever been published. Indeed, back in the 1980s Hall *et al.* (1987) demonstrated how growth of hi-technology industries along the M4 corridor west of London had been driven to a significant degree by UK defense investment, and other public infrastructure developments such as the M4 motorway itself, rather than as part of a national spatial strategy. Similarly, the various big projects described previously emerged in piecemeal fashion, usually through transport sector plans, and often with long delays between the original advocacy for the scheme and its realization. All the schemes have been subjected to forms of cost–benefit analysis, and strong technical cases have been presented to justify them. In moving toward decisions, policymakers have therefore had copious supplies of evidence, though usually that evidence has been contested by opponents of the particular scheme. Part of the argument has often been about how adequately, or otherwise, negative externalities such as air pollution, airport noise levels, loss of countryside, or damage to communities have been assessed.

Decisions (and non-decisions) have also been shaped by constraints. In this respect, the decision to defer Crossrail after the 1993 financial crisis was significant in comparison to the way that China used investment in major infrastructure to combat the effects of international economic downturns. This suggests that constraints are interpreted through ideologies, while the 1980s commitment to reconstruction of London's Docklands arguably demonstrated ideology trumping evidence and constraints. Other constraints have been political, with local Members of Parliament opposing the Heathrow extension and the high-speed rail line, to give just two examples. While I was writing these paragraphs a government Minister resigned in protest at the Heathrow runway go-ahead (Guardian, 2018)!

Provision of housing to keep pace with needs across the metropolitan region has proved to be a difficult challenge. This in part reflects the ideology of both Conservative and New Labour governments, who both relied on volume house-building companies to meet demand, regardless of the business models of such companies that rely on capturing land value increase, sustaining a surplus of demand over supply, and building out sites in a phased fashion so as to minimize fluctuations in requirements for labor and materials over time, and to avoid flooding the market with their products. However, a further constraint has been the opposition of local governments such as planning authorities to releasing land in the volumes and locations preferred by developers. This again reflects the political pressure placed on local elected politicians by their constituents. The result has been a chronic squeeze on access to affordable housing, particularly within London itself.

At a more local level, there was no strategic planning authority for London between 1986 when the Government abolished the Greater

London Council and 2000 when the New Labour government set up the Greater London Authority (GLA) and an elected mayor. The legislation creating the GLA required the plan to address three concerns: the health of Londoners, equality of opportunity, and its contribution to sustainable development in the UK. The first London Plan was then published in 2004. It celebrated London's economic success and sought to sustain it by further infrastructure investment: "The London Plan cannot realistically reverse these strong, deep-rooted factors driving change, nor does the Mayor wish it to do so" (Mayor of London, 2004, p. 3). Thus, the plan endorsed increased plot ratios and higher densities in the hope of capturing as much as possible of the growth within the boundaries of the administration. Subsequent iterations of the plan, under Mayors with different ideologies, have taken a similar stance. The latest plan (Mayor of London, 2017) notes the predictions of a 70,000 annual increase in population till 2040, and aspires to "Good Growth," claiming to break with previous plans by seeking community cohesion and social integration. "Growth at any cost … for too long has been the priority" (p. xiv).

Overall it appears that the growth of the UK's only real equivalent to a "metropolitan circle," the region of the Southeast of England centered on London, is best explained by the macro-economic policy of national government which, by deregulation in the 1980s, facilitated the boom in advanced producer services, which have then been driven forward by their own clustering and agglomeration economies. However, while lacking in coordination or an explicit national spatial strategy, the region has been supported by a series of seemingly separate major infrastructure projects: although some of these include private capital, the investment and underwriting role of the national state has been crucial to their delivery, though there have often been delays due to perceived financial or political constraints. The 2004 London Plan (p. 2) noted "Lacking its own strategic authority, London's economy developed and its population grew, without a clear vision of their place in the UK economy, without effective strategic planning, and without a clear assessment of the resources and policies required to deal with renewed growth."

Last but not least, we need to recognize the significance of the 2007–2008 banking and finance crisis — and the UK government's response to it — for the growth of the London region. The UK government opted to bail out the banks to avoid a complete breakdown of the system. This not only reflected a response to constraints but also an ideological choice to restore the supremacy of lightly regulated financial services. The UK government spent some £1.1 trillion between 2008 and 2011 in rescuing the banks, though some of the money has been recovered (National Audit Office, 2018). In spatial terms the chief beneficiary of this huge investment was London, where, as shown earlier, banking and finance is highly concentrated. The debt incurred has been the basis for a decade of austerity nationwide which has seen deep cuts in public spending, especially at local government level: in other words, a transfer of resources has taken place that has benefited London disproportionately, at the expense of other regions.

7. Greater Manchester

As noted previously, Britain's second largest metropolitan region is based in Manchester, some 180 mile north of London. However, as with London and the Southeast, the definition of the boundaries of the region is not clear. From 1974 to 1986 (when it was abolished by the UK government) there was a Greater Manchester Metropolitan Council (GMMC), which covered the area of 10 lower-tier District Councils; even then the more affluent commuter suburbs were not part of the GMMC. Most of the 10 District Council areas centered on a town that was once physically free-standing and based on the cotton industry. Suburban growth and the collapse of the textiles industry in the 20th century created what could be seen as an "accidental metropolitan area." The boundaries of the administrative city of Manchester itself are tightly drawn, and the city's population is only around 500,000, though the total population of the 10 Districts combined is around 2.5 million, with about another half million in the southern suburbs. The functional commercial area at the heart of the metropolitan region straddles the boundaries of three local authorities, Manchester, Salford, and Trafford.

Rees and Harding (2010) analyzed the agglomeration economies in this metropolitan region. From the 1960s to the 1990s the area suffered from decline in its traditional industries, with deindustrialization particularly severe in the 1980s. It was not until the late 1990s that the growth of service jobs began to create positive employment growth overall. Rees and Harding found that this service-led growth, and in particular financial services, was most evident in the regional core area of Manchester–Salford–Trafford, while elsewhere employment growth was "modest or negligible" (p. 14). A north–south divide began to consolidate within the conurbation. This continued after the financial crisis of 2007: as in London the financial services sector which looked most immediately at risk actually fared much better than expectations, while recovery was hardest for the outlying former manufacturing towns. A more fine-grained analysis by the same authors found a number of "hot spots" that dominated the regional economy. This is illustrated in Figure 5. Furthermore, this detailed analysis, supported by interviews, revealed that there did appear to be agglomeration advantages to service sector firms operating in the metropolitan core, and to a lesser extent close to Manchester International Airport. However, while there was clustering of high value activity in these locations, it did not lead to a ripple effect of lower value service growth in more peripheral locations. Growth in the engineering sector was much lower, but also more widely distributed, with locations close to transport infrastructure a key factor.

Thus, market-based agglomeration effects did assist the core of the metropolitan region to recover from the deep problems experienced in the 1980s, which themselves had been in part linked to macro-economic policies of the UK government (high exchange rates for sterling as oil began to flow from the North Sea). In addition, the concentration of higher education institutions in large urban centers benefited those cities when the UK government supported an expansion of higher education in the 1990s, and as the role of universities in regional development became more significant in a knowledge economy.

Public sector policymakers within the Manchester metropolitan area had little direct control, but their supporting role should not be overlooked. As Williams (1995), Quilly (2000), and Rees and Harding (2010) recount, the politicians and city administrators in Manchester were very proactive in developing local actions, taking advantage of UK government programs, and even in initiating city region development arrangements. The precise chronology and listing of institutions is too extensive to describe here, but the city of Manchester built pragmatic

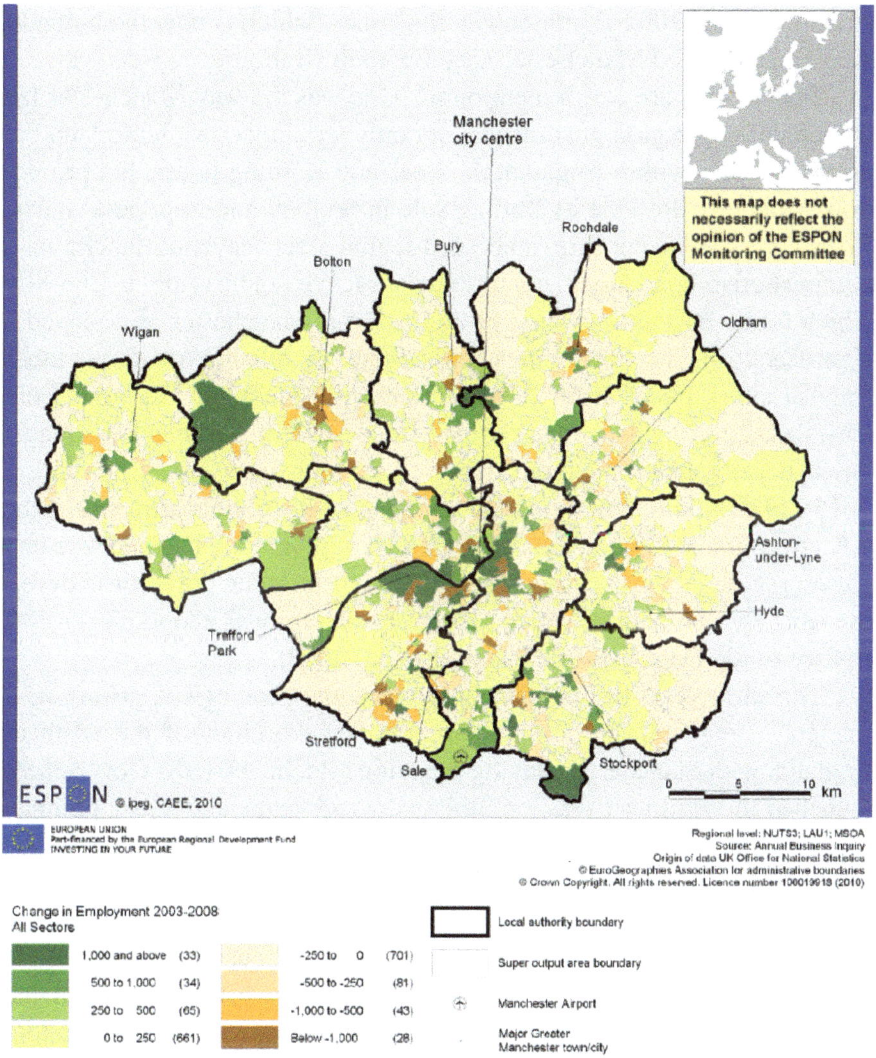

Figure 5. Greater Manchester employment change 2003–2008.

Source: Rees and Harding (2010, p. 16).

partnerships with the business community and had good links with the New Labour UK government (1997–2010). In particular, starting from an improbable bid to host the Olympic Games, they were able to receive government funding to restore derelict and polluted inner-city land for a stadium for the 2002 Commonwealth Games, which is now the home of Abu Dhabi-owned Manchester City Football Club.

Two aspects are worth mentioning. One was the way Manchester led the idea of city region governance, not only within its own hinterland but also nationally within England. As Rees and Harding noted, the promotion of the city drew on its leading role in football and in popular music in the early 1990s, but soon embraced spatial assets beyond Manchester's administrative boundaries, notably the attractive countryside of Cheshire which forms its southern suburbs and ex-urbs. Manchester also played a significant role in Core Cities, effectively an alliance of seven other English cities, plus Cardiff (the main city of Wales) and Glasgow. Core Cities made an evidence-backed case to the UK government for place-based development and more devolved funding (see, e.g., Core Cities, 2015). In addition, they were able to engage with key departments of the UK government, making the case based on agglomeration economies and clusters (without using those terms, though mentioning polycentric development) for the role of cities as drivers of regional economic growth (Office of the Deputy Prime Minister *et al.*, 2003).

The early years of the new century saw the peak of UK government interest in regional development, spurred by the cities of the north of England, with Manchester playing a leading role. In 2004, the Government launched the Northern Way, an initiative which came about as a political reaction from local governments and regional development agencies in the north to the announcement of £440 million government money for the Thames Gateway (i.e., the estuary area of the Thames adjoining London to the east) and further £170 million to address housing demand in the South-East of England. The Northern Way was to be a 20-year project that would take a pan-Northern view, bringing together three regional development agencies across the region, and creating city region plans based on eight major conurbations, including Manchester. Transport improvements were central to the vision, with priorities to improve connections to airports and sea ports and between the conurbations themselves (Northern Way Secretariat, 2006). Following a critical review of its performance, the Northern Way was restructured in 2008, to give it a stronger focus and less ambitious objectives — to change negative perceptions of the north rather than to narrow the productivity gap between the north and the southeast.

Although progress was reported by 2010 (SQW, 2011), the Conservative/Liberal Democrat government elected that year closed down the Northern Way.

Almost a decade on, the UK government has agreed a City Deal with the Greater Manchester Combined Authority (GMCA), the amalgam of the 10 former GMMC local authorities (though still not including the more prosperous areas in Cheshire to the south of the city, which are certainly part of the FUA). City Deal has been replicated in other parts of the UK, but the Manchester agreement was the first. It gives the GMCA greater discretion in the way it spends money from the central UK government.

The fact that the 10 authorities had agreed a Strategy "developed through a robust process, including analysis led by an independent panel of world-class experts" (GMCA, 2014, p. 7) was identified as a reason why the government entered the agreement. Thus, it appears that evidence played a part in the public policy-making process. However, constraints and ideology were also present: "The strategy demonstrates the critical link between economic growth and competitiveness and public sector reform: without addressing the latter and reducing the economic drag of dependency Greater Manchester will not achieve its full potential" (GMCA, 2014, p. 7). Taking the wider and more long-term view, Rees and Harding observed that "The enormous legacy of economic decline facing Manchester was crucial in focusing energy amongst city leaders" (p. 48): in other words, the path they followed from the 1980s was constrained by the circumstances in which the city found itself.

Despite its strengths, endeavors, and successes, the GMCA still has limited capacity to redress deep-rooted weaknesses in internal connectivity and transport infrastructure. While the High Speed 2 train line from London is planned to reach Manchester in 2033, reducing the journey time by an hour from the current 2 h and 8 min, heavy rail connections within the conurbation and between Manchester and the other northern cities are widely recognized as inadequate. The fastest rail journey from Manchester to Leeds takes 49 min for a distance of around 40 miles; the 31 miles in the opposite direction to Liverpool takes an hour or more. The northwest of England, which includes the GMCA, was getting £680 per capita for transport investment in 2016/2017; while this was better than other parts of the north of England, the London figure was £1940 (Institute for Public Policy Research, 2017).

8. Glasgow–Edinburgh

The final UK case study looks at the Central Belt — the traditional industrial heartland — of Scotland, with the cities of Glasgow (600,000) and Edinburgh (485,000) the poles separated by 45 miles. Between them are smaller towns that once were industrial centers, but now largely serve as commuter settlements, though there is also a planned New Town, Livingston (56,000) which has manufacturing and distribution employment, and is only about 15 miles from Edinburgh. The total population of the city region based on Edinburgh is about 1.4 million. There are also planned new towns at East Kilbride (75,000) and Cumbernauld (50,000). All three new towns were originally established to help improve housing and living conditions for people from Glasgow and the surrounding urban areas on Clydeside, though Livingston is closer to Edinburgh and was also intended to be a growth pole within the declining industrial area of West Lothian.

Edinburgh's economy has long been based on public services, education, financial services, and tourism. The financial services industries are closely linked to the legal profession, and the fact that the Scottish legal system is different from that in England has helped to glue these sectors to the city. Edinburgh's compact physical form and strong educational institutions helped to create a situation where clusters can develop. For a long time, the finance and legal services sectors were concentrated in the 18th century New Town in the heart of the city, but the advent of cabling and the availability of key sites saw a shift to a new hub just to the west of the city center. The Chief Executive of Scottish Financial Enterprise, the sector's organization, stated that "From my office I can, within a 20-min walk, meet most of our members" (Ballantyne, 2017). Bailey *et al.* (2002, p. 144) commented, "The concentration of employment in financial services reflects the general agglomeration economies for this sector and the prestige that many of the major Scottish financial institutions attach to an Edinburgh location."

More recently, there have been signs of the development of "fintech" clusters, with crossovers between the financial services and high technology sectors.

Glasgow, as Scotland's largest city and the core of a larger conurbation of around 1.8 million, has always had a significant role in consumer services. However, until late in the 20th century its reputation was as an industrial city, and from the 1930s onward it was seen as an industrial city in decline. The number of jobs in manufacturing in the city of Glasgow fell from 73,200 in 1981 to 30,300 in 2000, and as in Manchester the 1980s was a particularly severe period (Scottish Executive, 2002, p. 35). As production was shifted to cheaper labor locations globally, the interfirm linkages in sector supply chains unraveled. The loss of jobs in heavy industry was shared across the conurbation, and in addition the planned new towns (see earlier) attracted new firms and skilled workers, and contributed to a steep demographic decline in the older urban centers. Thus, the spatial aspect of regional development was significantly influenced by public policy. Population within Glasgow itself had fallen from 1.14 million in 1961 to roughly 600,000 by the end of the century, though much of the movement was to elsewhere in the city region (Scottish Executive, 2002, p. 24).

Finch and Cann (2013) summarized the contrasts in economic structures across the Central Belt. Wider Edinburgh was found to be strongly specialized in creative industries, life sciences, financial services, tourism, and higher education; whereas Wider Glasgow was most specialized in the sectors of energy and food and drink. This suggests a potential complementarity, in line with the arguments advanced to support polycentric development. However, it could equally be read as an obstacle to growing business to business linkages.

The idea that a metropolitanization strategy could connect Edinburgh and Glasgow to create an urban region with critical mass on a European if not a global scale, has been suggested at intervals, but never commanded serious public policy support. The reorganization of Scottish local government in 1975 produced regional-scale authorities, including Strathclyde Region based on Glasgow, and Lothian Region with Edinburgh its largest city. However, these two regions were competing with each other for finance from the UK government, rather than cooperating to produce better integration. Then in 1996 all Scotland's regional councils were abolished by the UK government, creating instead a system of 32 single-tier local councils. In 1997, the New Labour UK government passed legislation to devolve some internal affairs powers to an elected Scottish Parliament. That Parliament has not changed the local government structure it inherited. While it did provide for city region strategic plans in 2006 legislation, by 2017 it was seeking to abolish the requirement for such plans.

The regional structure plans produced by Strathclyde and Lothian between 1975 and 1996 did not prioritize stronger integration between their two regions. Each adopted a restrictive green belt policy to contain the spread of their urban areas, a policy in line with planning policy set for Scotland by the UK government (and continued under the Scottish governments to the present). In 2002, the Scottish government set up a review of Scotland's cities. This included work by an Academic Panel, whose members were well versed in the research on agglomeration economies. Our report (Scottish Executive, 2002, p. 11) argued that "as a hangover of last century thinking, we are currently underestimating and inhibiting the significance of cities for Scotland." However, its main focus was on functional regions and advocacy of the city region as a unit, with discussion of cross-boundary integration limited to local government boundaries within the identified city regions. The political response was to provide some ring-fenced additional funding to five city regions (Scottish Executive, 2003).

The Scottish governments have produced three National Planning Frameworks — a form of national spatial strategy — in 2004, 2009, and 2014. Over that period, they have developed with a stronger focus on infrastructure and major developments, but have not aspired to develop a "metropolitan circle" based on Glasgow–Edinburgh. One issue has been the constraints of geography and politics: Scotland has large rural areas, and this makes competition for transport infrastructure investment particularly problematic, since the Central Belt, by its centrality and urbanization, enjoys much better connectivity than other parts of the country.

Noone (2007, p. 4) argued that scale was increasingly important for international competitiveness, and could be "engineered," adding that "collaboration can reduce local 'zero sum game' competition by raising the growth prospects of all parties by focusing on complementary assets," a statement echoing ideas of polycentric development. However, the reality has contradicted these sentiments — because the Scottish Government exerts such significant control over local government finance, Scottish urban policy has been seen as a zero-sum game, and the potential to better integrate the Glasgow and Edinburgh city regions has not been seriously addressed. Edinburgh's (unpaid) "Design Champion," the distinguished architect Sir Terry Farrell, had told the Scottish Parliament in 2004 that "If Edinburgh and Glasgow can get their acts together, it could become the UK's second most important region after London" (Noone, 2007, p. 5). He continued this advocacy calling for a "spatial framework approach" (Farrell, 2008).

There was a Glasgow–Edinburgh Collaboration Initiative (GECI), which looked at the evidence base for better cooperation and experience from elsewhere in Europe. It was initiated in 2006 by Scottish Enterprise, Scotland's national economic development agency. GECI had the city councils of Edinburgh and Glasgow as partners, and was funded by money earmarked for the cities by the Scottish Executive after the Cities Review. The Chief Executive of GECI was quoted as saying, "To catapult the combined metro region of Glasgow-Edinburgh into Europe's first league of metropolitan regions, additional investments in transport infrastructure will be key, i.e., high-speed trains between Glasgow and Edinburgh supplemented by a thoroughly improved metro mass transit system leading to better connectivity also for sub-regions" (Jamieson, 2014).

GECI commissioned research, which found that 1.8% of Wider Glasgow's workers commuted from Edinburgh, while commuting in the other direction contributed 4.3% of Edinburgh's labor market. Furthermore, the researchers concluded that the quality of the transport network between the two cities was not hindering economic linkages between them, though in the longer term structural economic change and increased specialization of labor were likely to increase pressure on road and rail capacity (Finch and Cann, 2013). However, Noone (2007, p. 7) had argued that "a return journey by rail represents a considerable business time cost (up to half a working day when waiting times and connections at either end are considered), and the journey itself is slower and more prone to overcrowding than in the 1970s."

Over a decade later similar criticisms are still voiced frequently, and the train journey between the two city centers takes about an hour. A prominent Scottish journalist summed up what happened: "Meetings were held, papers produced, framework documents flourished and strategy agendas waved. It all fizzled out. Plans for a high-speed rail link foundered" (Jamieson, 2014).

Though a research case was made for growing Glasgow–Edinburgh as a metropolitan region, the idea has not been taken forward into public policy. Undoubtedly, the costs of dramatically improving the infrastructure were a constraint, especially after the onset of the 2007 financial crisis, and the subsequent imposition of austerity by the UK governments after 2010, since the finance for the Scottish government comes largely from the UK government as a percentage of UK-wide public expenditure. However, in contrast to what happened in Greater Manchester, the local level of government remained lukewarm about the scope for formal cooperation. Edinburgh, like London, and even more than Manchester, benefited from the UK government's bail out of the failed banks in 2008: the Royal Bank of Scotland, headquartered in Edinburgh was bust. The taxpayer-funded rescue has meant that over the past decade Edinburgh has continued to be an affluent city, where most residents enjoy a high quality of life. Rather than seeking growth through becoming part of a Glasgow metropolis, the public mood in Edinburgh is to keep things as they are.

The election of a Scottish National Party government, as a minority administration 2008–2012 and after 2016, but with a majority 2012–2016, was a factor in stalling pressures for Glasgow–Edinburgh metropolitan strategies. In 2008, the SNP heartland was in the northeast of Scotland, where constituents perceived the Central Belt, long the stronghold of the previous Labour-led Scottish Executive, as being unfairly favored in government spending.

9. Conclusion

The three case studies from the UK not only illustrate general points but also important differences. In all three cases, there is evidence of clustering and more general agglomeration economies. In each case, researchers or commissioned consultant reports have made persuasive cases to public

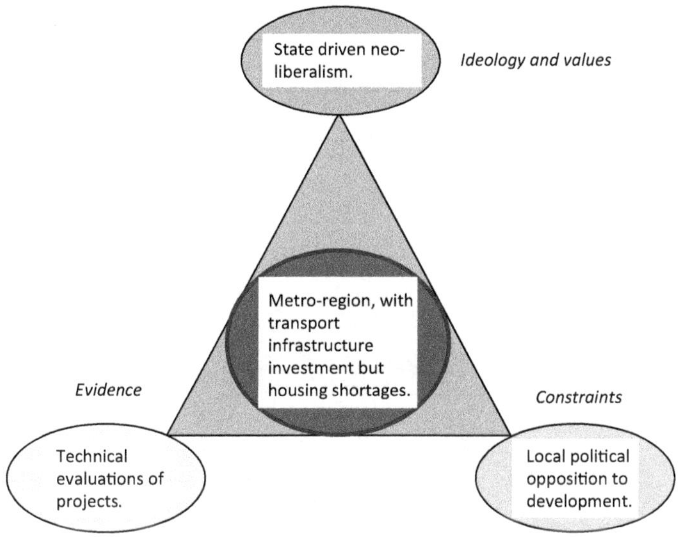

Figure 6. Key relationships and outcomes in the London metropolitan region.

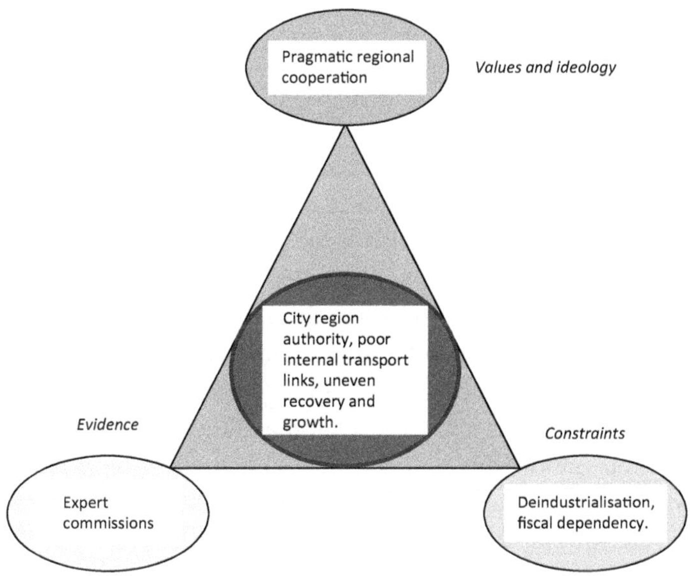

Figure 7. Key relationships and outcomes in the Manchester city region.

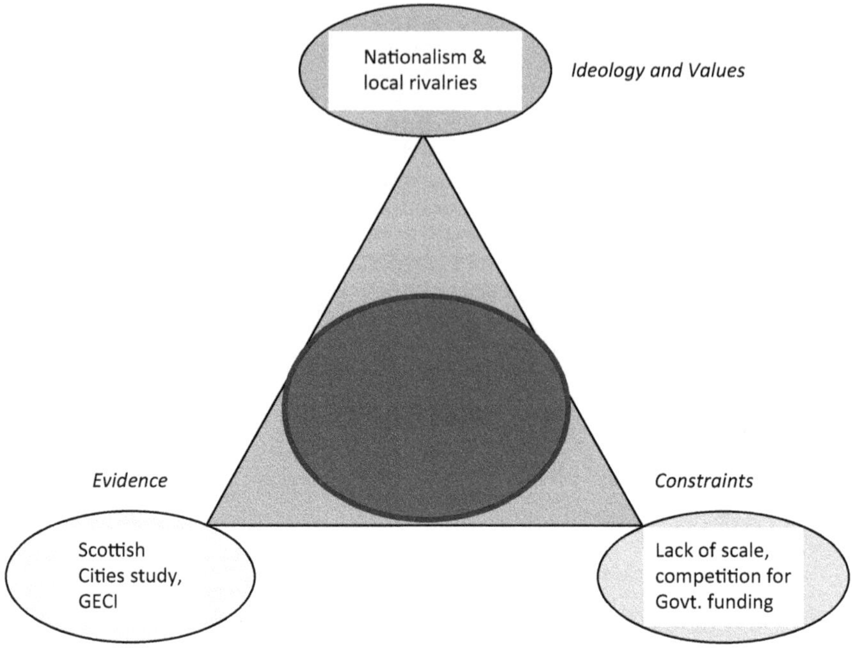

Figure 8. Key relationships and outcomes in Scotland's Central Belt.

policymakers that they should seek to accept and even promote agglomeration so as to grow the economy and enhance national and international competitiveness. The evidence appears to have had most impact in Greater Manchester, where it was used both to draw the 10 councils into agreeing to a Combined Authority, and also to help convince the UK government that the GMCA had a robust approach to public policy-making. In Scotland, somewhat similar advocacy through the Cities Review and the GECI, had some impact, in so far as the Scottish Executive set up a Cities Growth Fund and reinstated a city region scale of spatial planning after 2006. However, the Glasgow City Region and the Edinburgh City Region remain separate entities and both are smaller in population than the Greater Manchester City Region, even if the latter does not include some affluent commuter areas to the south of the main conurbation, an exclusion that is largely for political reasons. The truly metropolitan scale of London and the southeast of England has precluded the need for advocacy of creating

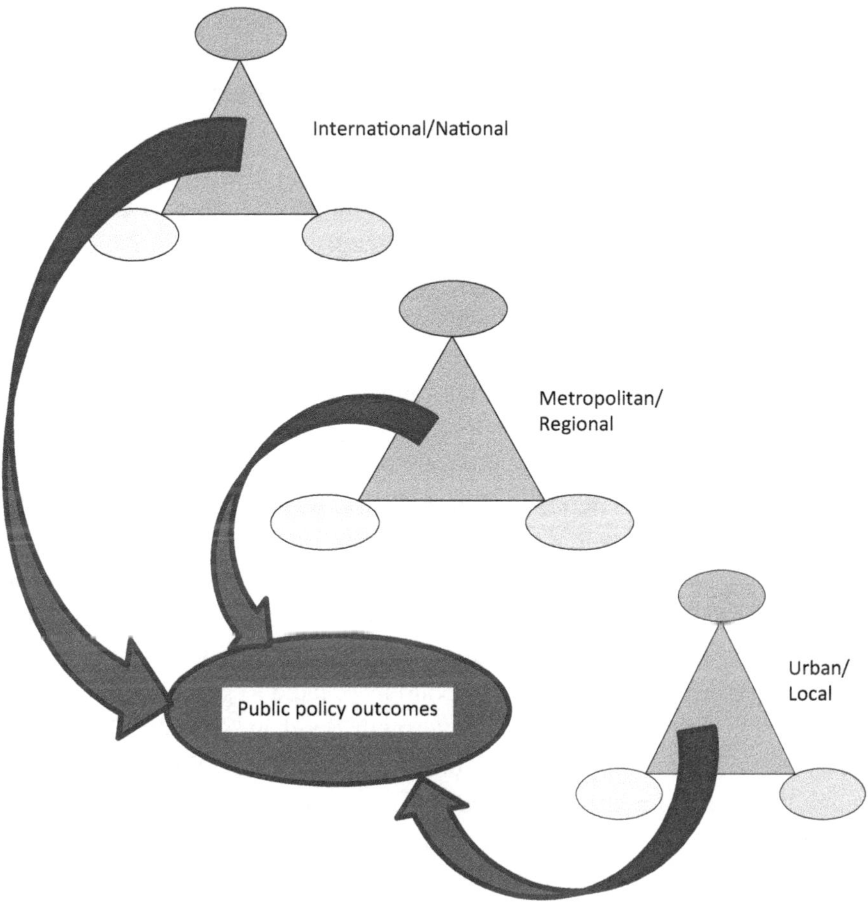

Figure 9. Spatial scales and public policymaking.

a metropolis. Research and evidence instead have largely been directed at making the (usually successful) case for specific infrastructure projects.

The idea of polycentric development, which was advocated by the EU during the 1990s and into the new century, was picked up by researchers in the UK and spatial planning policymakers were also familiar with it. However, ambiguities within the concept itself and the lack of a strong evidence base, meant that it never gained much traction in the UK, and after the financial crisis and the 2010 change of UK government, it virtually disappeared, along with England's Regional Development Agencies and the Northern Way. In none of the three case studies has a spatial strategy played a decisive role in driving metropolitan growth: the spatial dimension of the case for agglomeration has more usually been subsumed by arguments about skills, productivity, or business/tourism promotion.

Ideology has filtered the evidence, and also shaped perceptions of constraints. London, Manchester, and Edinburgh all had local administrations which in the 1980s stood out militantly against the ideology and actions of the Thatcher governments. A generation later they all had administrations that were "business-friendly" and pragmatic in tone. In Manchester, this conversion was central to the attempts to grow through creating market-friendly conditions (agglomeration) rather than through replacing the market with municipal interventions.

Ideology was vital to the interpretation and creation of constraints. Firstly, there were the actions of the Thatcher governments in creating the deregulation of finance that paved the way for "Big Bang" and the opening of London's Docklands to global capital through the work on the ground of the London Docklands Development Corporation. Then came the New Labour era, which showed more interest in Europe and in regional issues, and restored a strategic authority to London, created Regional Development Agencies in England and the City Growth Fund in Scotland. Most crucially New Labour opted to bail out the banks in the financial crisis, a move that most directly supported the largest urban areas, and was then followed after 2010 by austerity policies which held back infrastructure investment in Greater Manchester and in Central Scotland, while also marginalizing the role of strategic spatial planning. Similarly, the centralized nature of the UK state, and of the Scottish government, has ensured that the power of local-level governments to drive their own development agenda is very weak, compared to cities in Europe or North America.

However, not all constraints are rooted in ideology. History and geography have deeply defined the trajectories followed by our three case study regions. Thus, we have one truly global metropolitan region based on London, where successive governments have seen major investment in infrastructure as in the national interest. In Greater Manchester and the wider Northern Way, we have a city region, which is not completely a functional region and lacks connectivity to other city regions that could make them together a counter-pole to London within the UK. Then in Scotland we have two relatively small city regions, where only a spatial planning function in each separately defines them as city regions at all, and the government is proposing to abolish the requirement for such Strategic Development Plans.

Using the analytical framework proposed earlier in this chapter, we can summarize the situations of the three case studies as shown in Figures 6–8. Finally, the study demonstrates the significance and interrelation of different spatial scales in public policy-making, and the way that past policies and the institutional practices and mindsets associated with them can become constraints. This is summarized diagrammatically in Figure 9.

References

Bailey, N., I. Docherty and I. Turok (2002). Dimensions of City Competitiveness: Glasgow and Edinburgh in a UK Context. In *Urban Competitiveness: Policies for Dynamic Cities*, edited by I. Begg. Bristol: The Policy Press.

Ballantyne, E. (2017). A Fintech Cluster Greater Than the Sum of Its Parts. *City A.M.* Retrieved on June 28, 2018 from: http://www.cityam.com/267225/fintech-cluster-greater-than-sum-its-parts-.

Barca, F. (2009). *An Agenda for a Reformed Cohesion Policy: The Barca Report.* Brussels: European Commission.

Centre for Cities (2011). *Cities Outlook.* London: Centre for Cities.

Core Cities (2015). Unlocking the Power of Place, Manchester. *Core Cities.* Retrieved on June 28, 2018 from: https://www.corecities.com/publications/unlocking-power-place.

China Daily (2016). Shanghai to Have the World's Largest Metropolitan Circle in 3 to 5 Years: Report. *China Daily*, December 2, 2016. Retrieved on June 13, 2018 from: http://www.chinadaily.com.cn/m/shanghai/lujiazui/2016-12/02/content_27709315.htm.

Commission of the European Communities (1999). *European Spatial Development Perspective: Towards Balanced and Sustainable Development of the Territory of the European Union.* Luxembourg: Office for Official Publications of the European Commission.

Commission of the European Communities (2008). *Green Paper on Territorial Cohesion: Turning Territorial Diversity into Strength*. Retrieved on June 20, 2018 from: https://eur-lex.europa.eu/legal-content/EN/TXT/PDF/?uri=CELEX:52008DC0616&from=EN.

Davoudi, S. (1999). "Making Sense of the ESDP." *Town and Country Planning* 68, 367–369.

European Commission/UN-Habitat (2016). *The State of European Cities, 2016: Cities Leading the Way to a Better Future*. Brussels: European Commission.

Eurostat (2016). *Urban Europe: Statistics on Cities, Towns and Suburbs*. Luxembourg: Publications Office of the European Union.

Faludi, A. (ed.) (2002). *European Spatial Planning*. Cambridge, Massachusetts: Lincoln Institute of Land Policy.

Faludi, A. and B. Waterhout (2002). *The Making of the European Spatial Development Perspective No Masterplan!* London and New York: Routledge.

Farrell, T. (2008). Bringing Glasgow and Edinburgh Together. *Urban Realm*, June 2008. Retrieved on June 29, 2018 from: http://www.urbanrealm.com/features/190/Bringing_Glasgow_and_Edinburgh_together.html.

Finch, P. and Cann, R. (2013). Linking Glasgow and Edinburgh: The Glasgow–Edinburgh Collaboration Initiative. Paper to the Scottish Transport Applications and Research Conference, 2013. Retrieved on June 29, 2018 from: http://www.starconference.org.uk/star/2013/FinchCann.pdf.

French Presidency (2000). *Contribution to the Debate on the Long-term ESDP Polycentric Vision of Europe. Elaboration of a Long-term Polycentric Vision of the European Space*. Final Report, Volume 2. Paris: DATAR.

Greater Manchester Combined Authority (2014). *Greater Manchester City Deal*. Manchester: GMCA. Retrieved on June 28, 2018 from: https://assets.publishing.service.gov.uk/government/uploads/system/uploads/attachment_data/file/221014/Greater-Manchester-City-Deal-final_0.pdf.

Gu, C., W. Lia and I. Cook (2012). "Progress in Research on Chinese Urbanization." *Frontiers of Architectural Research* 1, 101–149, 10.1016/j.foar.2012.02.13. Retrieved on June 13, 2018 from: https://www.researchgate.net/publication/257737451_Progress_in_research_on_Chinese_urbanization.

Guardian (2018). Greg Hands Quits as Minister to Vote against Heathrow Third Runway. Retrieved on June 21, 2018 from: https://www.theguardian.com/uk-news/2018/jun/21/greg-hands-quits-as-minister-to-vote-against-heathrow-third-runway.

Habitat III (2016). *New Urban Agenda*. Retrieved on June 16, 2018 from: http://habitat3.org/the-new-urban-agenda.

Hall, P. and K. Pain (2006). *The Polycentric Metropolis: Learning from Mega-City Regions in Europe*, London: Earthscan.

Hall, P., M. Breheny, R. McQuaid and D. Hart (1987). *Western Sunrise: The Genesis and Growth of Britain's Major High Tech' Corridor*. London: Allen and Unwin.

Informal Meeting of EU Ministers Responsible for Urban Matters (2016). *Establishing the Urban Agenda for the EU*. Retrieved on June 16, 2018 from: http://ec.europa.eu/regional_policy/sources/policy/themes/urban-development/agenda/pact-of-amsterdam.pdf.

Institute for Public Policy Research (2017). New Transport Figures Reveal London gets £1500 per Head more than the North — but North–West Powerhouse Catching Up. Retrieved on June 28, 2018 from: https://www.ippr.org/news-and-media/press-releases/new-transport-figures-reveal-london-gets-1-500-per-head-more-than-the-north-but-north-west-powerhouse-catching-up.

Jamieson, B. (2014). Edinburgh Glasgow Vision Resurrected. *The Scotsman*, November 5, 2014. Retrieved on June 29, 2018 from: https://www.scotsman.com/news/opinion/bill-jamieson-edinburgh-glasgow-vision-resurrected-1-3595781.

Kloosterman, R. and S. Musterd (2001). "The Polycentric Urban Region: Towards a Research Agenda." *Urban Studies* 38(4), 623–634.

Mayor of London (2004). *The London Plan: Spatial Development Strategy for Greater London*. London: Greater London Authority.

Mayor of London (2017). *The London Plan: Spatial Development Strategy for Greater London*. Draft for Public Consultation, December 2017, London: Greater London Authority.

National Audit Office (2018). Taxpayer Support for UK Banks: FAQs. Retrieved on June 21, 2018 from: https://www.nao.org.uk/highlights/taxpayer-support-for-uk-banks-faqs/.

Noone, V. (2007). *Collaborating to Compete — Glasgow: Edinburgh*. Paper presented at Scotland House, Brussels, November 27, 2007. Brussels: Scotland Europa. Retrieved on June 29, 2018 from: https://portal.scotlandeuropa.com/file/download?id=792.

Nordregio *et al.* (2005). *Potentials for Polycentric Development in Europe*. Final Report of ESPON 2006 Project 1.1.1., Luxembourg: ESPON Monitoring Committee. Retrieved on June 15, 2018 from: https://www.espon.eu/programme/projects/espon-2006/thematic-projects/urban-areas-nodes-polycentric-development.

Northern Way Secretariat (2006). *Moving Forward: The Northern Way — Strategic Directions for Transport*. Newcastle-upon-Tyne: The Northern Way Secretariat. Retrieved on June 28, 2018 from: http://www.transportnorth.org.uk/wp-content/uploads/2014/08/Northern-Way-2007.pdf.

Office of the Deputy Prime Minister, H. M. Treasury, Department of Transport, Department of Trade and Industry, Core Cities and England's Regional Development Agencies (2003). Cities, Regions and Competitiveness. *Second Report from the Working Group of Government Departments, The Core Cities, The Regional Development Agencies*. London: Office of the Deputy Prime Minister.

Pain, K. and S. Vinciguerra (2012). The London Case Study. Working Paper 6, *Territorial Impact of Globalization for Europe and its Regions, ESPON 2013 Applied Research Project 2013/1/1*. Retrieved on June 20, 2018 from: https://www.espon.eu/programme/projects/espon-2013/applied-research/tiger-territorial-impact-globalization-europe-and-its.

Quilley, S. (2000). "Manchester First: From Municipal Socialism to the Entrepreneurial City." *International Journal of Urban and Regional Research* 24, 601–615.

Rees, J. and A. Harding (2010). *The Case for Agglomeration Economies in Europe: Appendix C2 — Manchester Case Study, ESPON 2013 Targeted Analysis Project 2013/2/1*. Retrieved on June 21, 2018 from: https://www.espon.eu/programme/projects/espon-2013/targeted-analyses/caee-case-agglomeration-economies-europe.

Scottish Executive (2002). *Review of the Cities: The Analysis*. Edinburgh: Scottish Executive.

Scottish Executive (2003). *Building Better Cities: Delivering Growth and Opportunities*. Edinburgh: Scottish Executive.

SQW (2011). *The Evaluation of the Northern Way, 2008–11: Final Report — Full Report*. Newcastle-upon-Tyne: One North-East.

Townroe, P. (1999). "Rising Real Incomes and Enough Jobs: The Contribution of a British National Spatial Planning Framework." *Town Planning Review* 70(3), 295–312.

Williams, G. (1995). "Prospecting for Gold: Manchester's City Pride Experience." *Planning Practice and Research* 10, 345–358.

World Bank (2009). "Reshaping Economic Geography." *World Development Report*, 2009, Washington, DC: The International Bank for Reconstruction and Development/The World Bank.

Zhang Laiming (2015). Substantially Improving the Development of Metropolitan Circle. *Development Research Centre of the State Council of the People's*

Republic of China. Retrieved on June 13, 2018 from: http://www.chinadaily.com.cn/m/drc/2015-07/28/content_21432070.htm.

Zhou Xian (2017). From Urbanization to Urban Agglomeration — Based on a Comparative Analysis of Population Density in Four Metropolitan Areas. *Development Research Centre of the State Council of the People's Republic of China*. Retrieved on June 13, 2018 from: http://www.chinadaily.com.cn/m/drc/2017-10/09/content_33017887.htm.

Chapter 4

Planning Mega-Regions in China and India

Xuefei Ren

Associate Professor of Sociology & Global Urban Studies,
Michigan State University, USA
renxuefe@msu.edu

1. Introduction

In June 2018, the *Economist* magazine ran an article about China's emerging mega-regions — large clusters of urban agglomeration sprawling over thousands of square kilometers and housing hundreds of millions of residents.[1] These mega-regions are engines of China's economic growth and they could transform the country into an affluent and innovative powerhouse (Figure 1). Some of the mega-regions are more organically integrated, such as the Yangtze River Delta (YRD) and the Pearl River Delta (PRD), some are less integrated, such as the Jing–Jin–Ji (Beijing–Tianjin–Hebei) region, and others are not yet formed and it is the central government's hope that these will develop into more integrated mega-regions in the near future, such as the urban clusters of Wuhan–Changsha–Nanchang in central China, and Xi'ning–Lanzhou in western China. The same article also highlights some of the unique features of Chinese

[1]Retrieved on July 5, 2018 from: https://www.economist.com/china/2018/06/23/china-is-trying-to-turn-itself-into-a-country-of-19-super-regions.

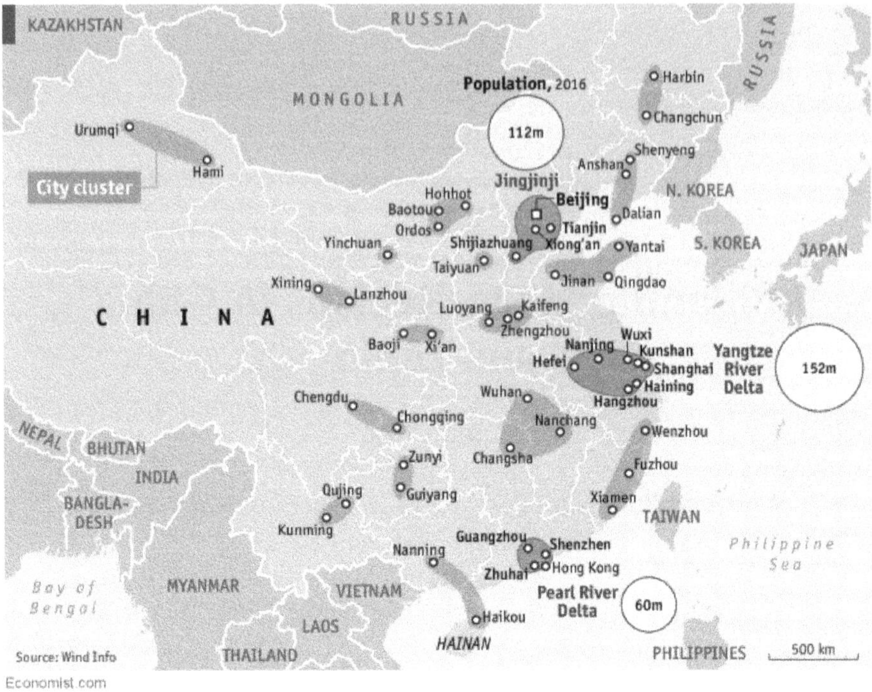

Figure 1. Mega-regions in China.
Source: Economist.

mega-regions: besides its gigantic scale, large population and vast territories, Chinese mega-regions also feature strong top-down intervention by the central government, as seen in the massive investment in high-speed rail that seamlessly links cities together, the building of new towns such as Xiong'an outside Beijing (Zou and Zhao, 2018), as well as various strategic plans promoting coordinated mega-regional development.

The scale of urbanization in China might be unprecedented, but the top-down approach to developing mega-regions is not unique to China. China's largest neighboring country, India, has also launched ambitious programs in recent years to develop economically competitive mega-regions. In the mid-2000s, the central government of India announced to build strategic industrial corridors that link India's major metropolitan cities such as Mumbai, Delhi, Chennai, and Bangalore, in order to improve infrastructure, promote manufacturing, and attract investment.

The leading initiative, Delhi–Mumbai Industrial Corridor (DMIC), is the largest infrastructure project in the world, and if completed, the Delhi and Mumbai metropolitan regions will be merged into one mega-region, with two dozen smaller (but not small) manufacturing cities and new towns built along the 1,500 km stretch in between the two metropolitan areas, attracting hundreds of millions of new urban residents. Since 2014, the DMIC has also been incorporated as part of the Modi government's "Make in India" campaign, the aim of which is to boost the country's manufacturing capacity and attract foreign investment. It is not unthinkable that DMIC will one day become a mega-region the size of China's YRD or PRD, with a dense cluster of networked cities.

Since the last quarter of the 20th century, China and India have experienced rapid urban growth. The combined urban population in both countries has topped 1 billion, and today one out of 6 people in the world lives in urban areas in China and India. Driven by migration and *in situ* urbanization, the two countries have seen rapid growth of cities of all sizes, and also the emergence of mega-regions of densely networked urban clusters (Figures 2 and 3). Mega-region planning in China and India have significant consequences not only for national and regional economic

Figure 2. NASA nightlight image, China.

Source: NASA (2016).

Figure 3. NASA nightlight image, India.
Source: NASA (2016).

development but also on the quality of life and social welfare of hundreds of millions of residents. This chapter compares mega-region planning and governance in China and India, by focusing on three major questions identified in the scholarship, that is, the rationale, key actors, and mechanisms of mega-region planning (Harrison and Holyer, 2014). First, why has mega-region development become a top priority for the national government of China and India in recent years? Second, who are the key decision-makers in mega-region planning and governance? And third, through what mechanisms are policies and projects of mega-region development implemented in each context? I will use the DMIC and Guangzhou–Shenzhen Innovation Corridor (GSIC) as examples to illustrate how China and India differently plan and govern their mega-regions.

The comparative analysis finds that in spite of the different regime types, that India is a democracy and China is not, the planning of mega-regions in both countries features a strong top-down approach, with the central government taking the lead and dominating major decision-making regarding when, where, and how to develop mega-regions. In India, the new initiatives of mega-region planning focus on manufacturing, while in China, mega-region planning serves multiple goals of industrial upgrading, promoting regional competitiveness, minimizing inter-city competition, and promoting environmental sustainability, as envisioned by the central government. At the sub-national level, however, the implementation of mega-region initiatives assumes two distinct trajectories, reflecting the different central–local governmental relations in the two countries. In China, where significant decentralization has taken place over the four decades of the market reform, municipal governments are vested with significant power to implement the central government's strategic plans for coordinated regional development; by comparison, in India where the devolution of power and authority from state to municipal governments has not advanced much, municipal governments are sidelined, and instead, state governments create new agencies comprising public and private partnerships to supervise mega-region planning and project implementation. Both models are unlikely to produce the ideal mega-regions that central planners in China and India are hoping for: competitive clusters of cities linked by efficient transportation infrastructure, which complement on each other's strength and together they provide good business climate and also high quality of living for residents. In China, despite the government rhetoric over "coordinated development" (协调发展), jurisdictional fragmentation and inter-city competition will continue to be the norm because of the lack of regional governing bodies with real power and authority and control over budgets. In India, not empowering municipal governments will turn mega-region planning into industrialization projects led by state governments, and the new residents of mega-regions will suffer from the old problem of poor infrastructure and service delivery if without an elected local government with substantive fiscal capacity.

I will briefly review the literature on mega-region planning and governance in the next section. Then I will discuss the different trajectories of urbanization and governance in China and India, focusing specifically on the uneven processes of decentralization and inter-governmental relations. This is followed by two case studies of mega-region planning — the DMIC and GSIC, with which I will examine how the mega-region planning is implemented differently in the two countries. The concluding section compares the governing structures, rationale, and mechanisms of mega-regional planning and discusses what the current approaches to building competitive mega-regions mean for the quality of life of urban residents.

2. From Megalopolis to Mega-Regions

The phenomenon of sprawling urban landscapes comprising interconnected metropolitan areas can be traced back to at least the mid-20th century. In his classical urban planning textbook, Jean Gottman coined the word "megalopolis" — derived from Greek, meaning very large cities — to describe the urbanized landscape of the East Coast in the United States that extends from Boston to Washington, DC (Gottmann, 1961). The megalopolis of the mid-20th century presented a new kind of economic scale of multiple metropolitan areas of central cities and their surrounding suburbs (Figure 4). After the 1980s, a number of other terms have been

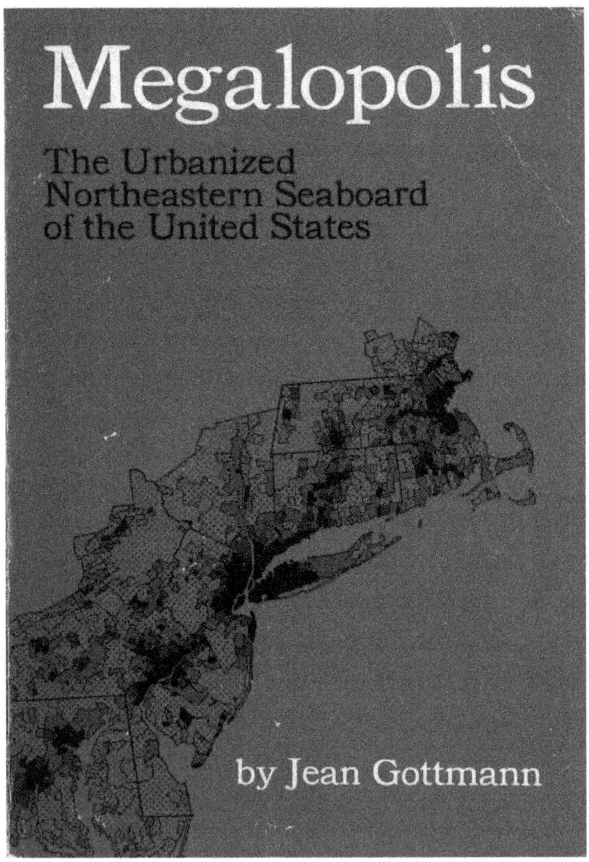

Figure 4. Megalopolis, Jean Gottman.

invented to describe the phenomenon of clustered urban networks and the role they play in the global economy, such as global city regions, mega-city regions, and mega-regions (Harrison and Hoyler, 2015). While global city regions (with more emphasis on their function) and mega-city regions (with more emphasis on their large population) refer to metropolitan areas of single urban systems — such as New York or Tokyo metropolitan region, mega-regions are often used to describe clustered urban networks of two or more urban systems, such as the Rio–Sao Paulo, Seoul–Pusan, and Tokyo–Osaka mega-regions (Harrison and Hoyler, 2015). In this sense, mega-regions are similar to what Jean Gottman had in mind when coining the term "megalopolis." In China, planners frequently use "urban clusters" (城市群) or "metropolitan circles" (都市圈) to denote mega-regions of two or more urban systems interconnected by transportation, infrastructure, and flows of people, capital, and economic activities. The largest mega-region in the world is the PRD in South China, comprising 9 major cities and more than 120 million residents (Xu and Yeh, 2011a). In India, policymakers and planners more often use metropolitan areas or mega-cities than mega-regions, partly because it is a relatively new thinking, on the part of the central government, to connect metropolitan areas with targeted infrastructure planning and turn them into continuous mega-zones of city regions.

If the phenomenon of continuous clusters of networked cities is not new, why have mega-regions attracted increasing policy and research attention in recent years? At least three reasons can be identified. First, in many countries, mega-regions are the engines of the national economy and they account for the majority of the national total economic output. This was the situation in the 20th century but in the early 21st century, the economic contribution of mega-regions to the national and global economy has become even more prominent. YRD, for example, occupies less than 6% of the national land, but produces more than 35% of China's GDP. Second, because of their increasingly powerful economic output, the stakes seem to be higher too, as many national governments are more involved in mega-region planning, often with multi-billion-dollar investment plans in infrastructure alone. Third, besides economic significance and central government intervention, some argue that the mega-region has also become a "new spatial format" of globalization, i.e., a particular scale at which the global economy operates (Sassen, 2009). In the introduction to a recently published book entitled *Megaregions*: *Globalization's New Urban Form?* geographers John Harrison and Michael Hoyler point out that mega-regions are the "latest episode in the long-running political-economic drama that is the search for a post-national spatial/scalar fix for globalized capital accumulation and organizing (inter)national space economies" (Harrison and Hoyler, 2015, p. 4). Mega-regions have attracted increasing attention, from both policymakers and academics, precisely because they present a novel scale and strategic terrain for global capital accumulation and state intervention (Xu and Yeh, 2011b).

Many believe that planning at the mega-region level can be a silver bullet serving multiple ambitious goals. These include strengthening regional competitiveness, attracting investment, planning integrated infrastructure, ensuring environmental sustainability, improving urban quality of life, as well as strengthening democratic values (Scott and Storper, 2003; Hall and Pain, 2006; Jonas and Ward, 2007). The advantage of mega-regions is not only about the agglomeration economy — bigger scale, more of the same, but rather, it is also because they contain a mixture of cities with different strengths, so that global firms can allocate their operations in these different cities to take advantage of what they can offer, for example, affordable housing market, lower manufacturing and labor costs in less developed cities, and advanced producer services and availability of a highly educated labor force in the more developed cities (Sassen, 2007). Sassen (2009) argues that global firms do not have to outsource more labor-intensive work to overseas if they can allocate their operations in smaller, cheaper cities or rural areas in mega-regions in the United States. In other words, the mega-region scale can connect "winners and laggards," and therefore, it can have some equalizing effect that the global scale does not have (Sassen, 2009).

In spite of the potential advantages, planning and governing at the mega-region scale has often been a challenge. In the United States, Regional Plan Association (RPA) launched *America 2050* project in 2005, identifying 11 mega-regions as prototypes for balanced and sustainable growth for the first half of the 21st century (Figure 5). The background for the initiative was lack of federal funding for large-scale transportation infrastructure, and by citing international examples such as high-speed rail investment in Europe and China, the RPA made policy

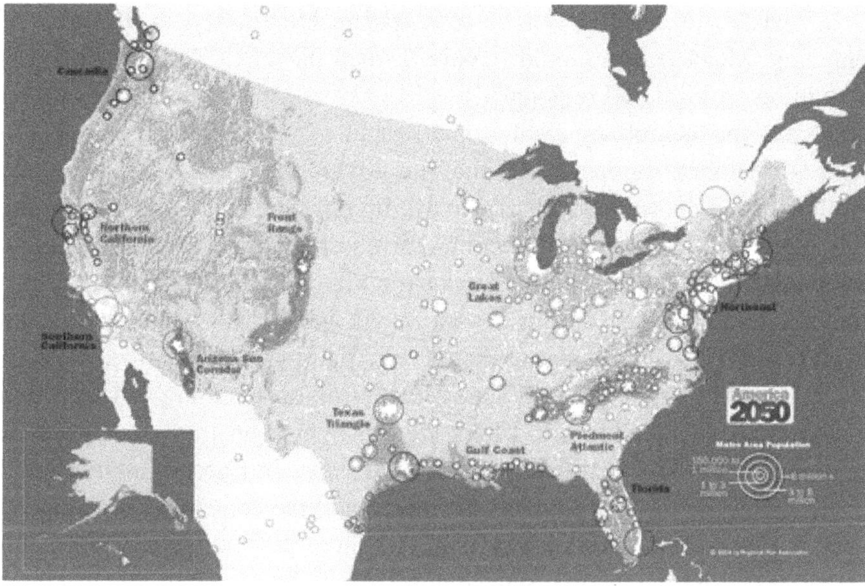

Figure 5. Mega-regions in the United States, by *America 2050.*
Source: Regional Plan Association.

recommendations on investing in high-speed rail in some of the identified mega-regions with large ridership (Ross, 2009). However, more than a decade has passed since the launch of *America 2050*, the RPA's recommendation still stays at the proposal stage, as there are no signs of any commitment from the federal government in mega-region infrastructure planning.

Some argue that integrated mega-regions as strategic actors in the US are unlikely to emerge. Instead, we will continue to see sprawling, polycentric urban areas internally fragmented under various jurisdictions (Wachsmuth, 2015). The critics of mega-region governance point out that the quotidian demands of American families — for jobs, healthcare, and quality schools — make mega-region planning rather abstract and that local communities are unlikely to show support for any initiative of planning at the mega-region scale (Glass, 2015). Yet, others question the many virtues afforded to mega-region planning, such as environmental sustainability. Wheeler (2015) wrote that, "rather than being seduced by mega-regional analysis and technologies such as high-speed rail, the need is for policymakers to develop visions of a sustainable society at all scales of planning. Mega-region should remain a small player … and the emphasis should be on local and regional" (p. 114). Overall, the critics point out, on one hand, the lack of any institutional structure in the US that is capable to plan at the mega-region scale (Schafran, 2014), and on the other hand, the neoliberal and boosteristic rhetoric in the discourse on mega-region planning that often prioritizes economic competitiveness, increased mobility, global integration over qualify of life for local communities. Uncritical development of infrastructure, some critics warn, will lead to more urban sprawl and even social and climate catastrophe (Hesse, 2015; Wheeler, 2015).

Compared to the United States, mega-region planning is much less abstract in Europe and Asia, where there is a stronger tradition of spatial planning at the supranational and national scale. In Europe, international spatial planning has long been legitimized and the concern over balanced regional growth, as exemplified in the notion of polycentric development, continues to dominate the discussion in spatial planning (Faludi, 2009). In Asia, many central governments actively intervene in forging competitive mega-regions, by formulating strategic plans and allocating funding for infrastructure investment (McGee and Robinson, 1995; Douglass, 2000; Yang, 2009; Li and Wu, 2012a; Park, 2013). One early example from the 1960s is Tokyo–Osaka mega-region, linked by high-speed rail and producing much of Japan's national economic output. More recent examples are China and India, both of which are trying to forge their own competitive mega-regions with state-of-the-art infrastructure that will hopefully become the magnets for global investment.

Can China and India build their dream mega-regions with balanced division of labor among cities, as Sassen (2007, 2009) articulated, mega-zones that can provide different advantages for global firms to locate their various operations? Different from the US, metropolitan areas in China and India present a very different portfolio of cities, from global cities with significant agglomeration of advanced producer services, to less developed cities with cheaper land, housing, and low-wage labor. But in order to forge a competitive mega-region, it is not enough just to have different kinds of cities, and what is also needed is to build innovative governing frameworks at the mega-region level. The current inter-governmental relations in both countries present significant challenges for any governing framework at the mega-regional level to emerge — in China, municipal governments have too much power, and in India, they have too little power and it is the regional state governments that control urban affairs including mega-region planning. The next section will examine in more detail the inter-governmental relations in each country, which provide the large context for the challenges of mega-region planning and governance.

3. Urbanization and Governance in China and India

Both China and India have witnessed significant restructuring in urban governance in the last few decades, with the central government devolving substantial power and authority to the sub-national governments. But devolution in China took place under the single-party system and it has advanced much more than that in India. After the market reform was launched in China in 1978, decision-making power and authority has been gradually but steadily shifted from central ministries to local territorial authorities, especially municipal governments. By comparison, in India the central government devolved power and authority to the regional state governments, but the state governments did not relinquish or share power with their municipal governments. As a result, urban affairs — including infrastructure, land, and housing development — are still firmly under the control of state governments. The difference in the extent and degree of devolution provides the larger contexts for understanding why mega-regions in China and India are planned and governed differently and what specific challenges they face.

In the socialist period (1949–1978), the Chinese governing regime was organized along a vertical system of government ministries and horizontal territorial authorities, such as provinces, prefectures, and cities. This system, widely referred to as "tiaotiao-kuaikuai" (条条块块), constituted the basic administrative grid that governed from the socialist period through the reform period (Lieberthal, 2004). In terms of territorial authorities, China's administrative hierarchy was characterized by a two-level structure composed of central and local governments. All major national policy decisions were made by the central government. The local encompassed a wide range of administrative ranks from provinces, prefectures, and cities, to counties, towns, and villages. During the socialist planned economy, local governments had little real power even in the decision-making of development policies in their own territories.

In the market reform era beginning in 1978, the reorganization of state power has gradually taken place along both vertical and horizontal administrative lines. The central government shifted decision-making and financial responsibilities away from central ministries to lower levels of state administration, although it still maintains control over local governments through legislative and personnel appointing systems. The central government gave municipal governments more autonomy over urban policy so that they can attract investment and promote local economic development. From the 1980s, many empowered municipal governments began to annex their surrounding rural counties, through mechanisms such as "converting counties to cities," "city-administering counties," and "turning counties into urban districts" (Ma, 2005; Shen, 2005, 2007). The annexation of rural counties opened new frontiers for municipal governments to promote property development, generate more revenue through land leasing, and also tap into the resources of their hinterlands. It also facilitated the development of mega-regions as cities extend their industrial, construction, and other activities from the central districts to the urban periphery.

Despite similar efforts made by the Indian central government to devolve power to municipal governments, the authority and resources required for urban development remain in the hands of state governments. In 1992, the central government adopted the 74th Amendment to the Indian Constitution, in order to devolve substantive power and resources to municipal governments. Yet India's municipalities and metropolitan regions remain largely disempowered. Although the framers of the Indian Constitution identified federalism as one of the five core elements of the independent Indian nation state (along with sovereignty, democracy, socialism, and secularism), the three-tier federalist structure was left incomplete, defining responsibilities only for the central and state governments (Corbridge and Harriss, 2000; Tummala 1992; Verney 1995). Concerned about regional fragmentation along religious, ethnic, or linguistic lines, they granted considerable power to the regional states, in part to hold the union together (Stepan, 1999). Urban development — including housing, infrastructure, economic development, and poverty alleviation — was a field to be financed and implemented by the regional states. Although regional states could choose to devolve power and resources to municipalities, most did not. The competitive stance between regional states and municipalities arises in part from inter-party competition. While devolution in China is simplified by the unified party structure, the rescaling of power in India often entails the handing of power from one political party to another. But some observe that even when state and municipal governments are ruled by the same party, state-level politicians still jealously guard their power and are unwilling to share power with lower-level municipal governments (Ren and Weinstein, 2013).

The political weakness of India's municipal governments also stems from colonial legacies and an inherent fear of the local. Prior to independence, municipalities were organized to carry out basic service-delivery functions, while the more substantive powers were retained by the colonial (presidency) government, particularly the land use powers and industrial policy, which would directly impact the colonial economy. When power was handed from the British Raj to the independent Indian nation state in 1947, the real authority over urban municipal bodies was transferred from the colonial presidencies to the regional state governments, while municipalities remained primarily service-delivery bodies (Pinto and Pinto, 2005). The decision not to empower the local scale was also a deliberate one, rooted in an anti-local bias. Although Gandhi famously asserted that India "lives in her villages," most of the English-educated delegates to the Constitutional Assembly, including the first Prime Minister, Jawaharlal Nehru, perceived India's villages to be backward, archaic, and inherently corrupt. They believed that local elites (in both villages and cities) organize power on the basis of communal sentiments, rather than on enlightened democratic principles. The less local the political system, the more democratic many believed it would be (Corbridge and Harriss, 2000).

Beginning in the 1980s, however, the pressure to devolve authority and resources to the local level began to emerge from two disparate corners: pro-democracy social activists and pro-liberalization economic reformers. In the mid-1980s, development economists and social activists began making the connection between India's rampant inequalities and the lack of political representation at the local level (Drèze and Sen, 1995, 2002; Plummer, 2000; Heller, 2005). Democratic deepening, it was argued, would ensure political participation and more equitable resource allocation. In the wake of India's adoption of economic liberalization reforms in 1991, the political movement to empower India's municipalities was reinvigorated; this time recast as a component of structural adjustment. Included in the package of reforms advocated by the International Monetary Fund (IMF), political decentralization was identified as a precondition for liberalization, diminishing the authority of the central government, introducing a greater role for the private sector, and enabling more openness to foreign investment. With support from these strange political bedfellows, the 73rd and 74th Amendments, defining a wider scope of authority for rural localities and urban municipalities, were adopted in 1992. Yet with the central government merely encouraging implementation of the amendments, few regional states have chosen to enact the reforms. This is particularly true in the domain of urban development, where regional states have chosen to retain the budgets and many key powers associated with land, housing, and infrastructure schemes (Ren and Weinstein, 2013).

The different processes of state rescaling — power reshuffling among different scales of the state — are also shaping how China and India plan and govern their mega-regions. In China, with decision-making power and authority over urban affairs largely concentrated in the hands of municipal governments, they are the key actors that implement the central government's strategic plans for coordinated mega-regional development. When the interests of specific cities are not well represented, or in conflict with the central government's strategic plans, municipalities often refuse to incorporate the central government's spatial policies in their own municipal plans. In India, with state governments as the leading actors for mega-region planning, municipal governments are sidelined and excluded from major decision-making. The next section will use two case studies to examine how the top-down approach to developing mega-regions in China and India is differently implemented.

4. The World's Largest Infrastructure Project: DMIC

The Indian government launched a number of industrial corridor projects in the mid-2000s, to promote export-oriented manufacturing, improve infrastructure, and attract foreign investment. With an estimated investment of $90 billion, the DMIC is the largest industrial corridor planned in India, and also the largest infrastructure investment project in the world.[2] The project aims to build a series of industrial clusters, residential new towns, and logistic hubs in a buffer zone of 150–200 km on either side of the Western Dedicated Freight Corridor linking Delhi and Mumbai, two of the most developed metropolitan areas in the country.[3] The corridor expands over six states, including both economic powerhouses such as Gujarat, Maharashtra, Haryana, and some less developed states such as Uttar Pradesh, Rajasthan, and Madhya Pradesh (Figure 6). One of the major goals of the project is to create a competitive manufacturing belt to attract global capital investment, by utilizing the comparative advantages of the fast-growing states and laggard states. The DMIC is the flagship program of Modi's "Make in India" campaign launched in 2014. It is introducing a new scale of urban settlement in India, that of mega-regions. With 24 industrial zones and 8 smart cities currently under planning, it will accommodate an additional urbanized population of 231 million by 2030 (Mukhopadhyay, 2017).

The industrial corridor projects are the latest attempts by the Indian government to foster manufacturing capacity to attract investment. Following the East Asian model of export-oriented manufacturing, India has long been trying to improve its manufacturing sector to enhance its economic competitiveness. In the early 2000s, it experimented with Special Economic Zones (SEZs), following the footsteps of China and other Asian countries, but SEZs in India did not deliver the results of boosting export-oriented industrial production, as hoped by planners and policymakers. One major hurdle was land acquisition, which was left for private developers and investors and the process was often wrought with difficulty and contention (Chakravorty, 2013; Ren, 2017; Balakrishnan, 2019). To address the issue of land acquisition, the central government decided to have state governments take the lead of land provision, and the industrial corridor projects emerged from this context, with state governments, instead of private sectors, in

[2]Other industrial corridor projects in India include Bengaluru–Mumbai, Amritsar–Kolkata, Chennai–Bengaluru, East Coast, and Visakhapatnam–Chennai Industrial Corridors.
[3]http://dmicdc.com.

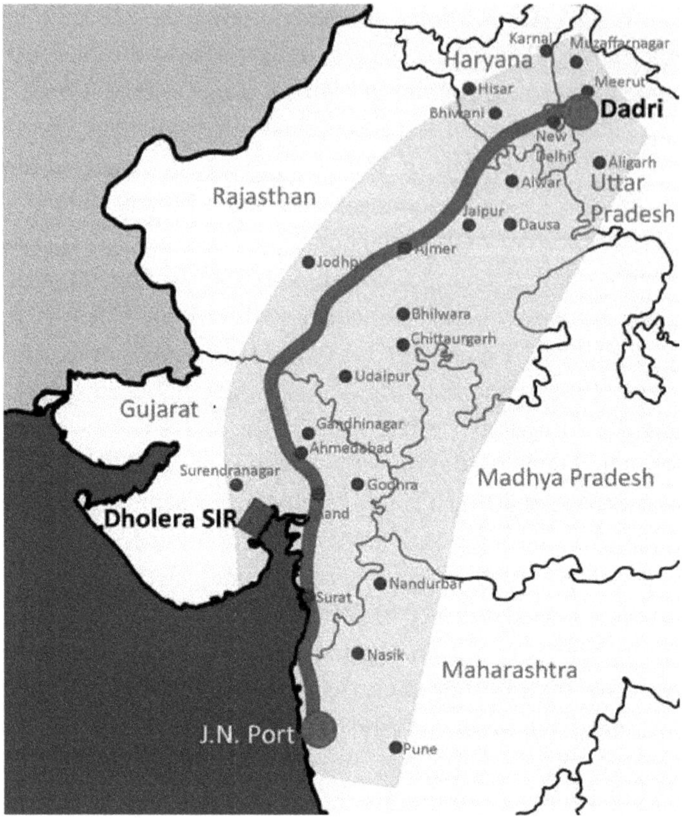

Figure 6. Delhi–Mumbai industrial corridor.
Source: DIPP.

charge of land acquisition. Some are critical of the industrial corridor projects, as the critics argue that India cannot really compete with China and other East Asian countries in export-oriented manufacturing, and it also faces new rivals such as Vietnam and Bangladesh that offer competitive labor costs for low-end manufacturing; India should certainly grow its manufacturing capacity but the target should be the domestic instead of the global market (Rajan, 2014). But in spite of the critics, the central government is determined to proceed with the industrial corridor projects and a few major industrial townships are already under construction as part of the DMIC.

The governing structure of DMIC features two layers of the central and state governments (Figure 7). At the central level, the Department of Industrial Promotion and Policy and the Ministry of Commerce and Industry take the lead and they decide the scope of investment and locations of the planned investment areas in each of the six states. In spite of the rhetoric of promoting urbanization, the Department of Urban Development is not included as a supervising agency for the DMIC (Anand and Sami, 2016). A Special Purpose Vehicle (SPV) — DMIC Development Corporation — has been set up and acts as the nodal agency overseeing the planning and implementation of the project. The DMIC Development Corporation is a public–private partnership, comprising the Department of Industrial Policy and Promotion, Japan Bank — Japan is a major donor for the project, Housing and Urban Development Corporation, India Infrastructure Finance Company, and Life Insurance Corporation of India as shareholders (Figure 7). Different state governments have appointed special agencies to supervise project planning and implementation within their states, such as the Gujarat Infrastructure Development Board (GIDB), the Bureau of Investment Promotion in Rajasthan, and the Maharashtra Industrial Development Corporation. The central government provides seed funding to finance the first phase of the development, and it is hoped that subsequent stages of development will be financed with land value appreciation.[4] International consultants and private–public partnerships play important roles too, becoming new partners in the emerging governance structure, and the central and state governments have to engage and coordinate with these new actors (Anand and Sami, 2015, 2016).

This two-layered institutional framework does not leave much space for including municipal governments in the decision-making. There is little coordination between state governments and the cities that will be affected by the DMIC project. As most decision-making takes places at the central and state levels, planners and policymakers in individual cities located within the DMIC are often not aware of how they are going to be affected. Local planning authorities did not modify their master plans anticipating the impact of DMIC (Anand and Sami, 2015, 2016). To avoid

[4] *Ibid.*

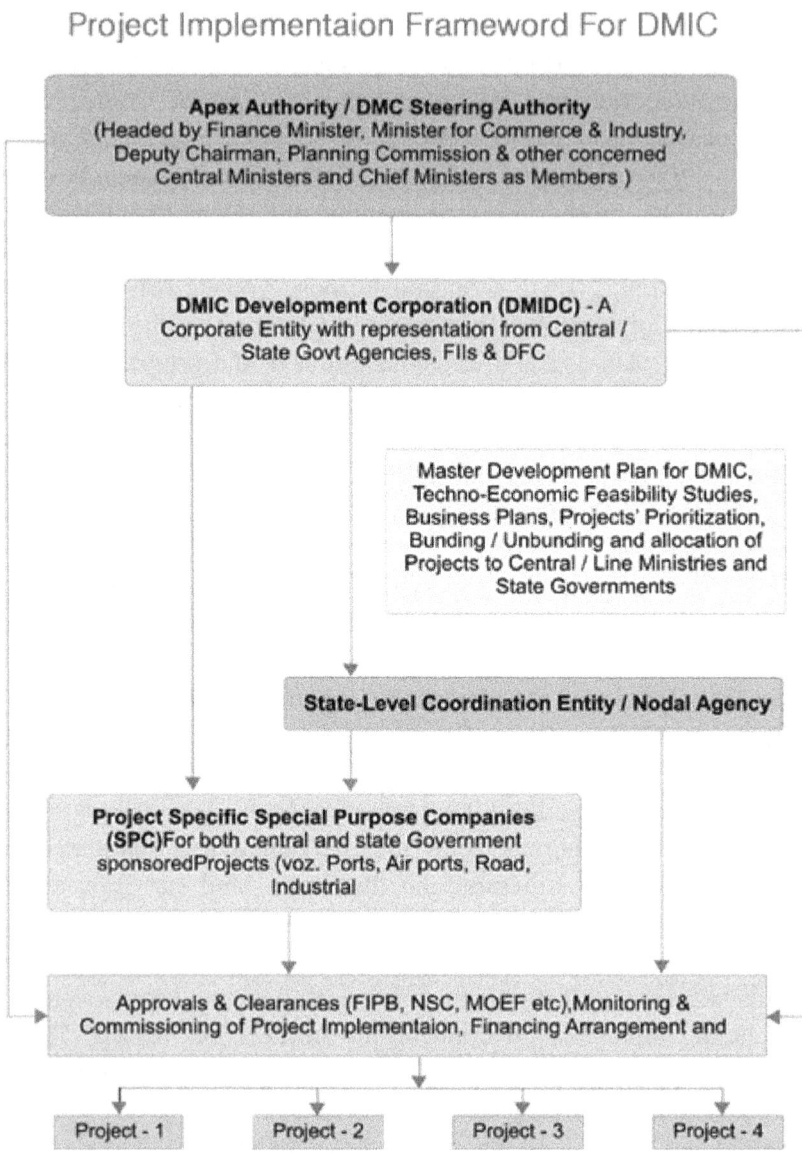

Figure 7. The governing structure of the Delhi–Mumbai industrial corridor.
Source: DMIC Development Corporation.

the difficulty with land acquisition, much of the investment is directed to greenfield sites. When new cities are planned on greenfield sites, no elected governments are formed and it is the regional development authorities, with their members appointed by the state governments, which oversee the investment and construction activities in these new cities developed along the industrial corridor (Anand and Sami, 2016). City-level SPVs are set up, acting as a single window for facilitating approvals required from private investors and developers, but these SPVs are also controlled by state governments.

Dholera, a newly planned Special Investment Region in Gujarat, illustrates how the two-layered governance structures works. Located in the Ahmedabad district, Dholera was designated by the central government in 2009 as a Special Investment Region and a global manufacturing hub is going to be constructed here with world-class infrastructure. Dholera is also hailed as India's first smart city, and at the 2013 Vibrant Gujarat Investors Summit, Prime Minister Modi commented that Dholera would be developed better than Delhi and six times bigger than Shanghai.[5] The nodal supervising agency in charge is the state-level GIDB headed by the Chief Minister. Core functions of the GIDB include approvals of land use plans, town planning schemes, and development plans of the Special Investment Region. Under this apex authority, the Dholera Industrial City Development Ltd. — an SPV of public–private partnership — was set up to supervise investment and project implementation. The central government provides seed funding and the state government is responsible for land acquisition. The projected development period is from 2016 to 2024, during which dozens of infrastructural projects such as ports, airports, expressways will be constructed within an area of 920 km^2. In its glossy brochure, it states that the joint venture company between central and state governments will also be "vested with municipal powers" and "eventually mature into a full-fledged local body for the city."[6] This implies that there is little effort to establish an elected local governing body for the new city, and the state-level nodal agency will continue to manage all aspects of urban affairs in this India's

[5] https://www.dholera-smart-city.com.

[6] *Ibid.*

first smart city. Mega-region planning, as illustrated in this case, is purely an undertaking by the central and state governments, and municipalities are largely absent, in a paradoxical way, from the planned urban mega-region of the DMIC.

5. Building China's Silicon Valley: The Guangzhou–Shenzhen Innovation Corridor

Similar to India, there has been growing interest in China for mega-regional planning since the mid-2000s. But different from India where manufacturing is the main focus for the planning of industrial corridors, in China, mega-regional planning serves multiple ambitious goals, such as upgrading the economy from low-end to advanced manufacturing, coordinating regional economic development, minimizing inter-city competition, and promoting environmental sustainability (Wu and Zhang, 2007; Wu, 2016). Such interest for planned mega-regional development is especially strong in the YRD and the PRD, the two largest mega-regions with densely networked clusters of cities. Compared to the YRD (Zhang, 2006), where cities fall under different jurisdictions such as Shanghai municipality, Jiangsu, Zhejiang and Anhui provinces, all major cities in the PRD are in the same Guangdong province, and being under the same provincial leadership has made it easier to plan and coordinate economic activities within the PRD mega-region. The PRD has thus become the pioneer in mega-region planning in China and its various strategies for coordinating regional development have been well studied (Xu, 2008; Xu and Yeh, 2010; 2011a; Ye, 2013, 2014; Zhang, 2015).

The central government and municipal governments are the two leading actors in mega-region planning in the PRD. Through formulating and approving strategic plans, the central government is interested not only in enhancing the competitiveness of the region but also in regaining some control over regional economic development, especially regarding land use planning (Xu, 2008). In 2008, the State Council approved is the "Outline Plan for the Reform and Development of the PRD 2008–2020" (Guangdong Provincial Government, 2008), which identifies a list of key projects aimed for regional integration and coordinated development — ranging from transportation infrastructure investment, environmental protection, urban–rural development to service delivery (Ye, 2013, 2014). Different from the central government, municipal governments are more concerned with economic growth within their jurisdictions, but they are incentivized to follow the Outline Plan, because this way they can garner support from the central government for various development projects in their cities. High-speed rail construction is such an example — transportation planning is an integral part of most strategic plans for mega-regional development, and local governments compete with one another to seek the central government's support to link their cities with the national high-speed rail network. To implement the Outline Plan, a special task force was set up at the provincial level, with members including the provincial chief and all of the nine prefecture-level city mayors in the PRD. Time-bound targets were set up and city officials are evaluated annually by provincial-level officials over the progress of implementation of the key projects in their cities (Ye, 2013).

What is missing from the two-tiered governance structure is a set of regional governing institutions with substantive decision-making power and control over budgets. Without such regional-level institutions, integrated mega-regional development is unlikely to be achieved. But under China's current administrative hierarchy, neither the central government nor municipal governments are willing to concede power to any regional-level governing institutions even if they are set up. As there is little interaction and information exchange between cities, local governments tend to fall back to the old norm of competition instead of collaboration (Luo and Shen, 2008; Cheung, 2012; Li and Wu, 2012b).

The GSIC is the latest attempt of promoting regional competitiveness by coordinating urban development in the PRD. The project illustrates the leading role of municipal governments in implementing the centrally approved strategic plans. At the 19th Plenary Meeting of the Chinese Communist Party (CCP) in 2017, Xi Jinping identified innovation as the driver for sustainable national economic development in the coming years. Xi used the word "innovation (创新)" more than 50 times in his three-hour speech, emphasizing the importance of science and technology in the transitioning of the Chinese economy — from a high-speed to a high-quality phase anchored on advanced manufacturing and services. Since the 19th Plenary, innovation has become the new buzzword in the national and local strategic planning documents. Following Xi Jinping's call for innovation, in 2017 Guangdong provincial government acquired the approval of the central government to develop an innovation corridor linking three major cities in the PRD — Guangzhou, Shenzhen, and Dongguan (Figure 8) — in the period of 2017–2030 (Guangdong Provincial Government, 2017; Ye, 2018). The rationale behind the innovation corridor project is to upgrade the regional economy from labor-intensive to advanced manufacturing, in order to maintain the competitiveness of the PRD region in the global manufacturing chain. The three cities of Guangzhou, Shenzhen, and Dongguan occupy 0.1% of national land, but 6% of the national GDP, and their per capita GDP has

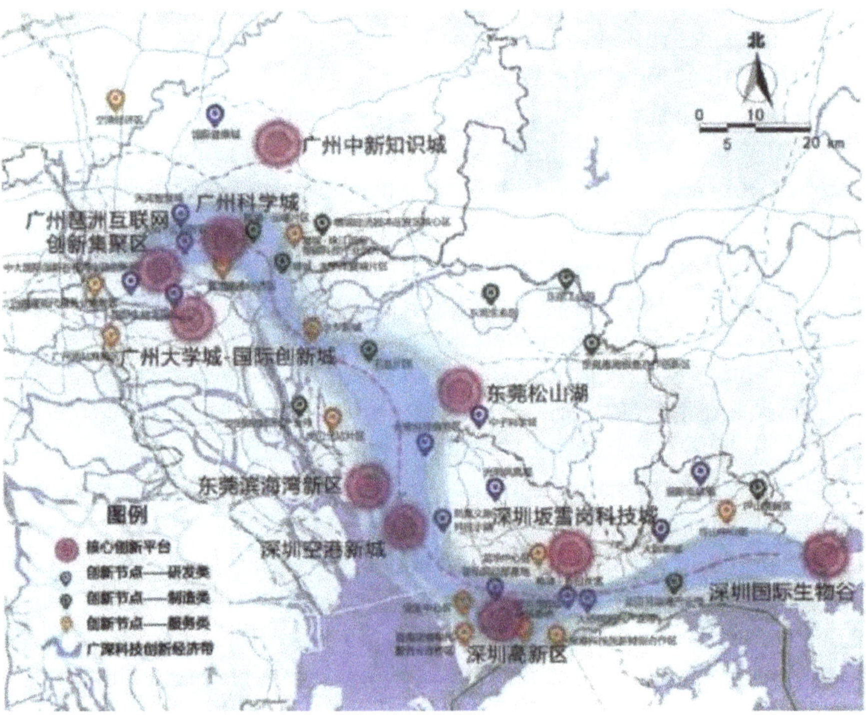

Figure 8. Guangzhou–Shenzhen innovation corridor.

Source: Guangdong Provincial Government (2017).

exceeded \$20,000. They also concentrate 78% of the high-tech companies in the PRD region, including the high-tech giants such as Huawei and Tencent. The three cities are already linked by Guangzhou–Shenzhen expressway, as well as Guangzhou–Shenzhen–Hong Kong high-speed rail and inter-city rail. Building on the existing advantage, the goal of the innovation corridor project is to develop 11,836 km^2 area covering the three cities and their in-between regions into China's Silicon Valley — a competitive region of R&D, innovation, and high-tech manufacturing, which can compete with San Francisco bay area and Boston area.

For each of the three cities, the 2017 Plan identifies its advantages and specifies its function in the innovation corridor: Guangzhou, because of its numerous universities and research institutes, will become a "national innovation urban center and international science and technology hub"; Shenzhen, with its agglomeration of high-tech companies, will become an "international innovation city and base for high-tech manufacturing," and Dongguan, with its advantage of cheaper labor and land costs, will be the major manufacturing base for various high-tech companies (Guangdong Provincial Government, 2017). The Plan also specifies the targets to be achieved by 2020 and 2030 in various sectors, such as the percentage of R&D investment in GDP and the percentage of high-tech manufacturing in the total industrial output. Following the spatial layout of "one corridor, ten centers, and multiple nodes," 10 centers such as science and technology parks are planned along the corridor, together with multiple nodal projects of smaller scale. As for funding, the provincial government will provide funding and city governments will provide additional matchup funds — the three cities are encouraged to put aside special funds and pool resources together for the development of the innovation corridor, and to further attract private investment. Under the initiative, the three cities are actively seeking support from the national government to invest in inter-city transportation infrastructure, so that all nodal projects can be connected within an "one-hour economic zone."

The GSIC project exemplifies many of the key characteristics of how mega-region planning is carried out in China. The central government identifies the direction of regional development, provincial governments provide funding and policy guidance, and local governments take the lead in the implementation of various projects endorsed by the higher-level governments. The overarching goal is to enhance regional competitiveness, and specifically, in the sector of high-tech and innovation, in this case. With a strong top-down approach, the central government specifies the functions of each of the three cities in the corridor with input from the provincial government, hoping to minimize race-to-bottom competition and utilize their comparative advantage. The three city governments are incentivized to implement the 2017 Plan for GSIC, as this can further promote economic development within their boundaries. Informal governing frameworks are encouraged, such as mayors' forums, but no formal governing institution will be set up to supervise the implementation of the innovation corridor. Without formal channels for interaction, exchange, and coordination among cities, however, it remains to be seen how the three cities will cooperate (instead of competing with one another for funding and resources) in the making of China's Silicon Valley in the next decade.

6. Building Mega-Regions in China and India: A Discussion

The comparative analysis demonstrates that mega-regions are not only competitive nodes of capital accumulation for global firms but are also products of diverse processes of state intervention, which leads to different outcomes in geographical, social and institutional terms (Xu and Yeh, 2011b). This section revisits the three questions raised at the beginning of the chapter, and compares who is constructing the new urban space of mega-region in China and India, what are the rationales behind, and how these new urban spaces are produced.

In spite of the different regime types, in both China and India, the central government plays a leading role in the planning of mega-regions in order to boost regional competitiveness. In India, the primary goal behind the central government's industrial corridor projects is to enhance the national capacity of manufacturing and to attract global investment, just like what the SEZs did for East Asian countries. In China, mega-regional planning in the PRD region is also to boost competitiveness, but by way of upgrading the economy from low-end to high-tech manufacturing and developing the technology sector. In spite of the different emphases on the industrial sectors — manufacturing vs. science and technology, both countries adopt a top-down approach to forge globally competitive mega-regions of densely networked cities.

At the sub-national level, however, China and India differ in the ways by which mega-regional planning is implemented. In India, state governments take full control of implementation, and by setting up Special Investment Vehicles, state governments directly supervise the construction of newly planned industrial and residential townships. Existing municipalities on the industrial corridors are not invited in the decision-making, and new townships will not have locally elected governing bodies anytime soon. In China, provincial governments provide funding and policy guidance for mega-regional planning, but the implementing bodies are municipal governments, which are highly incentivized to participate if they can benefit from the central government's initiatives for coordinated regional development, and are likely to resist if they do not benefit. In both cases, we do not see any innovative forms of governing arrangements emerging at the mega-regional scale yet, and existing forms of governance continue to characterize mega-regional planning. This can be explained by the reluctance toward power sharing — in India, from state governments, and in China, from municipal governments. With the top-down approach, neither the state government-led nor the municipalities-led mega-regional planning is conducive to building horizontal ties and fostering collaboration and exchange between cities, which is crucial for balanced regional development with networked cities complementing each other's strength.

Which localities are included or excluded from the emerging mega-regions? The leading mega-regional planning initiatives have targeted the most advanced regions, such as the Delhi–Mumbai corridor in India and the PRD in China. Although the idea behind the coordinated regional development is to link winner cities with laggard cities (and states, in the Indian case), economically powerful cities and states are likely to benefit more from infrastructure investment brought by mega-region planning. In the Indian case, previous studies have shown that more affluent states can better negotiate with the central government on the location choices of DMIC-related projects (Anand and Sami, 2016), and in the Chinese case, the latest attempt for coordinated development in the PRD targets the two most developed cities — Guangzhou and Shenzhen. Thus, in spite of its rhetoric of balanced development, mega-regional planning in China and India is likely to lead to more uneven development both within the mega-regions and across the country at large.

Finally, if we shift the lens to local communities, it is questionable how ordinary residents are likely to benefit from the ambitious mega-regional planning initiatives. In both China and India, ambitious mega-regional projects such as the industrial and innovation corridors will impact the lives of tens of millions of people. Land acquisition, undertaken by the state in order to build industrial townships, new towns, and science and technology parks, will continue to be contested by current landowners and users in rural areas. For the middle class, the "world-class" urban living is not guaranteed in the residential new towns being constructed on the Delhi–Mumbai corridor, without locally elected municipal governments with control over budgets and service delivery. For middle-class residents in the PRD, they will likely benefit from the better connectivity between major cities with the intensified investment in transportation infrastructure, but beyond faster trains and shorter travel time to the airports, the benefits of projects such as GSIC remain unclear for the everyday life of residents. If the project succeeds, and the corridor indeed becomes China's Silicon Valley, then the soaring housing prices will make the region one of the most unaffordable places to live in the country — just like the Bay Area in the United States. In both China and India, mega-regional planning emphasizes building competitiveness and attracting investment, and does not invite local input and ignores quality of life questions. To truly achieve sustainable development, in both social and environmental terms, it seems that the ambitious plans for building China's and India's mega-regions have to consider quality of life issues, and they need to coordinate with planning at the scales of the city and community.

References

Anand, S. and N. Sami (2015). *Urban Corridors: Strategies for Economic and Urban Development*. Bangalore: Indian Institute for Human Settlements.

Anand, S. and N. Sami (2016). "Scaling up, Scaling down: State Rescaling along the Delhi–Mumbai Industrial Corridor." *Economic & Political Weekly* 51(17), April 23.

Balakrishnan, S. (2019). *Shareholder Cities: Land Transformations along Urban Corridors in India*. Philadelphia: University of Pennsylvania Press.

Chakravorty, S. (2013). *The Price of Land: Acquisition, Conflict, Consequence*. New Delhi: Oxford University Press.

Cheung, P. T. Y. (2012). "The Politics of Regional Cooperation in the Greater Pearl River Delta." *Asia Pacific Viewpoint* 53(1), 21–37.

Corbridge, S. and J. Harriss (2000). Reinventing India. Cambridge: Polity Press.

Douglass, M. (2000). "Mega-Urban Regions and World City Formation: Globalisation, the Economic Crisis and Urban Policy Issues in Pacific Asia." *Urban Studies* 37(12), 2315–2335.

Drèze, J. and A. K. Sen (1995). *India: Economic Development and Social Opportunity*. Delhi: Oxford University Press.

Drèze, J. and A. K. Sen (2002). *India: Development and Participation*. Delhi: Oxford University Press.

Faludi, A. (2009). The Megalopolis, the Blue Banana, and Global Economic Integration Zones in European Planning Thought. In *Megaregions: Planning for Global Competitiveness*, edited by Catherine Ross. Washington DC: Island Press, pp. 18–34.

Glass, M. (2015). Conflicting Spaces of Governance in the Imagined Great Lakes Megaregion. In *Megaregions: Globalization's New Urban Form?* edited by John Harrison and Michael Hoyler (eds.). Cheltenham, UK and Northsampton, MA: Edward Elgar, pp. 119–145.

Gottmann, J. (1961). *Megalopolis: The Urbanized Northeastern Seaboard of the United States*. New York: Twentieth Century Fund.

Guangdong Provincial Government (2008). *Outline Plan for the Reform and Development of the Pearl River Delta, 2008–2020* (珠三角地区改革发展规划纲要, 2008–2020 年). Guangzhou: Guangdong Provincial Government.

Guangdong Provincial Government (2017). *Guangzhou–Shenzhen Innovation Corridor Masterplan* (广深科技创新走廊规划). Guangzhou: Guangdong Provincial Government.

Hall, P. and K. Pain (2006). *The Polycentric Metropolis: Learning from Mega-City Regions in Europe*. Earthscan: London.

Harrison, J. and M. Hoyler (2014). "Governing the New Metropolis." *Urban Studies* 51(11), 2249–2266.

Harrison, J. and M. Hoyler (2015). *Megaregions: Globalization's New Urban Form*? Cheltenham, UK and Northsampton, MA: Edward Elgar.

Heller, P. (2005). Reinventing Public Power in the Age of Globalization: The Transformation of Movement Politics in Kerala. In *Social Movements in*

India: Poverty, Power and Politics, edited by R. Ray and M. Katzenstein. New York: Rowman and Littlefield, pp. 79–106.

Hesse, M. (2015). Mega-urban Regions: Epistemology, Discourse Patterns, Big Urban Business. In *Megaregions: Globalization's New Urban Form?* edited by John Harrison and Michael Hoyler. Cheltenham, UK and Northsampton, MA: Edward Elgar, pp. 29–50.

Jonas, A. E. G. and K. Ward (2007). "Introduction to a Debate on City-Regions: New Geographies of Governance, Democracy and Social Reproduction." *International Journal of Urban and Regional Research* 31(1), 169–178.

Li, Y. and F. Wu (2012a). "The Transformation of Regional Governance in China: The Rescaling of Statehood." *Progress in Planning* 78(2), 55–99.

Li, Y. and F. Wu (2012b). "Towards New Regionalism? Case Study of Changing Regional Governance in the Yangtze River Delta." *Asia Pacific Viewpoint* 53(2), 178–195.

Lieberthal, K. (2004). *Governing China: From Revolution through Reform*. New York: W. W. Norton.

Luo, X. and J. Shen (2008). "Why City-Region Planning Does Not Work Well in China: The case of Suzhou-Wuxi-Changzhou." *Cities* 25(2), 207–217.

Ma, L. J. C. (2005). "Urban Administrative Restructuring, Changing Scale Relations and Local Economic Development in China." *Political Geography* 24(4), 477–497.

McGee, T. G. and I. Robinson (1995). *The New Southeast Asia: Managing the Mega-urban Regions*. Vancouver: University of British Columbia Press.

Mukhopadhyay, C. (2017). "Is the Delhi Mumbai Industrial Corridor (DMIC) an emerging 'megaregion' in India?" *Planning Theory & Practice* 19(2), 305–309.

Park, B. G. (2013). "State Rescaling in Non-Western Contexts." International *Journal of Urban and Regional Research* 31(1) 1115–1122.

Plummer, J. (2000). *Municipalities and Community Participation: A Sourcebook for Capacity Building*. Sterling, VA: Earthscan Publications.

Pinto, M. and D. A. Pinto (2005). *Municipal Corporation of Greater Mumbai and Ward Administration*. Delhi: Konark Publishers.

Rajan, R. (2014). Make in India, Largely for India. Bharat Ram Memorial Lecture, New Delhi, December 2. Retrieved from: https://www.bis.org/review/r141215a.htm. accessed on June 15, 2018.

Ren, X. and L. Weinstein (2013). Urban Governance, Mega-Projects, and Scalar Transformations in China and India. In *Locating Right to the City in the Global South*, edited by Tony Samara, Shenjing He, and Guo Chen. New York: Routledge.

Ren, X. (2017). "Land Acquisition, Rural Protests, and the Local State in China and India." *Environment and Planning C: Politics and Space* 35(1), 22–38.

Ross, C. (2009). *Megaregions: Planning for Global Competitiveness*. Washington DC: Island Press.

Sassen, S. (2007). Megaregions: Benefits beyond Sharing Trains and Parking Lots? *The Economic Geography of Megaregions*, edited by S. Goldfeld. Princeton, NJ: The Policy Research Institute of the Region, pp. 59–83.

Sassen, S. (2009). Novel Spatial Formats: Megaregions and Global Intercity Geographies. In *Megaregions: Planning for Global Competitiveness*, edited by Catherine Ross. Washington DC: Island Press, pp. 219–249.

Schafran, A. (2014). "Rethinking Mega-Regions: Sub-Regional Politics in a Fragmented Metropolis." *Regional Studies* 48(4), 587–602.

Scott, A. and M. Storper (2003). "Regions, Globalization, Development." *Regional Studies* 37(6–7), 579–593.

Shen, J. (2005). Space, Scale and the State: Reorganizing Urban Space in China. *Restructuring the Chinese City: Changing Society, Economy and Space*, edited by J. C. Ma and F. Wu. New York: Routledge, pp. 39–58.

Shen, J. (2007). "Scale, State and The City: Urban Transformation In Post-Reform China." *Habitat International* 31(3–4), 303–316.

Stepan, A. (1999). "Federalism and Democracy: Beyond the U.S. Model." *Journal of Democracy* 10(4), 19–34.

Tummala, K. K. (1992). "India's Federalism under Stress." *Asian Survey* 32(6), 538–553.

Verney, D. (1995). "Federalism, Federative Systems, and Federations: The United States, Canada, and India." *Publius* 25(2): 81–97.

Wachsmuth, D. (2015). Megaregions and the Urban Question: The New Strategic Terrain for US Urban Competitiveness. In *Megaregions: Globalization's New Urban Form?* edited by John Harrison and Michael Hoyler. Cheltenham, UK and Northsampton, MA: Edward Elgar, pp. 51–74.

Wheeler, S. (2015). Five Reasons Why Megaregional Planning Works against Sustainability. In *Megaregions: Globalization's New Urban Form?* edited by John Harrison and Michael Hoyler. Cheltenham, UK and Northsampton, MA: Edward Elgar, pp. 97–118.

Wu, F. (2016). "China's Emergent City-Region Governance: A New Form of State Spatial Selectivity through State-Orchestrated Rescaling." *International Journal of Urban and Regional Research* 40(6), 1134–1151.

Wu, F. and Zhang, J. (2007). "Planning the Competitive City-Region: The Emergence of Strategic Development Plan in China." *Urban Affairs Review* 42(5), 714–740.

Xu, J. (2008). "Governing City Regions in China: Theoretical Discourse and Perspective Regional Strategic Planning." *Town Planning Review* 79(2–3), 157–185.

Xu, J. and A. G. O. Yeh (2010). "Planning Mega-City Regions in China: Rationales and Policies." *Progressive Planning* 73(1), 17–22.

Xu, J. and A. G. O. Yeh (2011a). *China's Pan-Pearl River Delta: Regional Cooperation and Development*. Hong Kong: Hong Kong University Press.

Xu, J. and A. G. O. Yeh (2011b). *Governance and Planning of Megacity Regions: An International Comparative Perspective*. London: Routledge.

Yang, J. (2009). Spatial Planning in Asia: Planning and Developing Megacities and Megaregions. In *Megaregions: Planning for Global Competitiveness*, edited by Catherine Ross. Washington DC: Island Press, pp. 34–52.

Ye, L. (2013). "Urban Transformation and Institutional Policies: Case Study of Mega-Region Development in China's Pearl River Delta." *Journal of Urban Planning and Development* 139(4), 292–300.

Ye, L. (2014). "State-Led Metropolitan Governance in China: Making Integrated City Regions." *Cities* 41, 200–208.

Ye, L. (2018). The Mega PRD Region and Guangzhou–Shenzhen Corridor: A Preliminary Study. Paper presented at Urban Affairs Association conference, Toronto, Canada.

Zhang, T. (2006). "From Intercity Competition to Collaborative Planning: The case of Yangtze River Delta region in China." *Urban Affairs Review* 42(1), 26–56.

Zhang, X. (2015). Globalization and the Megaregion: Investigating the Evolution of the Pearl River Delta in a Historical Perspective. In *Megaregions: Globalization's New Urban Form?* John Harrison and Michael Hoyler (eds.), edited by Cheltenham, UK and Northsampton, MA: Edward Elgar, pp. 175–199.

Zou, Y. and W. Zhao (2018). "Making a New Area in Xiong'an: Incentives and Challenges of China's Millennium Plan." *Geoforum* 88, 45–48.

II. Urban Economy and Sustainability

Chapter 5

Land Redevelopment and the Built Environment in Third-Wave Cities: Review and Synthesis

Allen J. Scott

Department of Geography and Department of Public Policy,
University of California, Los Angeles, USA
ajscott@ucla.edu

1. Urban Land and Property in Question

This chapter takes the form of an extended essay in which I seek to synthesize a number of different approaches to issues of land redevelopment and the built environment in contemporary cities. My objective is to bring several somewhat disparate strands of thought regarding these issues into juxtaposition with one another so as to shed fresh light on the ways in which they operate, their relations to the functional structure of the city, and how they are currently reshaping patterns of urban development.

A complex scientific and political question about the valuation, appropriation, and use of urban land and property emerges endemically within cities in capitalist society (Roweis and Scott, 1978). The substance of this question can be discerned within the phenomenon of the urban land nexus in its substantive character as a mass of functionally interdependent assets such as factories, offices, houses, shopping facilities, public buildings, infrastructures, and so on, arranged in conjoint spatial patterns around a common center of gravity (Scott, 1980; Scott and Storper, 2015). Complex processes of redevelopment, piloted by intermediaries like property companies, real estate developers, and governmental agencies are constantly in operation at the interface between this mass of urban *relata* and the wider socio-economic context (cf. Guy and Henneberry, 2002; Hackworth, 2007; Topalov, 1974; Weber, 2015) though the ways in which these processes unfold vary significantly from one historical wave or phase of capitalism to another. In this chapter, I am concerned for the most part with urban redevelopment in the third and current wave of capitalism (with its primary expression in the new cognitive-cultural economy) in contradistinction to a first wave based on the 19th-century factory and workshop system and a second wave in the 20th-century focused on Fordist mass production (Scott, 2017).

Many of the most striking transformations proceeding in the urban land nexus today (including advances in so-called smart-city technologies) derive directly and indirectly from the technological, economic, and political logic of this third wave of capitalism (see also, Hutton, 2008; Folmer and Kloosterman, 2017). Three important examples of these transformations and their relationship to land redevelopment processes are dealt with specifically later in this chapter, namely, the functional and visual renascence of central business districts (cf. Fainstein, 2001; Kaika, 2010), the intensifying gentrification of low-income neighborhoods in the inner city (Clark, 2005; Lees *et al.*, 2007; Scott, 2018), and the formation of extended polycentric postsuburban spaces (Hall and Pain, 2009; Keil, 2018). Local government organizations, too, have been subject to significant restructuring, notably by reason of the spirit of deregulation that has penetrated deeply into contemporary political life. These organizations are hence nowadays much given to an entrepreneurial mode of functioning that differs sharply from the more rigid Keynesian-welfare statist orientation of local government in the Fordist era (Harvey, 1989; Raco and de Souza, 2018). At the global level, tidal waves of liquid cash have been unleashed by corporate and governmental entities, and are being fed down to the urban level by means of contrived fiduciary instruments managed by financial and property-development interests (Aalbers, 2012; Halbert and Attuyer, 2016). Much of the current ferment in the urban land nexus can be traced directly to these huge infusions of liquidity into the built environment. Caught up in this maelstrom are the lives of ordinary citizens, some of whom benefit greatly from the new state of play but vast numbers of whom pay a heavy price both in terms of their entrapment in the lower reaches of the cognitive-cultural economy and in terms of the displacement and disruption to which they are subject as those in control of the land redevelopment sector pursue their own peculiar version of creative destruction.

2. Land and Property Investment Decisions

Investment decisions in urban land and property typically revolve around a complex combination of variables including location, land rent, built structures, the costs of any prospective rebuilding or renovation activities, and financial conditions in the economy at large. Investors will also usually want to assess the effects of prospective changes in the urban environment on the eventual resale price of any property that they take over. We now consider these matters by first dealing with the specific case of land dedicated to commercial pursuits and by then treating the slightly more complicated case of land used for residential purposes. The argument that follows is couched in informal and descriptive language, but a more rigorous treatment will be found in the Appendix, and the reader should turn to that section of the chapter for a more detailed technical exposition.

2.1. *Redevelopment for commercial purposes*

Let us begin by building on some elementary ideas about investment in land that date back at least to the time of Marshall (1890) and then extending the argument by reference to some ideas drawn from Von Thünen's theory of land use and land rent (Scott, 1976).

Consider a situation where some given parcel of land in the city can be significantly revalorized by means of judicious investment and redevelopment. Let us suppose that an independent development company acquires the parcel. If, for the moment, we overlook anticipations about future land-use changes, the sale price to the company will consist of two basic quantities, namely, the present discounted value of all future rents that the land commands in its current state of development, and the depreciated value of any existing improvements (Munneke, 1996; Rosenthal and Helsey, 1994). If the company engages in renovation or construction activities on the site, additional investment of money will be required, including charges for dismantling all or part of the existing structures. Obviously, the prospective resale price of the property after redevelopment must be such as to allow the company to recover the total acquisition cost plus all renovation or construction costs and to earn at least a normal profit on resale. At the same time, redevelopment may also generate a surplus amount or rent over and above this profit, and any such surplus will be commandeered by the development company as (interim) owner of the parcel.

Any such surplus will itself arise from changes, due to redevelopment, in the quantity of output produced on the land in relation to market prices together with changes in costs of production (see Appendix for details). More precisely, the surplus represents an increment to overall rent originating from the enhanced operational capacity of the parcel after redevelopment. Additionally, the surplus is equivalent to an opportunity cost on redevelopment, and this amount must be greater than or equal to zero before the company will proceed with the project. Redevelopment may also induce a material change of land use, but for simplicity we will take it that the same type of productive activity continues on the parcel after redevelopment as before. Two generic outcomes are now possible with respect to the use of the parcel. One of these can be designated as "land-use intensification," meaning that redevelopment leads to rising total production or revenue per unit land area. The other we shall refer to as "extensive land-use conversion," a special and — given the stringency of the conditions that render it feasible — an almost certainly less common type of change characterized as it is by diminished total production or revenue per unit land area (see Appendix). Land-use intensification of any parcel can occur in combination with either falling or (given offsetting increases in productivity) rising unit costs of production due to redevelopment. Extensive land-use conversion is feasible only where costs of production are falling, and even then, they must fall below a certain threshold level before redevelopment will be pursued. In theory, both types of land-use change can occur at any location in the city. Two main points must now be made.

First, redevelopment via land-use intensification is a common phenomenon across the whole of the urban land nexus. Even the transformation of agricultural land into urban land is normally an exercise in land-use intensification. However, this type of land-use change typically appears in its most assertive forms at highly accessible locations such as the central city and associated satellite centers. Locations of these sorts already generate high rents per unit of output, which means *ceteris paribus* that any increases in production will yield additional rents at the same high value. In short, any unit of increased output at these locations will earn a rent at the going rate and this will accordingly augment the rent per unit area. Provided that the costs of production can be kept from rising unduly as a result of redevelopment, there will thus be an especially strong incentive to intensify land use at central, high-rent locations (notably by means of increases in floor space and building height).

Second, profitable redevelopment by means of extensive land-use conversion can only be accomplished in circumstances where production costs are sufficiently reduced to compensate for lowered output per unit area. Conditions like these are almost certainly less likely to occur in modern cities than those that encourage land-use intensification, but a hypothetical illustrative scenario might unfold where a property developer succeeds in assembling several individual parcels of land occupied by easily convertible buildings into a single unit of ownership. Economically viable conversion of the enlarged unit under conditions of reduced output and reduced operating costs might then be possible if the land is equipped with inexpensive improvements, perhaps with substantial open areas for outdoor storage. To the extent that extensive land-use conversion can be observed within the urban land nexus, it is probably confined for the most part to fringe areas where rents are already relatively low and where existing densities of development are minimal so that the costs of conversion are likely to be not too onerous (see Appendix).

Once the intensive or extensive redevelopment of any given parcel of land has been completed, the price of the parcel will be equal to the developer's acquisition cost (see earlier), plus all expenditures on renovation or reconstruction, plus the present aggregate value of all future land-rent increases ascribable to redevelopment.

2.2. *Redevelopment for residential purposes*

Redevelopment for the purposes of erecting residential properties for sale or rent is in its essentials already covered by the argument set out previously. But what of the individual householder who is intent on purchasing and rehabilitating a property for purely personal use? As in the case of a company that redevelops a property for commercial reasons, our householder must always, at a minimum, defray the cost of land acquisition as well as the cost of any reconstruction or renovation activities. However, we cannot in this instance identify a quantity of revenue created by redevelopment, and thus there is a question as to how we define the opportunity cost. The way around this dilemma, without invoking the circularity of an argument based on utility maximizing processes, is to use the expected resale price of the property when redevelopment is completed as a proxy measure for revenue. We then calculate the opportunity cost by subtracting the cost of acquisition and redevelopment from this amount. The expected price will itself be an estimate based in part on an assessment of the interplay of many different variables, including the quality of the improved property, its overall accessibility, and the assortment of neighborhood externalities that Sampson (2012) refers to as "collective efficacy." Despite the inevitably speculative element in any *ex ante* estimate like this, informed assessments can usually be made by reference to general market conditions. To be sure, there is always the further possibility that the householder, for personal reasons, will invest in the project to the point where the opportunity cost defined in this manner becomes negative. In these circumstances, the full amount of the monetary outlay on acquisition and renovation will be recoverable — if at all — only at some future date. Against this extra cost we must set the presumably added satisfaction of the householder over the time horizon defined by that future date.

2.3. *Temporal pathways and capital switching in the redevelopment process*

The durability of the urban built environment implies that important leads and lags are likely to make it difficult for actors in the property market to optimize the scheduling of their buying and selling decisions (Brueckner, 1980; Capozza and Li, 1994; Miron, 2017). By the same token, the need to assess the economic viability of any redevelopment project in advance of its actual completion always introduces a degree of speculation into the decision-making process. One high-risk dimension in this regard concerns the amount of time that is allowed to lapse between purchasing a parcel of land and the initiation or completion of redevelopment operations. Thus, a developer may purchase a parcel at one point in time but may wait to redevelop the site until a later period if future upward shifts of prices in the surrounding urban environment are anticipated. A decision-making strategy of this sort, as Nowlan (1977) has shown, necessitates complex front- and back-end calculations in any attempt to make a finely tuned assessment of the optimal amount of floor space or the type of building to be installed. A successful type of strategy, for example, would be to buy the land when prices are low, but to delay redevelopment until changing market conditions allow the improved property to generate sufficient revenue to sustain its profitable operation. Clearly, the amount of time that is allowed to lapse between parcel acquisition and project completion will tend to vary inversely according to the current interest rate with its direct impact on any carrying costs.

Cities almost always display many physical traces of these calculated delays between parcel acquisition and the completion of conversion activities. Parts of the city adjacent to the CBD are markedly prone to this syndrome in view of their susceptibility to the eventual outward expansion of high-density land use. One of the commonest expressions of the syndrome is the apparently paradoxical existence of empty spaces close to the CBD that are either boarded up or that serve as parking lots in the interim between land acquisition and redevelopment. The length of the interim itself is partly conditional on the local property-tax regime, and will tend to be prolonged where, as in many American cities, taxes are assessed on the basis of actual rather than potential land use. Alternatively, in cases where the land reserved for redevelopment is already equipped with structures capable of generating at least some level of income, the existing activities on the site may be allowed temporarily to function, and thus contribute to cutting overall costs. Little effort is likely to be dedicated to maintaining these structures, and hence they are liable to deepening blight prior to redevelopment.

The timing of land-acquisition and redevelopment decisions is also strongly sensitive to overall patterns of expansion and contraction in the property market. These patterns typically exhibit strongly cyclical behavior, especially in the office-construction sector (Ball, 1986; Barras, 1994; MacLaren, 2003). In a widely cited publication, Harvey (1985) has proposed a hypothesis that seeks to link this cycle in property development, or what he calls the "secondary" circuit of capital investment, to the changing fortunes of the "primary" sector, i.e., commodity production as a whole. The main thrust of the hypothesis is that new capital investments will be "switched" from commodity production into property development when overaccumulation starts to become evident in the former segment of the economy, signaling a looming business downturn. In this manner, the property sector is presumed to act as a sort of safety valve by temporarily staving off a deepening crisis of profitability. There has been little empirical examination of this hypothesis, and the few extant attempts to test it focus on symptomatic expressions of switching rather than explicit examination of overaccumulation as such. Beauregard (1994), basing his analysis on comparisons of trends in US real estate markets with the performance of rest of the economy over the 1970s and 1980s, finds little or no evidence in favor of the hypothesis; Christophers (2011), who examines British data on the changing share of real estate investments in pension funds from 2000 to 2007, claims to have discovered positive (but indirect) evidence in its favor. As it happens, a counter-argument to Harvey's hypothesis can be constructed on the basis of the literature in general which reveals the existence of a strong if irregular positive relationship between real estate cycles and the economic cycle as a whole (cf. Barras and Ferguson, 1985; Jadevicius *et al.*, 2017; Leamer, 2015). The evident deduction that can be drawn from this information is that the inter-sectoral rebalancing of profit rates will in all likelihood have occurred long before the appearance of any over-accumulation crisis in the wider business environment. In brief, the switching idea remains a bold hypothesis, but there are also reasonable grounds for a degree of skepticism as to its ultimate validity.

3. Real Estate Markets and Finance

Over much of the period since the end of World War II, funding for real estate construction and purchase in the United States was largely undertaken by highly regulated commercial banks and savings and loan institutions via mortgage agreements with prospective property owners. As third-wave capitalism has forged ahead in recent decades, bringing with it the rise of a powerful globalized financial sector underpinned by advanced data processing and communications technologies, important changes in these funding arrangements have come about with major repercussions on urban structures, not just in the United States but in other parts of the world as well (Aalbers 2012; Christophers, 2015; Haila 2016; Harvey, 2012; Rutland, 2010). In particular, the deregulation of the US banking sector since the early 1980s, combined with snowballing innovation in financial engineering, has unleashed a stream of new investment practices in the built environment, not all of them benign (Fernandez and Aalbers, 2016). In the United States, one of the first intimations of the potentially negative impacts of these shifts was the savings and loan crisis brought on by relaxation of lending standards in the second half of the 1980s.

The main impetus for this relaxation was the repeal of the Glass–Steagall Act in 1999, and the consequent move to effective banking deregulation. Among the many other effects ascribable to the repeal of the Act was the removal of impediments to the fusion of the business operations of commercial banks and financial institutions. This fusion was then accompanied by a deepening engagement of financial institutions in mortgage lending and in the financialization of real estate assets. The overall strategy of financialization was accomplished by means of comprehensive income-generating securities or collateralized mortgage obligations (CMOs) such as mortgage-backed securities (MBS) and structured investment vehicles (SIVs) based on the aggregation of large numbers of individual mortgages into massive investment pools (Gothan, 2012; O'Neill, 2018). The new-found ability to securitize real estate debt in this way offered enormous windfall profits to financial institutions, including global giants like Bear Sterns, Lehman Brothers, Merrill Lynch, J. P. Morgan, and Wachovia (Crosby and Henneberry, 2016). Institutions like these, in partnership with commercial banks, issued commercial paper that in effect shifted money from the international financial system down to individual real estate purchasers and then transferred the concomitant interest payments back up to holders (many of them insurance companies and large pension funds) of the paper. Financialization was further reinforced by the rise of real estate investment trusts or REITS acting as both managers of physical properties and as investors in real estate construction projects. Waldron (2018), Aalbers (2017) and Gothan (2012), among others, have pointed out how all these different currents have transmuted immobile property into a mirror state of placeless financial liquidity. The deepening integration of financial and real estate markets and the easy credit that ensued led to an explosion of mortgage debt and property investment not only in the United States but also in other countries that pursued aggressive deregulation after the 1980s. The accelerated pace of land redevelopment that accompanied the resulting property boom had major impacts on the urban landscape. Important symptoms of this trend were rapid upward shifts in rates of home ownership, major expansion of business premises in CBDs, and the flowering of urban mega-projects, many of them in old industrial quarters such as the Zürich West development (Dörry *et al.*, 2016), the Docks of St. Ouen in the suburbs of Paris (Guironnet *et al.*, 2016) and the Bicocca Technocity in Milan (Kaika, 2016). These latter projects illustrate another important feature of third-wave urbanization, namely, the assertive recycling and upgrading of derelict Fordist industrial sites in pursuit of property-led urban regeneration.

To many observers in the early years of the 21st century, this figurative liquefaction of real estate into financial assets held out the promise of significant improvements in the operational efficiency of urban property markets and all the more so given its basis in advanced digital technologies. With the aid of these technologies, market makers could supplement their practical capacity to digest vast amounts of information, enabling them constantly to reevaluate changing economic conditions. For a while, it seemed as though property markets might continue indefinitely to operate at this new tempo as they entered into a period of full-blown expansionary thrust after the turn of the 21st century, though at the cost of rapidly soaring house prices. The data displayed in Figure 1 clearly illustrate the course of the housing-price bubble in the United States over the 1990s and through the early years of the 21st century. As shown in the figure, the total value of outstanding mortgages (less farm mortgages) as a percentage of GDP increased from 48.1% in 1980 to 63.6% in 2000, and then, as the global credit boom intensified, rose sharply over the next several years before flattening off in the period from 2007 to 2009 (reaching an absolute

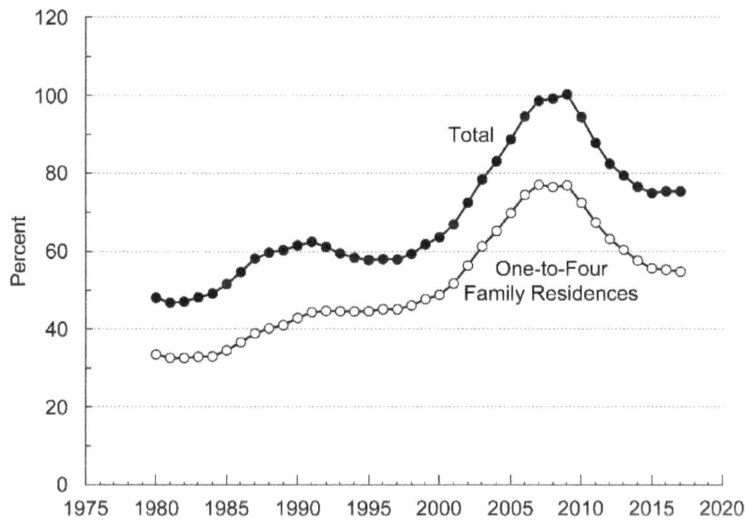

Figure 1. Total mortgage debt (omitting farm mortgages) and mortgage debt on one-to-four family residences in the United States; both series are expressed as a percentage of US GDP.

Source: Federal Reserve Board and Bureau of the Census.

peak of 100.3% in 2009) to be followed by a massive and extended downturn. Figure 1 also indicates that the relative value of mortgages for one-to-four family residences in the United States runs in parallel with these aggregate data. Concomitantly, house prices increased from a value of 92.7 on the Case–Shiller US National Home Price Index in January 1999 (the year the Glass–Steagall Act was repealed) to a peak of 184.6 in July 2006, a total increase of 99.1% or just over 13.0% a year (cf. Kim and Renaud, 2009). From this peak to February 2012, house prices nationwide declined by 27.4%, and the peak itself was not to be surpassed again until December 2016. To compound matters, the collapse ignited a massive and widespread economic crisis, initially in the United States (Ashton, 2009), and then in other major capitalist countries, though at different rates and intensities given national differences in housing markets and housing finance systems (Fernandez and Aalbers, 2016; Kim and Renaud, 2009).

One of the major causes of the breakdown of real estate prices after 2009 can be traced back to the increasingly indiscriminate disbursement of mortgage funds by lending institutions in response to deregulation. As the boom gathered momentum, more and more subprime mortgages were incorporated into commercial instruments that were then sold over financial markets. In earlier times, banks and savings and loan institutions had typically exercised considerable caution in their mortgage-lending practices, but in this new more liberal climate, lenders calculated that by bundling together mortgages issued to a mix of individuals with poor and high credit ratings they could fine-tune risk levels without compromising the marketability of the corresponding financial instruments. Discretionary caution was accordingly relaxed, and commercial banks along with their financial partners greatly expanded their mortgage lending programs while simultaneously tapping into new markets among low-income minority borrowers by means of widespread predatory lending (Dymski, 2012). The application of discriminatory red-lining methods had traditionally limited the degree to which these borrowers could gain access to mortgage funding, but they were now being actively encouraged to take out loans even in cases where their ability to sustain payments over the long run was clearly in doubt. These predatory lending programs remained generally viable as long as interest rates were falling and house prices increasing so that the equity in the hands of individual homeowners continued to rise, but both lenders and borrowers rapidly encountered severe headwinds as reverse trends began to appear. In view of these trends, more and more mortgage holders were unable to meet their debt obligations, and mounting defaults and foreclosures started to impose considerable stress on the banking and financial system (Ashton, 2009). In many instances, over-leveraged homeowners, especially in low-income neighborhoods, simply abandoned their houses to their creditors (Halbert and Attuyer, 2016). The end result was widening distress in the housing market and rapid diffusion of recessionary conditions through the rest of the economy.

In response to these and allied problems, the federal government of the United States passed the Dodd–Frank Wall Street Reform and Consumer Protection Act in 2010, in an attempt to improve financial stability, and, by means of Title XIV of the Act, to reign in predatory mortgage-lending practices. The Act also reintroduced elements of the earlier Glass–Steagall legislation by limiting financial speculation on the part of commercial banks. Despite this attempt at remediation, many of the stipulations of the Dodd–Frank Act are currently under high-pressure attack in Washington, and at least some watering down of the main thrust of the Act seems likely. Even if the Act remains fully in force, the overall trend toward deregulation and financialization in the last few decades has introduced a new and troubling degree of instability into urban real estate markets, and has contributed significantly to amplifying the gap between the fortunes of those at the top and those at the bottom of the income ladder.

4. Municipal Policy Tools and Initiatives

Public authorities have always played a role in shaping capitalist urbanization processes, and their efforts have always been intensely focused on two broad goals, namely, the correction of market failures in the urban land nexus when these lead on to socially and politically unacceptable outcomes, and the pursuit of collective projects deemed necessary or desirable for urban growth and social order. It follows that municipal oversight of land redevelopment and property conversion projects is typically a major component of these efforts. This oversight also invariably reflects the influence of political demands exerted by different urban constituencies. In American cities in particular, powerful formal and informal growth coalitions repeatedly bring pressure to bear on municipal decision-making in general, and perhaps most forcefully in regard to issues of real estate investment and development (Molotch, 1976; Stone, 1987).

All that being said, the modalities of governance and collective action in the urban land nexus vary significantly over historical time. In the era of Fordism, they were deeply inflected with the spirit of Keynesian-welfare statism. In North America and much of Western Europe, this meant that public intervention in issues of land redevelopment and the built environment was heavily directed to urban renewal programs, infrastructure planning, public housing investments, and the provision of sundry social facilities. Large-scale urban renewal in the United States was initiated by the 1949 Housing Act and was implemented for the most part in order to deal with the urban ravages directly and indirectly brought on by the accelerating flight of industry and employment from central cities (cf. Brenner, 2004). Much public housing was constructed by city governments in inner-city areas and elsewhere at this time in order to accommodate working-class families displaced by clearances of blighted neighborhoods.

With the waning of the Fordist regime in the late 1970s and early 1980s, and the formation of the early stages of third-wave capitalism, many of these Keynesian-welfare statist policy arrangements were severely curtailed and alternative strategies of governance focusing on deregulation and the extension of market order were implemented in their place. Along with this sea change came a mounting concern with efficiency and urban economic development issues that was all the more urgent in view of the damage wrought by the collapse of Fordism and the spreading influence of global capitalism. Harvey (1989) was an early and astute observer of these turn of events, which he diagnosed in terms of a shift from managerialism to entrepreneurialism in urban governance. Harvey also suggested that a prime symptom of this shift was the rising importance of private–public partnerships involving local government and diverse business interests in the search for increased rates of urban and regional growth. In the three decades that have elapsed since Harvey published these ideas, the creed of entrepreneurialism — or perhaps, better yet, project-oriented planning — has continued to extend its hold over the practices of local governments as manifested in a multifaceted array of policy tools and incentives devoted to facilitating private investment in large-scale urban development projects and other ways of promoting urban prosperity and repute, including city branding operations. Iconic building designs by celebrated international architects are a striking symptom of this city-branding urge (Fainstein and Fainstein, 2015), as represented, for example, by the classical cases of the Bilbao Guggenheim Museum inaugurated in1997 and Kuala Lumpur's Petronas Towers, officially opened in 1999. Initiatives of these sorts enrich the stock of built forms of the city while simultaneously serving as beacons that help to guide inflows of capital and skilled migrants from elsewhere.

Land redevelopment and property conversion processes are, of course, deeply intertwined with urban growth and land-use change, and public agencies work intensely to channel them into desired configurations.

The specific policy resources at the command of these agencies include traditional planning instruments like zoning and land-use regulations as well as more recently devised financial provisions that among other things facilitate the ability of municipalities to operate in customized collaborative relationships with private developers and construction companies. Local governments also typically have selective authority to override rights of private ownership that might otherwise create bottlenecks to urgent or socially imperative tasks of redevelopment. Continued, if relatively restrained investment in public housing and other welfare arrangements, but the most active engagement of these agencies in the matter of land redevelopment and property conversion today is devoted to promoting a dynamic urban economy with strong competitive advantages at the national and global scales. A common form of this activity is property-led regeneration, especially in cities with extensive tracts of land that have been left in a state of dilapidation as a legacy from the old Fordist regime. Public participation in land and property upgrading for the purposes of regeneration extends across the entire range of land use types from commercial real estate to residential neighborhoods. On the one side, public agencies are increasingly involved in subsidizing and promoting land-use changes calculated to boost local participation in dynamic third-wave sectors like business and financial services, the cultural economy, and technology-intensive industries, particularly in parts of the city such as the CBD, decaying warehouse and factory districts, and extensive peripheral areas suitable for business centers and science parks (cf. Kaika, 2010; Ponzini and Nastasi, 2011; Scott, 2011). On the other side, policy measures such as building clearances, rezoning, property-tax increases, and the abolition of rent controls are frequently brought to bear on low-income residential districts in efforts to promote neighborhood redevelopment. These measures in turn are apt to accelerate the gentrification processes that are increasingly evident in third-wave cities (Hamnett, 2003; Ley, 1986; Zukin, 1982).

Much of this private–public intervention in the built environment is nowadays coordinated by urban development corporations with wide powers of intervention. Corporations of this type are familiar elements of governance structures in cities in the United States and Britain where they function above all as agencies of property-led regeneration. In France, analogous institutions exist in the guise of government-sponsored *Etablissements Publics d'Aménagement* (EPA), or Public Planning Agencies, whose work is facilitated by long-standing legal arrangements that empower municipalities to designate given tracts of land as *Zones d'Aménagement Concerté* (ZACs) or Collaborative Planning Zones. The powers invested in these French institutions make it possible to establish flexible partnerships between local authorities and private corporations in the tasks of land assembly, infrastructure provision, and construction (Bonneval and Pollard, 2017). Financial packages involving both public subsidies and private investments typically play an important part in mobilizing ventures like these.

In addition to the forms of public support for property development as described earlier, tax increment financing agreements or TIFs are now widely and increasingly deployed by local governments in the United States as a way of stimulating private intervention in the built environment. TIF-based redevelopment procedures begin with the official designation of a specific site or area in the city as a target of renewal and regeneration. The actual redevelopment of a given parcel of land can usually be expected to generate increases in tax revenues, and TIF agreements are designed precisely to securitize these increases. Thus, once a given parcel in the city is designated for rehabilitation under a TIF agreement, the municipality enters into a contract that assigns the tax revenue increases to a developer, or a consortium of developers, in exchange for specified construction and improvement work. "In this way," as Weber (2010, p. 258) writes, "cities obtain capital by turning the rights to their own … property tax base into standardized tradable assets," (see also Pacewicz, 2013; Savini and Aalbers, 2016). TIFs, moreover, not only serve as a technique for subsidizing private construction operations but also as a means of keeping the relevant monetary transfers off the municipal budget and hence of depoliticizing at least some of the redevelopment process. The property boom of Chicago that lasted from 1996 to 2007 can in large degree be ascribed to the widespread implementation of TIF agreements, and by 2008, Chicago had 160 different TIF districts covering as much as 30% of the city's land area (Weber, 2010, 2015).

5. Composite Outcomes: Three Illustrative Vignettes

Each historical phase of capitalism triggers specific kinds of readjustments in the built environment together with definite forms of social disruption and political contestation. The current expansionary phase of third-wave capitalism has also brought in its train a series of very specific shifts in modalities of physical redevelopment and in the character of the built environment. In the discussion thus far, I have mostly focused on analysis of the discrete systematic elements that make up these modalities. In the present section, by contrast, I offer an illustrative triad of more synthetic views that bring these elements into mutual inter-relationship in complex aggregations of built forms. The argument proceeds with special reference to land-use intensification in CBD areas, gentrification in downtown neighborhoods, and the geography of postsuburbia. These cases illustrate, each in its own peculiar way, how land markets together with private and public redevelopment processes both shape and respond to the functional dynamics of cities.

5.1. *The CBD: Aestheticized land-use intensification*

The CBDs of capitalist cities have always been susceptible to insistent redevelopment via land-use intensification, i.e., the multiplication of the ground area of any given site by means of increasing floor space. This multiplication is a response to the elevated land rents that can be extracted as a consequence of the location of central business districts relative to the rest of the urban land nexus. The physical signs of this condition are evident in the ever-changing array of high-rise buildings that typify these districts. Hoyt (1933, p. 335) recounts that in the Chicago of his day "thirteen story skyscrapers with a structural life of a century or more have been torn down to give room for twenty-two or forty-four-story tower buildings." These processes of property clearance in the CBD and the construction of newer and more efficient structures tend to proceed in a cyclical rhythm, and, as Barras (1994) shows, are usually most apparent at times when the economy is booming.

The buildings of the CBD are almost always the highest, most visible, and most expensive edifices in the urban land nexus. They also house many of the most prestigious business, financial, and service functions in the city, forming dense concentrations of generally high-level professional, managerial, and administrative employment. These functions have always dominated CBD economies in capitalist cities, but they have taken on augmented importance in the current cognitive–cultural era where high-level intellectual and affective forms of labor lie at the core of much of the productive system. This combination of visibility and prestige in so many of the buildings in the CBD is conducive to another distinctive feature, namely, the profusion of architectural signs and symbols that adorn these buildings and that testify to their special status as icons of power and wealth. The built structures of the CBD thus tend to embody more dramatically than any other part of the city the distinctive forms generated by the synthesis of prevailing construction technologies and aesthetic motifs (often encoded in ideologies of architectural practice) that reflect the dominating temper of the times (Cuthbert, 2006). Each historical generation of CBD building activity leaves a unique mark of this sort. Consider Figure 2, which portrays three different generations of quintessential central-city buildings, each of them imprinted with a historically-specific set of design principles. The chunky Marshall Field Wholesale Store in Chicago with its exterior load-bearing walls is an example of vigorous land-use intensification in the late 19th-century and a forthright statement of the doctrine that form should follow function. The soaring curtain-walled Seagram Building in mid-20th-century New York proclaims, for its part, the Miesian doctrine that less is always more. The neo-baroque Swiss Re Building in the 21st century London exhibits the enhanced construction capabilities opened up by new digital technologies in combination with advanced building materials while capturing expressive possibilities appropriate to an icon of global corporate finance. Each of these buildings illustrates how, at different historical moments, the search for profitable self-assertion at the pinnacle of capitalist enterprise gives rise to processes of aestheticized land-use intensification that in turn beget a landscape of robust functionality and high symbolism.

Sklair (2005, 2010) has observed that styles of architectural expression in the cores of major world cities today also convey something of the self-conception of the transnational capitalist class whose members circulate with increasing frequency across the globe from one major bastion of

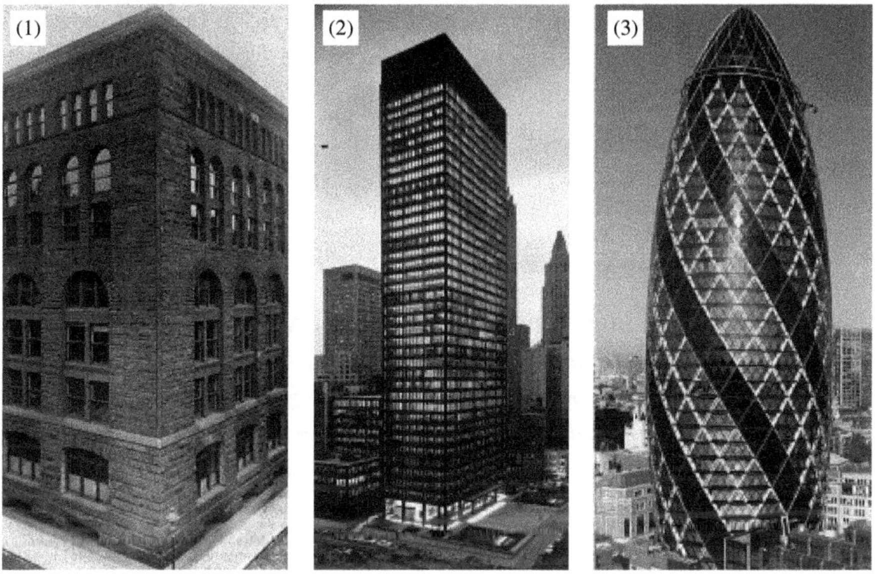

Figure 2. Three generations of land-use intensification and architectural form. From left to right: (1) Form follows function: Marshall Field Wholesale Store, Chicago, Henry Hobson Richardson, (1887). (2) Less is more: Seagram Building, New York, Mies van der Rohe, (1958). (3) Global icons of the 21st century: Swiss Re Building, London, Norman Foster and Partners, (2003).

Source: Illustrations by courtesy of the Creative Commons.

finance, business, and culture to another. In addition to the Swiss Re Building already cited, spectacular instances of the monumental structures that constitute these bastions at the cores of major metropolitan areas in North America and Western Europe are One World Trade Center in New York, London's Canary Wharf, and La Défense in Paris. Each of these buildings also testifies to the power and influence of governmental agencies in motivating private developmental forces. Burgeoning city regions of the Global South participate actively in this trend as well, with striking illustrations being offered not only by Kuala Lumpur's Petronas Towers but also by the Taipei 101 skyscraper in Taiwan, and the Burj Khalifa in the United Arab Emirates (cf. Schmid *et al.*, 2011). Additionally, CBD areas are prime sites for ostentatious cultural projects such as Disney Hall in Los Angeles, the Shanghai Cultural Plaza, London's Royal Opera

House or Tokyo's National Arts Center, all of which affirm their individuality by means of assertive symbolic gestures. These projects, in combination with other design-intensive CBD buildings, exert powerful branding effects that endow their cities with a strong global image (Anttiroiko, 2014; Dinnie, 2011).

5.2. *Gentrification of residential property*

Just as the CBDs of numerous major cities are undergoing dramatic transformation via land redevelopment and reconstruction in recent decades, so too residential neighborhoods in the inner city and elsewhere are experiencing significant rehabilitation. One of the commonest instances of this process is the peculiar form of residential land-use intensification generally referred to as gentrification.

"Gentrification" is a term that has taken on a multitude of different meanings since it was first coined by Glass (1964) in reference to the London housing market in the early 1960s. It is now widely applied to virtually any form of property conversion that entails upgrading, including the redevelopment of commercial properties. In this discussion, however, I restrict the term to its original use as defined by Glass to signify a change of land use where higher socio-economic groups appropriate and upgrade housing vacated — compulsorily or voluntarily — by lower socio-economic groups. Gentrification in this sense is mostly to be found in inner-city neighborhoods that have traditionally been occupied by working-class and low-income families. As such, it entails the replacement or modification of existing buildings and the construction of more capacious and more expensive structures in their stead. In many cases, the gentrification of a given neighborhood proceeds in a piecemeal manner by private individuals who purchase single properties and renovate or restore them on an individual basis; in other cases, professional investors and developers operating at a relatively large scale also foster gentrification, notably by redeveloping land for high-rent multiple-family apartment complexes. Municipal authorities frequently encourage these activities by means of land clearances and the offer of subsidies to developers.

In a series of influential papers, Smith (1979, 1987) claimed that the basic impulse motivating individuals and professional developers to engage in gentrification in US cities derives from the existence of a depression or gap in the urban land-rent surface. According to Smith, this "rent gap" is an observable datum that regularly makes its appearance in low-income residential neighborhoods close to the city center, i.e., in sections of the urban land nexus where rents are lower than the theoretical level they would achieve if the land were given over to what Hurd (1903) called its "highest and best use." Smith suggests that the rent gap then encourages gentrification by making it possible for investors to earn speculative gains by means of property conversion. Certainly, where rent gaps are present, they would tend to reinforce the proclivity to property upgrading, yet it must also be pointed out that rent gaps are neither necessary nor sufficient for gentrification to occur (cf. Hamnett, 1991). This claim can be validated at once by reference to both the earlier discussion of the economic rationale behind land redevelopment and to the more analytical argument presented in the Appendix. In brief, the incentive to redevelop property is not just a function of the rent or price of the land, but also, and critically, of two other variables, namely, the monetary value of the existing improvements on the land, and, more importantly, the projected value of the land and its improvements once reconstruction and/or renovation have been accomplished. Moreover, if the opportunity cost is positive, even initially high-rent land is susceptible to redevelopment or gentrification (as exemplified by land that is sufficiently densely occupied by low-income families as to command a high rent per unit area). Incidentally, this is not an argument against the empirical existence of rent gaps as such, and in fact there is much evidence of their presence in American cities (Scott, 2018); but it *is* an argument to the effect that rent gaps are not, as Smith (1979) avers, the *sine qua non* of gentrification.

In order to close the analytical circle, we need to inquire as to why it is that opportunity costs on gentrification are currently positive at many given inner-city locations whereas the same locations remained impervious to gentrification in earlier decades, with or without the presence of a rent gap. In this regard, there is now a mounting body of theory and evidence suggesting that the essential logic of inner-city gentrification can be captured by reference to the changing employment structures of third-wave cities. To begin with, there has been a very marked increase, both absolutely and relatively, in the numbers of white-collar workers in major cities as the cognitive–cultural economy has grown apace and significant proportions of the employment opportunities for these workers are concentrated in CBD areas. Concomitantly, residential neighborhoods possessing high levels of accessibility to these areas are becoming more and more attractive as foci of housing for white-collar workers (Hamnett, 2003; Ley, 1986; Zukin, 1982). A detailed statistical analysis of these relationships is presented in Scott (2018) for the case of Los Angeles. The *zeitgeist* of contemporary society is also undoubtedly influential in these matters, given the increasing disenchantment of many middle-class individuals with traditional suburban life in contrast to the widening appeal of central cities as hubs of cultural consumption and associated amenities (Bridge, 2001; Clark, 1992).

Then again, gentrification is rarely, if ever, a purely neutral or apolitical affair, not only because it frequently results in involuntary displacement of families from traditional low-income communities but because even when the departure of these families appears to be purely voluntary, they are often driven to leave by locally rising land values, rents and taxes. Renters, above all, can be easily evicted on the termination of their lease. The use of physical threats and eviction on the part of unscrupulous landlords, eager to reap the benefits of higher property values, has also been widely documented. And, as analysts like Slater (2006) and Wacquant (2008) have shown, city councils intent on fostering property upgrading and increasing the tax base within their jurisdictions are often all-too-willing to participate in measures that favor gentrification in deprived neighborhoods at the expense of long-standing residents. Policy measures that function in these ways include the abolition of rent controls, the tightening of building codes, rezoning for single-family houses, increases in property taxes, and the offer of subsidies to first-time house purchases in "under-served" areas. It is no surprise, then, to note that when municipal agencies, private households, or development companies begin to gentrify a given neighborhood, the predictable outcome is political mobilization and protest on the part of low-income residents who are typically at risk of being penalized by this turn of events (see, for example, Blomley, 2003 and Lees *et al.*, 2015).

5.3. *Suburbia, postsuburbia, and sprawl*

For a century and more, the expanding suburban fringe of American cities has been a prime terrain of land redevelopment by both public and private interests. The suburbs in the early decades of the 20th century were principally given over to low-density residential communities where much of the growing white-collar fraction of Fordist society lived, though life in these communities was never as homogeneous as it is sometimes claimed to have been. The suburbanization of white-collar residential activity was a locational arrangement that offered effective geographic and social distance from the predominantly blue-collar neighborhoods of the inner city combined with a hospitable environment in which to satisfy what were then taken to be the domestic needs of the white-collar fraction, including detached and semidetached housing in spacious lots. With increasing urban population and ever-rising rates of car ownership the suburbs expanded relentlessly outward, a trend that was facilitated more often than not by the policies of compliant municipalities in support of the acquisition and conversion of agricultural land and investment in basic infrastructure.

By the late 1940s, large property-development companies were also assertively facilitating suburban expansion. Levittown, built between 1947 and 1951 outside New York, was a pioneering large-scale planned community in the suburbs, as was Lakewood, built between 1949 and 1953 in Los Angeles County by the Lakewood Park Company. These two projects were archetypes of postwar mass-produced suburbs in America with their low costs per residence made possible by economies of scale based on the synchronized redevelopment of extensive tracts of land. Analogous projects proceeded in Britain and France in the 1950s and 1960s via both suburban housing construction and the development of new towns to accommodate the expansion of London, Paris and other major urban centers. In France, much of this suburban expansion took the form of high-rise, rent-subsidized HLMs (*Habitations à Loyer Modéré*) constructed by private–public partnerships set up within the framework of the ZAC legislation described earlier (see also Preteceille, 1973). High-rise construction in the French suburbs made it possible not only to achieve economies of scale in construction but also to achieve relatively high levels of efficiency in infrastructure provision by means of augmented population density at designated sites.

Despite the role of public authorities in North America and Western Europe in helping to accelerate the pace of suburbanization in the decades following World War II, selectively remedial attempts were also made to restrain the outward expansion of cities and to limit the negative effects of sprawl. Perhaps the most ambitious but also one of the most controversial remedial efforts in this direction was the British Greenbelt legislation, first formalized in the Town and Country Planning Act of 1947 and subsequently imitated in a number of other countries. Greenbelt regulations are normally designed to preserve the countryside in designated swaths of land around the city by severely limiting the amount of space that can be converted to building use. In more recent times a variety of so-called smart-growth policy measures have also sought to curtail suburban sprawl by such means as regional transport plans that put constraints on car usage while encouraging the expansion of rapid transit systems. These and other anti-sprawl measures are currently subject to forceful debate between partisans of high-density urban development and a growing body of critics who argue that anti-sprawl policies are driving up property prices in many cities, thereby creating a crisis of affordable housing and hampering economic growth (cf. Cheshire *et al.*, 2014).

Notwithstanding widespread attempts to limit the outward expansion of cities, sprawl typically continues to advance steadily outward, often in a leapfrog fashion wherever obstacles are put in its way. The outward expansionary thrust of the urban periphery is accompanied and complemented by the growing heterogeneity of land uses in the suburbs as exhibited by the growing social variation of residential neighborhoods together with the continued growth and diversification of industrial, office, and retail activities. In addition, some of the most ambitious cases of recent land redevelopment in the suburbs are focused on major recreational and tourist attractions with global appeal such as the Disneyland parks and resorts (descendants of the original Disneyland in suburban Los Angeles) that have been established in Marne-la-Vallée, Hong Kong, Shanghai, and Tokyo. The expansive technology and software parks, new office complexes, university and college campuses, malls, shopping plazas, sports stadia, convention centers, and upscale gated communities that now thrive in suburban areas, too, represent advanced elements of this developmental model in the peripheries of global city regions (Teaford, 1997). So great is the contrast between much of suburbia in this third-wave of capitalist development and its classical form in the pre-War period that it is nowadays often referred to as a *postsuburban* phenomenon (Keil, 2018; Kling *et al.*, 1991; Phelps, 2015). In many respects, indeed, the evolving built environment of postsuburbia with its emergent polycentric structures and its deepening internal socio-economic differentiation is increasingly coming to resemble a sort of fractal echo of the city as a whole.

6. The Contradictory Logic of Urban Redevelopment

I have argued in this chapter that the fountainhead of much of the turbulent redevelopment and rebuilding activity that is proceeding in the urban land nexus today coincides with the restoration of rapid but uneven urban growth in the 21st century in the context of the distinctive socio-economic dynamics of third-wave capitalism. The same dynamics are revealed in and partially fashioned by the land uses and built forms that constitute the physical expression of urban life in this version of capitalism. These phenomena are produced by diverse structures of agency responding to both market and political signals, most notably the property development sector and financial institutions, together with local government organizations with their growing preference for entrepreneurial–interventionist procedures. These trends are most visible in North American and Western European cities, but they are apparent in many other areas of the world as well, including parts of Asia and above all China. To be sure, there is currently much debate about the validity of cross-cultural referencing in urban studies, and, in a recent paper, Wu (2016) has correctly pointed out that the shape and form of China's cities have many unique features that reflect the country's very distinctive institutional and political character (see also, Roy 2009). Contrariwise, and in purely formal terms, China's cities are evidently coming to display at least some of the broad developmental outcomes described in this chapter, such as aestheticized land-use intensification, gentrification, and postsuburban growth (see, for example, He, 2010; Lin and Zhang, 2017; Liu *et al.*, 2018; Wu and Phelps, 2011; Zacharias and

Yang, 2016). This is not the place to attempt to resolve this particular debate, except perhaps to say that as capitalism extends its hold over the global economic order, so certain basic forces and trends of land development (including ever closer cooperation between local governments and financial interests) can be identified across a far-flung swath of cities. The continuing diversity of institutional and cultural contexts from one city and one country to another means that these pressures typically play out in very different kinds of empirical detail, but more in the way of speciation within a wider generic category than as symptoms of absolute incommensurability (cf. Scott and Storper, 2015; Storper and Scott, 2016).

Land redevelopment is, and always has been a highly lucrative sector of the economy. In third-wave cities, in particular, enormous profits and rents are being extracted from the multiple opportunities for property construction and conversion in the urban land nexus. The monetary gains acquired in this manner have served to swell the coffers of banking and financial institutions, property owners, development corporations, building contractors, real estate investors, land assembly agencies, and the like. At the same time, a significant portion of the risks that these parties face is socialized by governmental agencies, which, in the current conjuncture, are prone to offer generous subsidies and other cost-reducing incentives for redevelopment activities. The benefits that flow from these arrangements are almost never apportioned out in socially equitable ways. Equally, vast numbers of low-income families have paid a heavy price as inner-city neighborhoods have been redeveloped to make way for residential gentrification and new commercial ventures. Many low- and medium-income families, too, have been severely disadvantaged by the subprime mortgage-lending fiasco that began in 2007. The social dislocations wrought by these events are compounded by the escalating property values and the persistent shortages of affordable housing in large urban areas at the present time. Third-wave cities are to all intents and purposes locked into a *modus operandi* that systematically endows some portions of intra-urban space with cachet and glitter while others are condemned to marginality and decline (Currid-Halkett and Scott, 2013). Municipal authorities may offer grudging remedial measures in response to the social dislocations that are engendered by these trends, but in the absence of root-and-branch reform, the profit-driven evolution of the urban land nexus seems destined to pursue its customary logic through endless endemic predicaments and political conflicts.

APPENDIX: The Elementary Principles of Property Redevelopment

In order to simplify matters, the discussion here will be limited to considerations of decision-making with regard to the upgrading of purely commercial non-residential property.

Consider any parcel of urban land that yields the quantity x of a given type of output every year. The annual rent earned by *each unit of output* from the parcel is

$$r = \pi - c, \tag{1}$$

where π is the market price and c is the unit production cost including normal profit; c also incorporates any location-dependent quantities such as transport costs.

The market value or acquisition cost, R, of the land (net of any improvements) will be equal to the discounted present value of all future rents accruing to the parcel, i.e.,

$$R = \rho/i = xr/i, \tag{2}$$

where ρ is annual rent *on the whole parcel* and i is the rate of interest (Williams, 1997).

Now let V be equal to the current (depreciated) value of all existing improvements on the land. The aggregate acquisition cost of the land and its improvements will therefore be

$$C = R + V. \tag{3}$$

Suppose that the land and its existing improvements are destined for redevelopment. Let Y equal the cost of redevelopment operations. For present purposes, Y can range from the expense of simple renovation to the cost of wholesale clearance of the land and the erection of new built structures. We can take it that Y also includes carrying costs of the land between its initial acquisition and its resale. Accordingly, the total capital advanced to purchase and redevelop the land will be

$$K = C + Y = R + V + Y. \tag{4}$$

We will temporarily assume that redevelopment entails only change in the quantity of physical output from the parcel, but no change in the nature of the output itself. Total annual output after redevelopment can be identified as $x^* = x + \Delta x$ and its unit production cost as $c^* = c + \Delta c$, where Δx and Δc can take on either positive or negative values. Thus, we can have either increasing or decreasing production quantities combined with either increasing or decreasing costs as a result of redevelopment. Any given shift is equivalent to a switching of production techniques à *la* Sraffa (1960) with important implications for land rent.

In formal terms, redevelopment of the land is economically feasible only when the total rent generated on the converted parcel exceeds the total rent earned on the parcel in its original condition. The difference between these two quantities (assuming that the market price, π, remains unchanged) can be written as

$$\Delta\rho = x^*(\pi - c^*) - x(\pi - c) = x^*r^* - xr, \tag{5}$$

where r^* is rent per unit of output after redevelopment. As it happens, $\Delta\rho$ is also the overall opportunity cost on redevelopment, and the developer has an incentive to proceed if this quantity is positive. Given that x^* and c^* must necessarily be estimated *ex ante* the decision to develop will always comprise a speculative element.

Equation (5) can be re-written in a way that explicitly identifies the relationship of $\Delta\rho$ to Δx and Δc, i.e.,

$$\Delta\rho = (x + \Delta x)\,[\pi - (c + \Delta c)] - x(\pi - c) = \Delta x\,[\pi - (c + \Delta c)] - x\Delta c. \tag{6}$$

Consider Figure 3, which traces out three isolines, $\Delta\rho_1$, $\Delta\rho_2$, and $\Delta\rho_3$, each of each represents a constant opportunity cost as a function of Δx and Δc. Note that $\Delta\rho_1 < 0$, $\Delta\rho_2 = 0$, and $\Delta\rho_3 > 0$. Therefore, any combination of Δx and Δc defining a point that lies above the isoline $\Delta\rho_2$ yields an opportunity cost that is negative; and any combination defining a point that lies below yields an opportunity cost that is positive. The points α, β, and γ, as shown in the figure all represent combinations Δx and Δc that

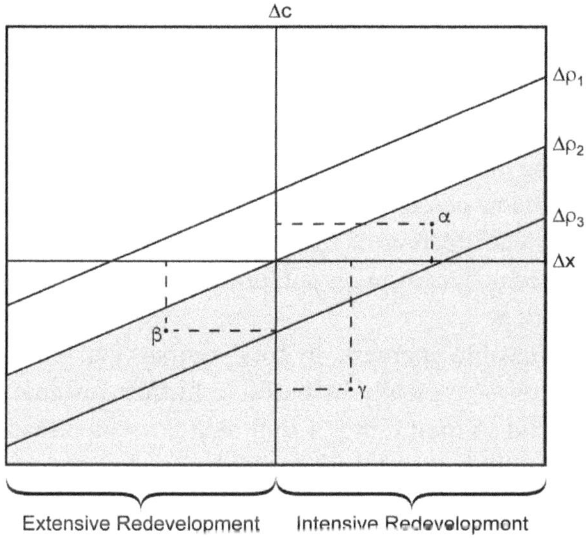

Figure 3. Opportunity costs on land redevelopment as a function Δx and Δc. The horizontal axis of the figure is defined by Δx and the vertical axis by Δc. The isolines $\Delta\rho_1$, $\Delta\rho_2$, and $\Delta\rho_3$ represent different levels of opportunity cost. Note that $\Delta\rho_1 < \Delta\rho_2 < \Delta\rho_3$. Only points that lie below the isoline $\Delta\rho_2$ yield positive opportunity costs; points lying above $\Delta\rho_2$ yield negative opportunity costs.

give positive opportunity costs and that represent viable redevelopment opportunities. Point γ identifies a situation where output increases and production cost declines after redevelopment, and in this case the incentive to redevelop is positive with respect to both Δx and Δc. Points α and β represent more complex situations. In the case of point α, total output from the parcel *increases* after redevelopment, but this advantage is partly offset by increases in production cost; in the case of point β, output *declines* but this is more than matched by a decline in cost.

These remarks now take us directly to issues of intensive and extensive land-use redevelopment. Whenever redevelopment of a given parcel results in $x^* > x$, land use per unit area becomes by definition more *intensive*, and where $x^* < x$ land use becomes more *extensive* (with the proviso in each case that the feasibility of redevelopment presupposes that x^*r^* is greater than xr). In both of these cases, the optimal form of redevelopment is given where the values of x^* and c^* are chosen to maximize the value of x^*r^*.

Intensive redevelopment and extensive redevelopment are in principle possible at any location in urban space. However, the more stringent conditions governing the economic feasibility of extensive redevelopment mean that it is almost certainly less likely to occur than intensive redevelopment. Further clarification of these issues turns on an analysis of the interaction between changes in output, production cost and rent relative to intra-urban location.

First, any feasible increase in total output via redevelopment at any given location — typically by building further upwards — will generate an increment to total rent per unit area. Provided that the value of c^* $(= c + \Delta c)$ can be kept within identifiable limits (so that the opportunity cost is positive) there will be an inducement to intensify land use at the same location. Given that land lying toward the center the city virtually always commands high rents per unit of output in advance of any specific redevelopment action, intensification on this land is thus likely to be especially profitable to the developer.

Second, it is also possible in theory to pursue profitable redevelopment projects by means of a strategy that lowers both output per unit area and its production cost. In this case the new level of output will be $x^* = x - \Delta x$, and the new unit production cost will be $c^* = c - \Delta c$. The rent differential or opportunity cost on redevelopment will again be given by Equation (5), and, if this is positive, redevelopment will be cost-effective. In view of the fact that extensive land-use redevelopment entails joint reductions in output and unit cost, this is evidently apt to be a rather special case.

Once redevelopment of any parcel is complete, the market value of the land (i.e., the present value of all future land rents) will be

$$R^* = R + [(x + \Delta x)\Delta r + r\Delta x]/i = R + \Delta\rho/i = R + \Delta R. \tag{7}$$

The full market value of the parcel (land plus improvements), or its price to the next purchaser, is then determined by the original capital invested by the developer plus the current value of all future increments to annual rent yielded by redevelopment, namely,

$$K^* = K + \Delta R = R^* + V + Y. \tag{8}$$

The quantity R^* will be appropriated by the developer in the sale price of the improved parcel because its constituent elements (R and ΔR) are attributable to the land and the building, both of which are under the developer's control before resale takes place.

It is an easy matter now to generalize the analysis by allowing for land-use change to occur not only with respect to density but also to type of output. Variations in market prices due to changing volumes of output as redevelopment diffuses through the urban land nexus can at this stage also be entered into the analysis (cf. Scott, 1976). As indicated in the main part of the chapter, dynamic extensions of the model are possible.

References

Aalbers, M. (2012). *Subprime Cities: The Political Economy of Mortgage Markets*. Chichester: Wiley-Blackwell.

Aalbers, M. (2017). "The Variegated Financialization of Housing." *International Journal of Urban and Regional Research* 41, 542–554.

Anttiroiko, A. V. (2014). *The Political Economy of City Branding*. Oxford: Routledge.

Ashton, P. (2009). "An Appetite for Yield: The Anatomy of the Subprime Mortgage Crisis." *Environment and Planning A* 41, 1420–1441.

Ball, M. (1986). "The Built Environment and the Urban Question." *Environment and Planning D* 4, 447–464.

Barras, R. (1994). "Property and the Economic Cycle: Building Cycles Revisited." *Journal of Property Research* 11, 183–197.

Barras, R. and D. Ferguson (1985). "A Spectral Analysis of Building Cycles in Britain," *Environment and Planning A* 17, 1369–1391.

Beauregard, R. A. (1994). "Capital Switching and the Built Environment: United States, 1970–1989." *Environment and Planning A* 26, 715–732.

Blomley, N. K. (2003). *Unsettling the City: Urban Land and the Politics of Property*. London: Routledge.

Bonneval, L. and J. Pollard (2017). "Promoteurs Immobiliers, Bailleurs Sociaux, Collectivités Locales: Des Acteurs Aux Frontières Des Marchés Du Logement." *Métropoles* 20, 1–15.

Brenner, N. (2004). "Urban Governance and the Production of New State Spaces in Western Europe." *Review of International Political Economy* 11, 447–488.

Bridge, G. (2001). "Bourdieu, Rational Action and the Time-Space Strategy of Gentrification." *Transactions of the Institute of British Geographers* 26, 205–216.

Brueckner, J. K. (1980). "A Vintage Model of Urban Growth." *Journal of Urban Economics* 8, 389–402.

Capozza, D. and Y. Li (1994). "The Intensity and Timing of Investment: The Case of Land." *American Economic Review* 84, 889–904.

Cheshire, P. C., M. Nathan and H. G. Overman (2014). *Urban Economics and Urban Policy: Challenging Conventional Policy Wisdom.* Cheltenham: Edward Elgar.

Christophers, B. (2011). "Revisiting the Urbanization of Capital." *Annals of the Association of American Geographers* 101, 1347–1364.

Christophers, B. (2015). "The Limits to Financialization." *Dialogues in Human Geography* 5, 185–200.

Clark, E. (1992). "On Blindness, Centerpieces and Complementarity in Gentrification Theory." *Transactions of the Institute of British Geographers* 17, 358–362.

Clark, E. (2005). The Order and Simplicity of Gentrification: A Political Challenge. In *Gentrification in a Global Context: The New Urban Colonialism*, edited by R. Atkinson and G. Bridge. London: Routledge, pp. 262–269.

Crosby, N. and J. Henneberry (2016). "Financialization, Valuation of Investment Property and the Urban Built Environment in the UK." *Urban Studies* 53, 1424–1441.

Currid-Halkett, E. and A. J. Scott (2013). "The Geography of Celebrity and Glamour: Economy, Culture and Desire in the City." *City, Culture and Society* 4, 2–11.

Cuthbert, A. R. (2006). *The Form of Cities: Political Economy and Urban Design*. Oxford: Blackwell.

Dinnie, K. (2011). *City Branding: Theory and Cases*. Houndmills, Basingstoke: Palgrave Macmillan.

Dörry, S., M. Rosol and F. Thissen (2016). "The Significance of Creative Industry Policy Narratives for Zürich's Transformation Toward a Post-Industrial City." *Cities* 58, 137–142.

Dymski, G. (2012). Subprime Crisis and Urban Problematic. In *Subprime Cities: The Political Economy of Mortgage Markets*, edited by M. B. Aalbers. Oxford: Wiley-Blackwell, pp. 293–314.

Fainstein, N. and S. S. Fainstein (2015). The Changing Character of Urban Redevelopment. In *The Oxford Handbook of Urban Planning*, edited by R. Crane and R. Weber. Oxford: Oxford University Press, pp. 587–608.

Fainstein, S. S. (2001). *The City Builders: Property Development in New York and London, 1980–2000.* Lawrence: Kansas University Press.

Fernandez, R. and M. B. Aalbers (2016). "Financialization and Housing: Between Globalization and Varieties of Capitalism." *Competition and Change* 20, 71–88.

Folmer, E. and R. C. Kloosterman (2017). "Emerging Intra-Urban Geographies of the Cognitive–Cultural Economy: Evidence from Residential Neighbourhoods in Dutch Cities." *Environment and Planning A* 49, 801–818.

Glass, R. (1964). Aspects of Change. In *London: Aspects of Change*, edited by Centre for Urban Studies, Report No. 3. London: MacGibbon and Kee, pp. xiii–xlii.

Gothan, K. F. (2012). Creating Liquidity Out of Spatial Fixity: The Secondary Circuit of Capital and the Restructuring of the US Housing Finance System. In *Subprime Cities: The Political Economy of Mortgage Markets*, edited by M. B. Aalbers. Oxford: Wiley-Blackwell, pp. 25–52.

Guironnet, A., K. Attuyer and L. Halbert (2016). "Building Cities on Financial Assets: The Financialization of Property Markets and its Implications for City Governments in the Paris City-Region." *Urban Studies* 53, 1442–1464.

Guy, S. and J. Henneberry (2002). *Development and Developers: Perspective on Property*. Oxford: Blackwell.

Hackworth, J. (2007). *The Neoliberal City: Governance, Ideology and Development in American Urbanism.* Ithaca: Cornell University Press.

Haila, A. (2016). *Urban Land Rent: Singapore as a Property State*. Chichester: Wiley-Blackwell.

Halbert, L. and K. Attuyer (2016). Introduction: The Financialization of Urban Production: Conditions, Mediations, and Transformations." *Urban Studies* 53, 1347–1361.

Hall, P. G. and K. Pain (2009). *The Polycentric Metropolis: Learning from Mega-City Regions in Europe.* London: Routledge.

Hamnett, C. (1991). "The Blind Men and the Elephant: The Explanation of Gentrification." *Transactions of the Institute of British Geographers* 16, 173–189.

Hamnett, C. (2003). "Gentrification and the Middle-Class Remaking of Inner London, 1961–2001." *Urban Studies* 40, 2401–2426.

Harvey, D. (1985). *The Urbanization of Capital: Studies in the History and Theory of Capitalist Urbanization.* Baltimore: The Johns Hopkins University Press.

Harvey, D. (1989). "From Managerialism to Entrepreneurialism: The Transformation in Urban Governance in Late Capitalism." *Geografiska Annaler* 71B, 3–17.

Harvey, D. (2012). "The Urban Roots of Financial Crises: Reclaiming the City for Anti-Capitalist Struggle." *Socialist Register*, 1–35.

He, S. (2010). "New-Build Gentrification in Central Shanghai: Demographic Changes and Socioeconomic Implications." *Population, Space and Place* 16, 345–361.

Hoyt, H. (1933). *One Hundred Years of Land Values in Chicago: The Relationship of the Growth of Chicago to the Rise of its Land Values, 1830–1833*. Chicago: Chicago University Press.

Hurd, R. M. (1903). *Principles of City Land Values*. New York: Record and Guide.

Hutton, T. A. (2008). *The New Economy of the Inner City: Restructuring, Regeneration, and Dislocation in the Twenty-First Century Metropolis*. London: Routledge.

Jadevicius, A., B. Sloan and A. Brown (2017). "Century of Research on Property Cycles: A Literature Review." *International Journal of Strategic Property* 21, 129–143.

Kaika, M. (2010). "Architecture and Crisis: Reinventing the Icon, Reimag(in)ing London and Rebranding the City." *Transactions of the Institute of British Geographers* 36, 453–474.

Kaika, M. (2016). "Land Financialization as a Lived Process: The Transformation of Milan's Bicocca by Pirelli." *European Urban and Regional Studies* 23, 3–22.

Keil, R. (2018). *Suburban Planet: Making the World Urban from the Outside In*. Cambridge: Polity.

Kim, K. H. and B. Renaud (2009). "The Global House-Price Boom and its Unwinding: An Analysis and a Commentary." *Housing Studies* 24, 7–24.

Kling, R., S. Olin, and M. Poster (1991). *Postsuburban California: The Transformation of Orange County Since World War II*. Berkeley: University of California Press,

Leamer, E. E. (2015). "Housing Really is the Business Cycle: What Survives the Lessons of 2008–09? *Journal of Money, Credit and Banking* Supplement to 47, 43–50.

Lees, L., T. Slater and E. Wyly (2007). *Gentrification*. London: Routledge.

Lees, L., H. B. Shin and E. López-Morales (eds.) (2015). *Global Gentrifications*. Bristol: Policy Press.

Ley, D. (1986). "Explanations for Inner-City Gentrification: A Canadian Assessment." *Annals of the Association of American Geographers* 76, 521–535.

Lin, G. C. S. and A. Y. Zhang (2017). "China's Metropolises in Transformation: Neoliberalizing Politics, Land Commodification, and Uneven Development in Beijing." *Urban Geography* 38, 643–665.

Liu, Y., P. Fan, W. Yue and Y. Song (2018). "Impacts of Land Finance on Urban Sprawl in China: The Case of Chongqing." *Land Use Policy* 72, 420–432.

MacLaren, A. (2003). Masters of Space: The Property Development Sector. In *Making Space: Property Development and Urban Planning*, edited by A. MacLaren. London: Arnold, pp. 7–62.

Marshall, A. (1890). *Principles of Economics*. London: Macmillan.

Miron, J. R. (2017). *The Organization of Cities: Initiative, Ordinary Life, and the Good Life*. Cham: Springer.

Molotch, H. (1976). "The City as a Growth Machine: Toward a Political Economy of Place." *American Journal of Sociology* 82, 309–333.

Munneke, H. J. (1996). "Redevelopment Decisions for Commercial and Industrial Properties." *Journal of Urban Economics* 39, 229–253.

Nowlan, D. M. (1977). The Land Market: How It Works. In *Public Property?* edited by L. B. Smith and M. Walker. Vancouver: Fraser Institute, pp. 3–37.

O'Neill, P. (2018). "The Financialization of Urban Infrastructure: A Framework for Analysis." *Urban Studies* 56, 1304–1325. doi 10.1177/0042098017751983.

Pacewicz, J. (2013). "Tax Increment Financing, Economic Development Professionals and the Financialization of Urban Politics." *Socio-Economic Review* 11, 413–440.

Phelps, N. A. (2015). *Sequel to Suburbia: Glimpses of America's Suburban Future*. Cambridge, MA.: The MIT Press.

Ponzini, D. and M. Nastasi (2011). *Starchitecture: Scenes, Actors and Spectacles in Contemporary Cities*. Turin: Umberto Allemandi.

Preteceille, E. (1973). *Production des Grands Ensembles*. Paris: Mouton

Raco, M. and T. M. de Souza (2018). "Urban Development, Small Business Communities and the Entrepreneurialisation of English Local Government." *Town Planning Review* 89, 145–165.

Rosenthal, S. and R. W. Helsey (1994). "Redevelopment and the Urban Land Price Gradient." *Journal of Urban Economics*, 35, 182–200.

Roweis, S. T. and A. J. Scott (1978). The Urban Land Question. In *Urbanization and Conflict in Market Societies*, edited by K. Cox. Chicago: Maaroufa, pp. 38–73.

Roy, A. (2009). The 21st-Century Metropolis: New Geographies of Theory." *Regional Studies* 43, 819–830.

Rutland, T. (2010). "The Financialization of Urban Redevelopment." *Geography Compass* 4, 1167–1178.

Sampson, R. J. (2012). *Great American City: Chicago and the Enduring Neighborhood Effect*. Chicago: University of Chicago Press.

Savini, F. and M. B. Aalbers (2016). "The Decontextualization of Land-Use Planning through Financialization: Urban Redevelopment in Milan." *European Urban and Regional Studies* 23, 878–894.

Schmid, H., W. D. Dietrich and J. Urry (2011). *Cities and Fascination: Beyond the Surplus of Meaning*. Farnham: Ashgate.

Scott, A. J. (1976). "Land Use and Commodity Production." *Regional Science and Urban Economics* 6, 147–160.

Scott, A. J. (1980). *The Urban Land Nexus and the State*. London: Pion.

Scott, A. J. (2011). "Emerging Cities of the Third Wave." *City: Analysis of Urban Trends, Culture, Theory, Policy, Action* 15, 289–321.

Scott, A. J. (2017). *The Constitution of the City: Economy, Society, and Urbanization in the Capitalist Era.* New York: Palgrave Macmillan.

Scott, A. J. (2018). "Residential Adjustment and Gentrification in Los Angeles, 2000–2015: Theoretical Arguments and Empirical Evidence." *Urban Geography,* early view from: https://doi.org/10.1080/02723638.2018.1500253.

Scott, A. J. and M. Storper (2015). "The Nature of Cities: The Scope and Limits of Urban Theory." *International Journal of Urban and Regional Research* 39, 1–15.

Sklair, L. (2005). "The Transnational Capitalist Class and Contemporary Architecture in Globalizing Cities." *International Journal of Urban and Regional Research* 29, 485–500.

Sklair, L. (2010). "Iconic Architecture and the Culture-Ideology of Consumerism." *Theory, Culture and Society* 27, 135–159.

Slater, T. (2006). "The Eviction of Critical Perspectives from Gentrification Research." *International Journal of Urban and Regional Research* 30, 737–757.

Smith, N. (1979). "Toward a Theory of Gentrification: A Back to the City Movement by Capital Not People." *Journal of the American Planning Association* 45, 538–548.

Smith, N. (1987). "Gentrification and the Rent Gap." *Annals of the Association of American Geographers* 77, 462–465.

Sraffa, P. (1960). *Production of Commodities by Means of Commodities*. Cambridge: Cambridge University Press.

Stone, C. N. (1987). A Study of the Politics and Urban Development. In *The Politics of Urban Development*, edited by C. N. Stone and H. T. Sanders. Lawrence: Kansas University Press, pp. 3–22.

Storper, M. and A. J. Scott (2016). "Current Debates In Urban Theory: A Critical Assessment." *Urban Studies* 53, 1114–1136.

Teaford, J. C. (1997). *Post-Suburbia: Government and Politics in Edge Cities*. Baltimore: The Johns Hopkins University Press.

Topalov, C. (1974). *Les Promoteurs Immobiliers: Contribution à l'Analyse de la Production Capitaliste en France*. Paris: Mouton.

Wacquant, L. (2008). "Relocating Gentrification: The Working Class, Science and the State in Recent Urban Research." *International Journal of Urban and Regional Research* 32, 198–205.

Waldron, R. (2018). "Capitalizing on the State: The Political Economy of Real Estate Investment Trusts and the Resolution of the Crisis." *Geoforum* 90, 206–218.

Weber, R. (2010). "Selling City Futures: The Financialization of Urban Redevelopment Policy." *Economic Geography* 86, 251–274.

Weber, R. (2015). *From Boom to Bubble: How Finance Built the New Chicago*. Chicago: Chicago University Press.

Williams, J. T. (1997). "Redevelopment of Real Assets." *Real Estate Economics* 25, 387–407.

Wu, F. (2016). "Emerging Chinese Cities: Implications for Global Urban Studies." *The Professional Geographer* 68, 338–348.

Wu, F. and N. A. Phelps (2011). "(Post)suburban Development and State Entrepreneurialism in Beijing's Outer Suburbs." *Environment and Planning A* 43, 410–430.

Zacharias, J. and W. Yang (2016). "A Short History of the Chinese Central Business District." *Planning Perspectives* 4, 611–633.

Zukin, S. (1982). *Loft Living: Culture and Capital in Urban Change*. Baltimore: Johns Hopkins University Press.

Chapter 6

Circular Economy and Metropolitan Circles in Europe — Case Study: Amsterdam

Mehri Madarshahi

Senior Economist (Emirata),
United Nations, New York, USA
president@culturelsglobal.org;
madarshahi@madarshahi.org

1. Introduction

Cities present a sustainability conundrum. While they are engines for economic growth, political power, hubs for innovation, and the most efficient means of service distributions, they remain large-scale consumers of water, energy, natural and processed products, and account for more than 80% of the world's greenhouse gas emissions (Figure 1).

According to the Food and Agricultural Organization (FAO) of the United Nations, the world's population will grow to nine billion people by 2050, and, as the world urbanizes, the demand on resources rises. This demand, combined with the finite supply of resources, will lead to scarcity and strong price fluctuations (Figure 2).

As cities grow, their increasingly complex infrastructures, population, and services undoubtedly will be threatened by the consequent spatial changes. This is a common problem for all metropolitan areas worldwide.

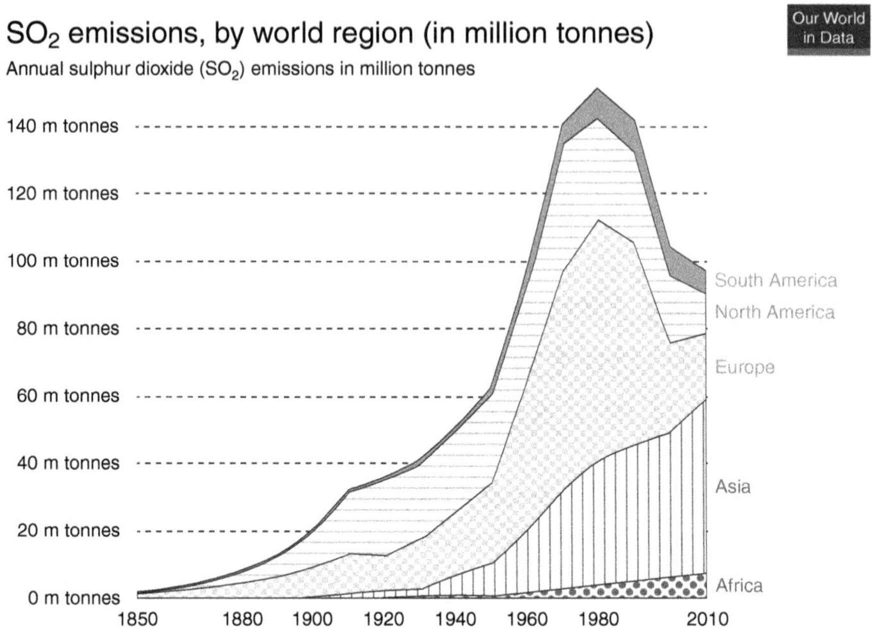

Figure 1. SO_2 emissions, by world region.

Source: https://www.stateofglobalair.org/data.

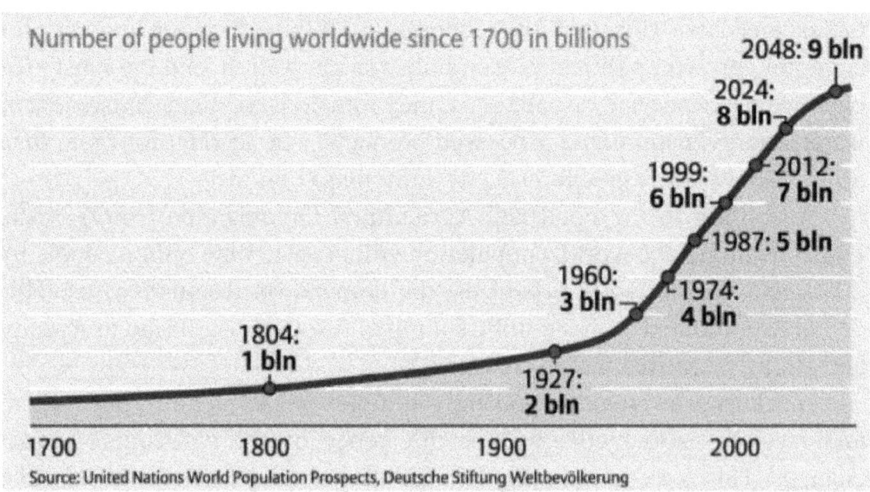

Figure 2. Population growth since 1900 and its rise in 30 years.

The present systems and infrastructures for the provision and management of essential services in cities are the result of several decades of evolution, despite the fact that the urban centers have continued to change both in size and density. In addition, advancements in technologies and new threats of discontinuity such as climate change and resource scarcity, among others, are increasingly giving rise to new challenges affecting the proper functioning of the cities. These problems are complex and call for a shift to a new paradigm, rethinking the present practice of economic models. Our linear way of producing and consuming is under pressure. Cities of today and tomorrow need novel and integrated metropolitan solutions that can focus on the exploitation of possible synergies at a mega scale ensuring a more resilient and integrated sustainable food, energy, water, and material nexus.

The new thinking must focus on "design for circular reuse" based on renewable sources, new services, and demand–supply matching through smart infrastructures. It must combine green–blue urban environments based on integrated water, nutrient and material recovery, shared services, and supply chain optimization.

The circular economy offers cities a systemic framework to address some of their most pressing challenges and to create new opportunities for building resilient and prosperous communities reconciling social, cultural, and environmental governance. Circular economy expresses an aspiration to get more value from resources and waste less, especially as resources come under a variety of pressures — price-driven, political and environmental. Delivering the circular economy can bring direct costs savings to businesses, reduce risk and offer reputational advantages, and can therefore be a market differentiator. Reallocation of cars in the urban systems and emphasis on walkability, bike-ability, and dedicated low-emission mobility require the adoption of new thinking by citizens. Technology and innovation are critical components for social integration and empowerment of citizens and are driving economic growth in the metropolitan circles.

2. Integration of Circular Economy in Metropolitan Circle

In Figure 3, the existing urban infrastructure and environment are redesigned to integrate not only consumption by but also production for

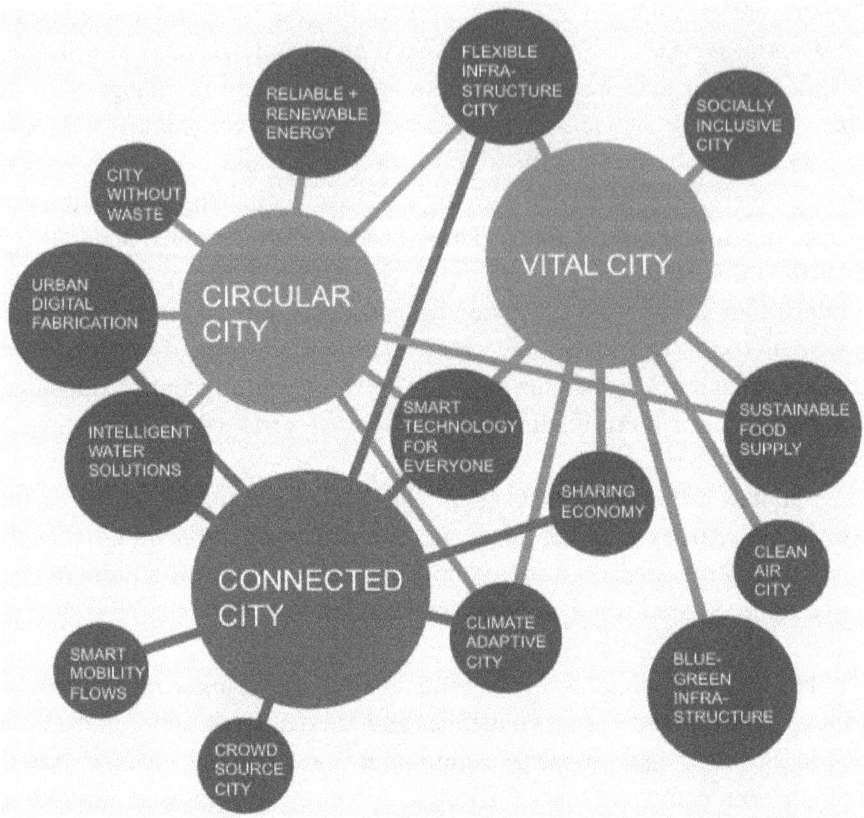

Figure 3. Integration of circular economy in metropolitan circle.

citizens in the context of, i.e., a circular city. In such a scheme, the redesign of urban green and blue morphologies and urban infrastructures must increase resilience to disruptive changes (both climate- and economy-related) and meet the health and biodiversity needs of metropolitan areas.

Metropolitan circles of the future are fully adapted to the consequences of climate change. They seek to eliminate the concept of waste, keep assets at their highest utility at all times, and are enabled by digital technology. They produce and promote use of renewable energy, adaptable infrastructure to the need of the cities and to its citizens and fully planned mobility to move from point A to B. Metropolitan circles embed the principles of a circular economy across all their functions, establishing an urban system that is regenerative and restorative by design.

The impact on how cities are conceived, materialized, and operationalized in a circular framework can hardly be overstated. Owing to the complexity of cities some impacts can be imagined and others, at best, can be anticipated. The implications of a circular agenda are thus significant, and we only just begin to fathom its magnitude.

In addition, the proliferation of various interpretations of the meaning of circularity and its new value systems by cities and citizens also has created difficulties for urban planners. Some interpretations are essentially linear processes to be made more efficient: examples are some European models and the Greater Bay Area (GBA) project in China. Certain interpretations may seem "too holistic" such as the proposed plan for Amsterdam where not only the formation of the city will change from linear to circular, but where also the whole value system of the citizens as well as their economic practices will be revamped.

3. Linear vs. Circular Models in City Planning

The most prevailing practices in city planning, which maintain a linear approach combined with some modifications, are found among a number of European countries such as Great Britain, Spain, and Italy. These cities aim at introducing an innovative crowd management, a better use of bike and pedestrian spaces, more robust and resilient public transport and a more efficient use of low emission cars, and other modalities such as water, energy, waste, data, and food. Many try to eliminate the concept of waste, keep assets at their highest utility at all times, and are enabled by digital technology.

A couple of examples cited in the subsequent paragraphs may highlight some of the ongoing efforts. While many cities share rides, London has taken the sharing model one step further, introducing a "Library of Things," where people actually share electronics and appliances. This is a congenial concept extending the useful life of many assets and vastly reduces the quantity of new products purchased and eventually discarded.

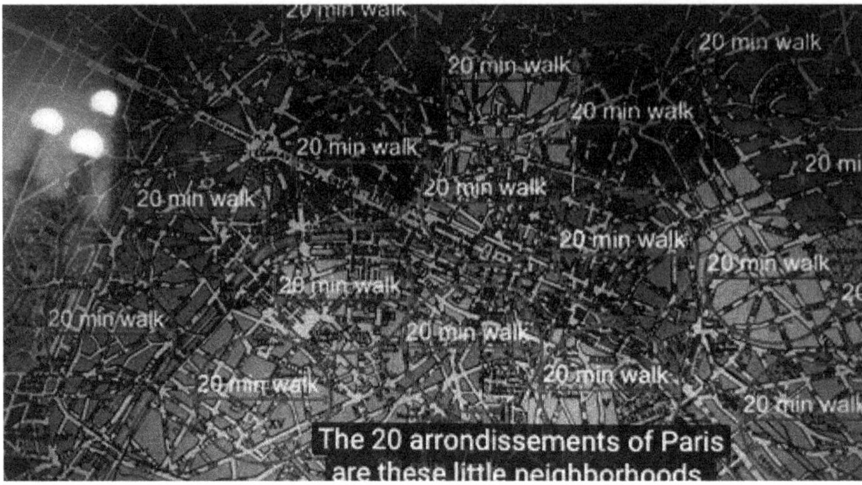

Figure 4. The circular structure in metropolitan Paris.

The city of Cremona in Italy is focusing its circular efforts on waste management, piloting door-to-door collection and citywide second-hand markets. The city has also introduced a tariff on any waste that cannot be collected. In just two years, Cremona has thus increased recycled waste from 53% to 72%.

This initiative is part of a larger roadmap explicitly connected with and building on the many plans that are already being or will be implemented.

Paris — on the other hand — provides a good example of a circular city in the European context. Originally, a series of little villages came together and created a circular structure with the present 20 arrondissements (Figure 4).

The French MAPTAM law (Modernization of Territorial Policy and the Cities) of January 27, 2014 created the Greater Paris Metropolis (GPM). The latter is organized into regional government agencies (EPTs) and will unite Paris with the municipalities of the inner suburbs (Haut-de-Seine, Seine-Saint-Denis, and Val-de-Marne départements), comprising 124 municipalities.

The GPM will thus have a population of nearly 7 million, or more than half of the inhabitants of the region. It will exercise four major functions: metropolitan area planning; local housing policy; economic, social and cultural development and planning; and air and environmental protection. The Metropolis will also be responsible for harmonizing electricity, gas, heating, and cooling distribution networks.

The French Agency for the Environment and Energy Management (ADEME) defined the circular economy according to seven pillars in order to uncouple economic growth and the consumption of natural resources: sustainable supply, eco-design, industrial and regional ecology (IRE), product-service system, sustainable consumption, extending the duration of use (reuse, repair, and re-utilization), and recycling.

The digitization of public and private life is imminent and the Internet of things will enable city planners to create a connected city and more intelligent urban infrastructure at scales that were previously unthinkable.

The Chinese model in creating the GBA project tries to present a new inter-connected transregional transportation network as a strategic corridor for accelerating smart development and safeguarding institutional innovations. It links Hong Kong and Macao with nine other cities into a hi-tech economic powerhouse. The core objective of this project is to bridge the gap between urban and rural development and to facilitate rural development. The Guangdong–Hong Kong–Macao (GBA) project was part of China's 13th Five-Year Plan (FYP). Since its introduction in March 2018, this concept has been embraced by much of the local business community.

In Europe, the Amsterdam region presents itself as the front-runner in circularity, and for transition to a circular economy. The region has many entrepreneurial and innovative businesses, citizens, start-ups, organizations and knowledge institutions that are already working within the framework of a circular economy. The economic activity of the Amsterdam metropolitan region amounts to €106 billion annually, of which €47 billion are accounted for by the city of Amsterdam (2013).

4. A Circular Amsterdam

A summary of the future vision for Circular Amsterdam and its roadmap is presented in the following paragraphs.

Amsterdam's focus is on a number of interconnected pathways that include: low emission development, resilient development, nature-based development, equitable and people-centered development, as well as circular development. It uses the circular economy as representing a new model for economic development based on redesign, reuse, repair, remanufacture, recycle, and restore resulting in high resource use efficiency. It seeks systematically to increase environmental capacity and to reduce its ecological footprint. Amsterdam plans to coordinate ecology and human life systematically by improving/redesigning its urban transportation, community development, and the integration of the built environment with smart concepts for the connection and mobility, energy generation, storage, and exchange. The design for a circular metropolitan area in Amsterdam entails moving toward radial sectors and belts via pathways into areas known as circulars or rings. Circular belts then subdivide the radial sectors which extend outward from a central point forming a

Figure 5. The circular metropolitan area in Amsterdam.

widening circular grid structure. As the circle widens more circular belts follow until the perimeter is reached where in the environment is allowed to return to wild nature without any form of sprawl (Figure 5).

5. Total City System

Through this experimentation, Amsterdam concluded the following:

- a circular scheme is more efficient than other city layouts (Figure 6);
- all facilities such as mass transit, medical, and other common needs could be located near the center;
- starting at one point one can travel a circle and eventually come back to the same point. In a linear city one has to travel back again to get to the same point;
- planned circular design minimizes the length of all transportation and distribution lines;

Figure 6. The city layouts of Amsterdam.

Source: Frans Lemmens via Getty images.

- in a circular city, one will be within a reasonable distance from all facilities in the city;
- in such a design, resources that drive human activities are by definition regenerative rather than linear or degenerative. Therefore, the focus shifts from gradual destruction of resource-value — "take, make, waste" — to value-creation through models based on cascades and cycles.

6. Deconstruction and Reuse

Research programs were an essential part of planning. Their focus was on three, strongly interrelated subthemes: materials and buildings, nutrients recovery, and urban energy systems. Each subtheme had its own research priorities. Each theme accentuated innovation in systems engineering and integration, energy storage, and information technology, adopting a citizen perspective (Figure 7).

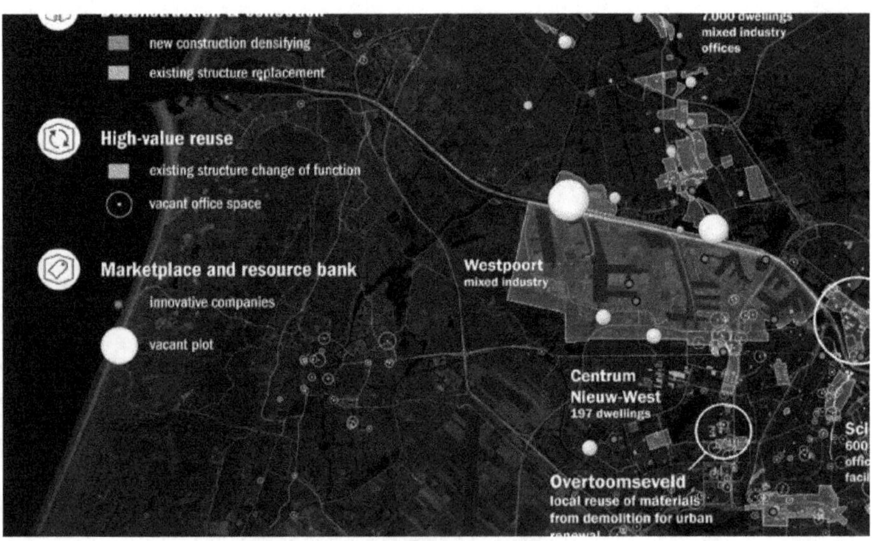

Figure 7. Deconstruction and Reuse.
Source: Amsterdam.nl. Circle Scan Amsterdam-Smart City Initiatives in the Netherlands (Smart City Embassy)

The practical application of this scheme resulted in the reduction of greenhouse gas emissions by half a million tons of CO_2 per year, equivalent to 2.5% of the current annual CO_2 emissions of the city of Amsterdam.

7. Recycling and Re-Use of Materials

Through its various experimentations Amsterdam has concluded that redesigning product and material supply chains can save the city €85 million per year in construction costs and €150 million per year through use of organic residual streams. The economic activity of the Amsterdam metropolitan region amounts to €106 billion annually, of which €47 billion is accounted for by the city of Amsterdam (2013) (Figure 8).

Figure 8. Recycling and re-use of materials.

Source: Urbantransfor.eu. Urban waste management an Recycling System (ECOFIL.SRL www.ecofil.IT)and Circle Scan Amsterdam-Smart City Initiatives in the Netherlands (Smart City)

8. Conclusion

This chapter briefly discusses that, due to its new nature, the concepts of the circular economy and of metropolitan circles are yet to be fully defined and their definitions and inter-relationships must be subject to an in-depth analysis. It is important to review systematically design processes in various urban settings to address the behavior and accessibility of systems and objects over time as well as to assess whether digital mechanisms for city infrastructures such as waste management, water, sanitation, and power supply can be better designed for future platforms.

Out of the various experiments it has become obvious that

- circular design means less to build and less to maintain and hence is more efficient;
- use of space: a circle provides the most efficient form of infrastructural elements;
- replicating the same access points and designs means fewer resources than conventional construction methods;
- such circular design is cost-efficient since it requires one central radial to be designed and then replicated throughout the radials.

New technologies and research findings can assist to make an urban center more livable and beautiful. In order to link cultural policy with industrial policy, urban planning, and environmental policy, the vertical administrative structure must be made horizontal, ordinary bureaucratic thinking must be eliminated, and organizational culture must be changed.

A long road lies ahead, but the difficulties are not insurmountable.

Reference

Gemeente Amsterdam (2013). *Towards the Amsterdam Circular Economy.*

Chapter 7

Current Conditions and Future Drivers of Mega-City Regions in the US, Focusing on the Los Angeles Metropolitan Area

Hilda Blanco

Price School of Public Policy and Center for Sustainable Cities, University of Southern California, USA
hblanco@usc.edu

1. Introduction

Beginning with a review of the concept of mega-city regions and of recent trends throughout the world, this chapter focuses on the Los Angeles–Long Beach Combined Statistical Area (CSA), the second largest CSA in the US with an estimated population of 18.8 million, and characterizes the suburban densities in different parts of this vast mega-city region.

China boasts of a national urban development policy, whereas the US lacks such a national policy. In the absence of a national policy on this issue, beginning in the 1960s–1970s, several states and cities in the US developed urban growth management policies to address such challenges. The section on urban growth management reviews the rationale for the movement and profiles Oregon's urban growth management system, often viewed as the most successful statewide growth management program. This is followed by a discussion of smart growth, a blending of growth management and new urbanism concepts, which emerged in the mid-1990s. The chapter then addresses the issue of whether urban growth management efforts have been effective in the US by reviewing major research on the topic, which has mixed results. It ends this section with a discussion of the major challenges to urban growth management in the US, including the lack of metropolitan governance, the difficulty of financing urban infrastructures, and the lack of adequate housing affordability strategies.

The chapter then focuses on how urban form affects GHG emissions and discusses syntheses of research that link different aspects of urban form, such as density or mix of uses to reductions in vehicle miles traveled (VMT) and greenhouse gas (GHG) emissions. It profiles California's legislation on Sustainable Communities and Climate Protection as a statewide growth management legislation focused on climate change mitigation.

Section 2 discusses two types of future drivers of urban form, technological and climate change impacts. Technological drivers examined include changes in commercial land uses, specifically, the decline of regional shopping malls in the US and the opportunities for their redevelopment, and the increasing automation of industrial processes. Climate change impacts are explored from the perspective of California's climate change research programs and increasingly evident extreme climate impacts, especially wildfires and floods. In conclusion, the chapter suggests that urban growth management efforts focused on avoiding areas vulnerable to extreme climate impacts, such as flood- or wildfire-prone areas, will become increasingly important over the 21st century.

2. Mega-City Regions: Evolving Concepts

Although current urbanization processes and speeds are unprecedented, the phenomenon of mega-city regions became widely recognized in the literature with Gottman's notion of megalopolis (Gottman, 1957, 1961). Gottman defined a megalopolis as a polycentric region with over 25 million people connected by transportation infrastructure. His prime example was the Boston–Washington corridor. Georg *et al.* (2016) in a recent paper reviewed various concepts coined to describe massive forms of urbanization and identified over a dozen related concepts. One of the major concepts to emerge more recently is the mega-city region, defined as a main city with a population of over 10 million and including 10–50 other cities interconnected by ITC infrastructure and commuting patterns (Hall and Pain, 2006). The mega-region concept is also polycentric, and the Pearl River Delta urban region is often cited as an example (Florida *et al.*, 2007).

The phenomenon of mega-cities and regions has been recognized by the United Nations. Its most recent report on World Urbanization Prospects (United Nations, 2015) compares and projects the number and size of mega-cities around the world. In its projection for 2030, it clearly recognizes the increasing size and agglomeration of cities within urban areas. Figure 1, drawn from their study, highlights the increasing number of coastal mega-cities, which will be increasingly vulnerable to the impacts of sea-level rise.

2.1. *Mega-city regions in the US*

In the US, a similar concept, megapolitan region, has been identified and applied to large regions with anchor cities that could be from 50 to 200 miles apart but connected by ITC and commuting patterns (Lang and Dhavale, 2005). Southern California or the Southland is identified as one such region, which includes Los Angeles and San Diego. However, commuting on a regular basis from Los Angeles to San Diego is not feasible, with the time taken to commute from one city to the other being 2 h by driving and more than 4 h by a combination of train and bus.

The most relevant mega-city region concept applied to the US is the US Census concept of CSAs. These regions contain multiple cities, large and small, and counties and are defined by commuting patterns. The great advantage of this concept is the availability of data provided by US Census on a periodic basis for these areas. Figure 2 provides the latest map identifying CSAs in the country.

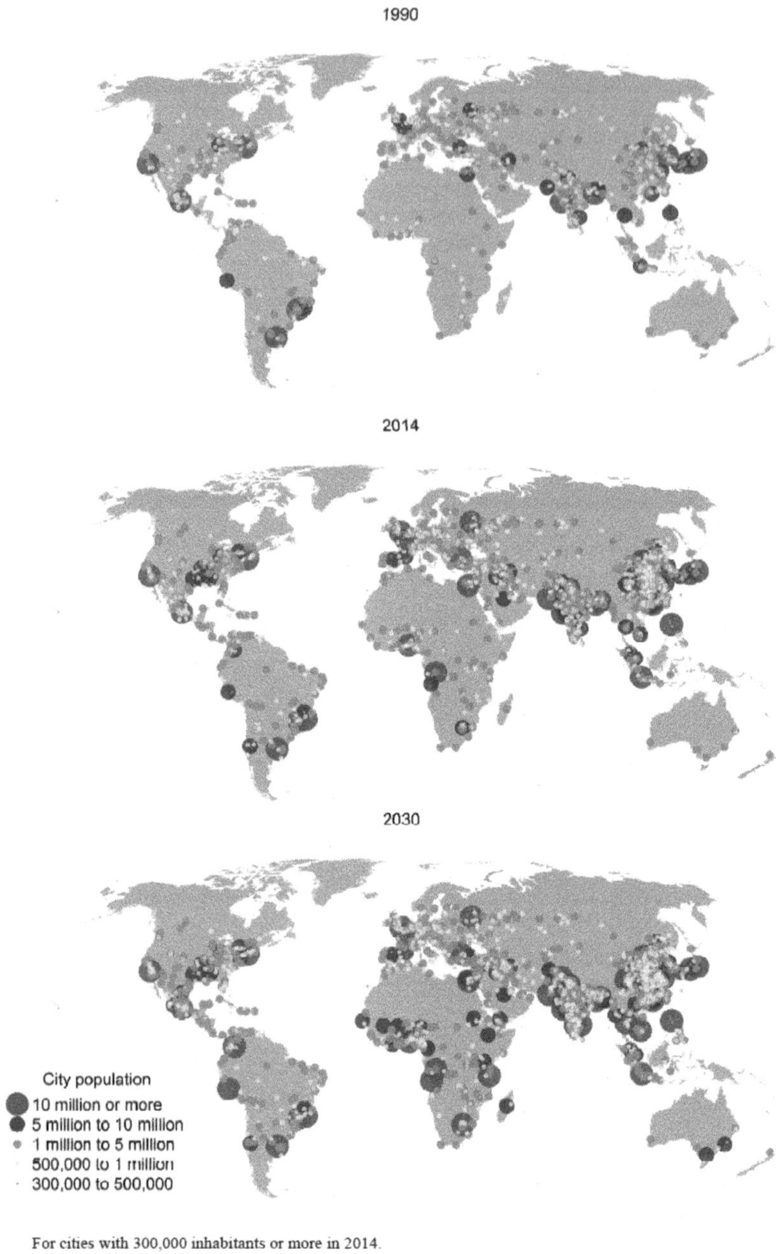

Figure 1. Cities by size and class of settlement, 1990, 2014, and 2030.

Source: United Nations (2015, p. 89).

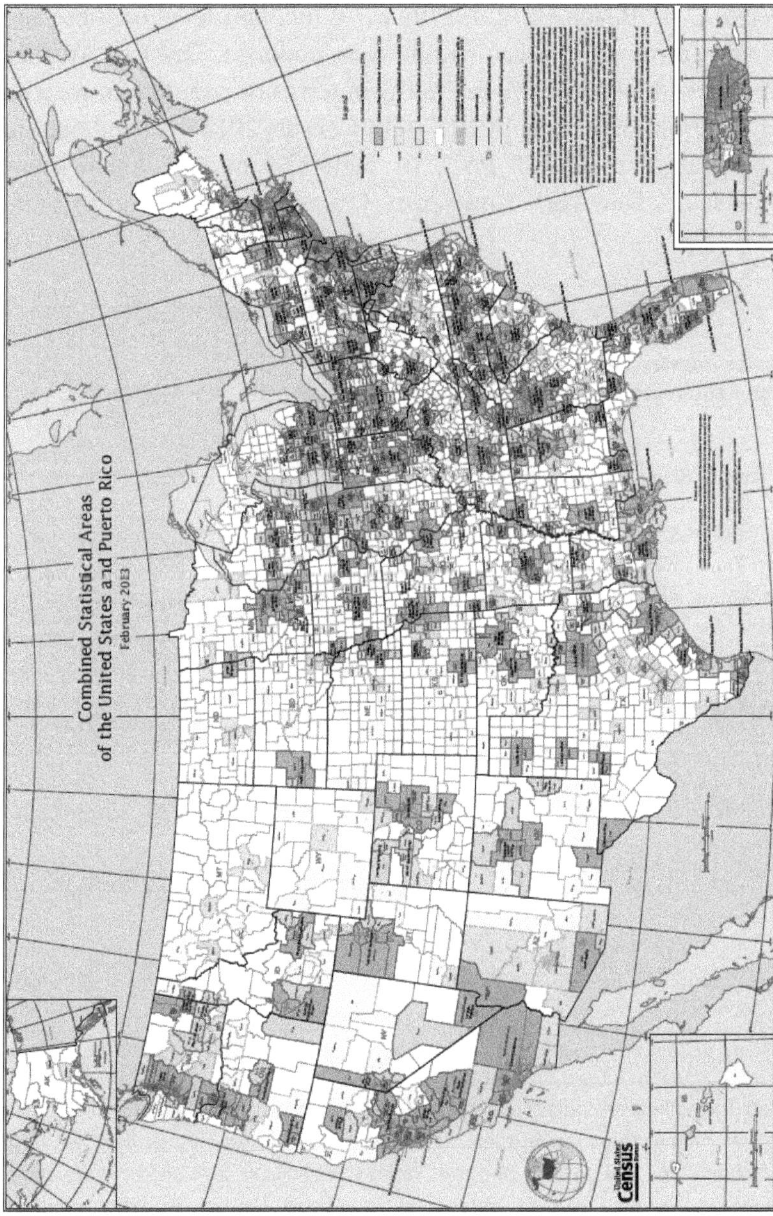

Figure 2. CSAs of the US and Puerto Rico.

Source: US Department of Commerce (2013).

2.2. *The Los Angeles–Long Beach CSA*

Los Angeles–Long Beach CSA, see Figure 3, includes five counties[1] and the cities and surrounding areas within those counties. The Los Angeles CSA is the second largest CSA in the US in terms of population, with an estimated 18.8 million people in 2017 (US Census, 2018), second only to the NY–Newark, NY–NJ–CT–PA CSA with 23.9 million which spans parts of four states, New York, New Jersey, Connecticut, and Pennsylvania.

5 Counties: Los Angeles, Orange County, Ventura, San Bernardino, Riverside Counties

Total Population (2017): 18.825 Million

•Los Angeles Co.:	88 cities	10.231 M
•Orange Co.:	33 cities	3.199 M
•Riverside Co.:	28 cities	2.383 M
•San Bernard. Co.:	23 cities	2.156 M
•Ventura Co.:	9 cities	0.856 M

City of Los Angeles **4.021 M**

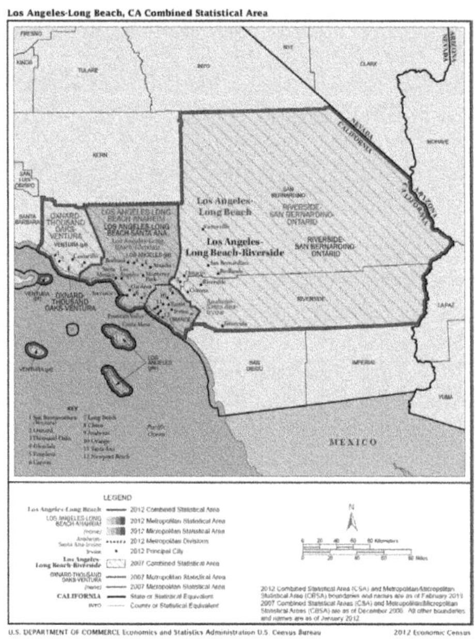

Figure 3. Los Angeles–Long Beach CSA, map, and selected statistics.

Sources: US Census (2012) for map; CA Department of Finance (2018) for population of counties and number of cities.

[1] Counties are the earliest administrative or political subdivisions of US states, which retain significant government functions in most states, especially in areas which have not been incorporated into cities. Their scope of power varies from state to state and between counties and incorporated cities. In California, cities have broad powers, including land-use regulatory powers over their territory, and counties retain land-use powers only over unincorporated areas of the county.

The third largest CSA is the Chicago–Naperville CSA, which straddles parts of the states of Illinois, Indiana, and Wisconsin, with an estimated 9.9 million people.

The metropolitan regions (CSAs) in the US are not homogeneous but are composed of a range of cities from large to small, vast suburban areas, as well as rural, and agricultural and natural resource lands. Within the region, Riverside and San Bernardino counties were major agricultural centers up to the 1950s and since then have become increasingly residential suburbs to LA and other cities within the metropolitan area. Table 1 shows a range of urban areas, many of which are suburban in character within the Los Angeles–Long Beach CSA.

Litman (2015, 12) provides useful equivalences that enable us to translate housing units per square mile to housing density per net acre to better understand the figures in Table 1, Columns 1–6. Zoning and housing density guidelines for transit are expressed in housing units per net acre. According to Litman's guidelines (p. 12), from a regional perspective, 8,000 residents per gross square mile taking into account all land in a region, including industrial areas and open space, are equivalent to 10 dwelling units per net acre. Using Litman's guidelines, the last column in Table 1, housing density per net acre, provides a better sense of net housing densities to compare the figures available from the Census to guidelines for effective transit. Referring to this column in Table 1, it is clear that densities within the two MSAs, Los Angeles–Long Beach–Santa Ana, and Riverside–San Bernardino–Ontario, can be considered suburban densities, at 3.3 du/net acre and 0.19 du/net acre, respectively. However, some cities within the Los Angeles–Long Beach–Santa Ana MSA, such as Los Angeles, Santa Ana, and Santa Monica, have overall net residential densities higher than 10 du/net acre. Also important to note is the vast territory in the Riverside–San Bernardino–Ontario MSA, the suburban densities even in the major cities, and the rural densities of its many smaller settlements. The low suburban densities across much of the CSA determine the use of private automobiles for work trips and make it difficult to provide efficient public transit, which typically requires 10–14 dwelling units per net acre (Litman, 2015, p. 50).

The metropolitan areas in the US are much more expansive, in terms of urban land cover or impervious surface area than those of China's, as the

Table 1. Population, housing units, and density in MSAs, principal cities, and not in principal cities in the Los Angeles–Long Beach CSA, 2010.

MSAs and selected cities in the Los Angeles–Long Beach CSA	Population	Housing units	Total area ($mile^2$)	Land area	Persons ($mile^2$)	Housing ($mile^2$)	Housing density per net acre
Los Angeles–Long Beach–Santa Ana MSA	12,828,837	4,493,983	5,699.01	4,848.45	2,646	926.9	3.3 du/acre
Los Angeles City	3,792,621	1,413,995	502.69	468.67	8,092.3	3,017.0	10.1 du/acre
Santa Ana City	324,528	76,896	27.52	27.27	11,900.8	2,819.9	14.9 du/acre
Santa Monica City	89,736	50,912	8.42	8.41	10,664.1	6,050.3	13.3 du/acre
Not a Principal City	5,757,532	1,919,933	4,664.79	3,882.01	1,483.1	494.6	1.85 du/acre
Riverside–San Bernardino–Ontario, MSA	4,224,851	1,500,344	27,408.25	27,263.42	155.0	55.0	0.19 du/acre
Riverside City	303,871	98,444	81.44	81.14	3,745.0	1,213.3	4.7 du/acre
Not a Principal City	3,005,146	1,081,232	26,976.26	26,834.06	112.0	40.3	0.14 du/acre

Source: US Census. Population, housing units, area and density: 2010 — County — County subdivision and place.
Note: The last column in the table, “Housing density per net acre” is calculated using Litman (2015, p.12) equivalences.

study by Kuang *et al.* (2014) makes clear. The study by Kuang *et al.* compared the three largest metropolitan regions in China — Beijing, Shanghai, and Guangzhou — to the three largest in the US — New York, Los Angeles, and Chicago — in terms of their urban expansion from 1970 to 2010. Their study makes clear that while the three Chinese mega-city regions have experienced significant expansion from 1970 to 2010, the US mega-city regions, especially the New York and Los Angeles regions, had established their extensive suburban footprints by 1970. The Chicago urban region, on the contrary, significantly expanded its suburban area during the 1990s. This comparison with Chinese mega-cities highlights the suburban nature of much of the mega-city regions in the US. The next section discusses how the suburban expansion in metropolitan areas established during the 1970s led to urban planning efforts to manage urban growth.

3. Growth Management in the US

Unlike China, especially as incorporated in its 11th and 12th Five-Year Plans (Ye, 2014), the US has no national urban development policy. To address this lack in policy, many states and local governments have developed state and local policies to deal with urban development problems. Since the 1970s, these types of policies have become known as urban growth management policies, or growth management policies.

Until the emergence of the growth management movement in the US, most urban planning programs were implemented at the local level through land-use regulations. Local governments typically provided public facilities after development took place. The provision of public facilities was not seen as a strategy to shape urban development, but rather as a government function to be provided as urban development occurred. Also hindering the use of infrastructure provision as an urban development tool was the typical fragmentation of city functions, that is, most cities have public works departments and transportation departments which conduct their own planning for infrastructure systems separate from city planning departments which develop land-use plans. However, since in the US most urban infrastructure is publicly financed, the provision of public infrastructures can be a powerful development tool, sometimes more powerful than the traditional land-use regulations. Government, through the provision and financing of infrastructure, has the opportunity to determine directly the following:

- **The value of land:** In the US, extending a road or sewer service through an undeveloped area multiplies the value of undeveloped land.
- **The location of development:** By extending infrastructure systems to particular locations and not to others, the location of development can be strongly influenced.
- **The type of development:** The scale of infrastructure provided can influence the type of development, for example, whether high or low density.
- **The timing/sequencing of development:** The provision of infrastructure could be phased in such a way as to influence the sequence of development in undeveloped areas.

The growth management movement in the US, with its roots in the environmental movement of the 1960s, began to emerge in the late 1960s and early 1970s (Porter, 1986). This movement within urban planning and environmental protection circles was aimed at managing the rapid growth that occurred after World War II and through the 1960s in the US. This growth was perceived as encroaching into rural and undeveloped lands and often lacked the infrastructure to support it. The movement represented the most positive incorporation of environmental concerns into land planning during the middle of the last century and extended the urban planning agenda to include the following:

- land-use regulation of the amount, location, sequencing, and character of development;
- comprehensive planning linked to capital investment — although urban planning in the US already incorporated comprehensive planning, capital investment in infrastructure systems often was handled by different state or city agencies; thus, the growth management approach combined land development regulations, infrastructure planning, and public capital financing.

Through the mid-1980s, growth management systems were primarily aimed at preserving natural and agricultural areas from the encroachment of urban development, that is, at the containment of urban areas to preserve non-developed areas. Beginning in the 1990s, there was a greater emphasis on controlling or managing sprawl. In the US, sprawl came to mean at least three types of development: strip development, leapfrog (or disconnected) development, and low-density, single uses. Suburban developments of detached low-density housing were recognized as the primary type of sprawl development.

Growth management in the US has been employed at two scales, the local and the state levels. Communities in states where there was no statewide growth management program, such as California or New York, could develop their own growth management programs. But local growth management programs were criticized early on because of the regional problems that they often worsened. For example, controlling growth in one municipality is likely to reduce affordable housing options in that municipality. This could contribute to regional traffic congestion and air pollution, since those who work in the municipality, not being able to live in that municipality, would need to commute from other localities (Dowall, 1984). In addition, growth management advocates saw local control of land use as a major cause of loss of agricultural and environmentally sensitive land and of the regional problems the nation faced (Bosselman and Callies, 1971). These advocates argued for state governments to take back the local powers over land-use regulation they had ceded to local governments since the turn of the 20th century.[2] Today, nine states in the US are widely

[2]Under the US Constitution, local governments are not recognized officially; only state governments are recognized. Outside of the federal powers that are stated in the Constitution, state governments retain all other powers. Local governments obtain their government powers from state governments. These powers, including land-use regulatory powers and fiscal powers, must be explicitly provided to local governments by the states through state statutes or by individual city charters. All local government powers flow to localities from the states. But land-use powers were provided by state governments across the US through enabling legislation beginning in the 1920s. Growth management advocates, beginning in the 1970s, claimed that in order to reduce sprawl and manage urban development more efficiently, state governments needed to take back some of the powers they had devolved to local governments. Thus, statewide growth management programs, in effect, provide more extensive state guidelines and oversight over regulatory activities which had been left to local governments since the 1920s. Although the state governments are the source of the original powers, it has proved very difficult for states to regulate local land-use powers, even under the most successful state growth management systems.

recognized as having some form of state urban growth management (Florida, Hawaii, Maine, Maryland, New Jersey, Oregon, Rhode Island, Vermont, and Washington) (Paulsen, 2013, p. 201). Section 3.1 will briefly review Oregon's system, one of the most successful statewide programs.

3.1. *Oregon's state growth management system*

Oregon's state growth management plans (1973) have several distinctive features: its Urban Growth Boundary (UGB) strategy, its linkage of infrastructure to land use, and Portland's metropolitan government (Metro).

3.1.1. *Senate Bill 100*

Oregon's statewide system was motivated by two major factors: Oregonians' feelings that the natural resources of their state should be protected and their fear of the state becoming another California. Then Governor Tom McCall led the call for state planning by decrying "sagebrush subdivisions, coastal 'condomania', and the ravenous rampage of suburbia in the Willamette Valley" (DeGrove, 1984, p. 235). Senate Bill 100 (SB 100), Oregon's growth management system, was passed in 1973[3] (Knapp and Nelson, 1992; Abbot *et al.*, 1994; Seltzer, 2013).

The state plan, which now includes 19 goals, is the core of the system. The state plan sets the standards for and is implemented by city and county plans. Local governments are required to develop local plans, zoning, and land division ordinances that are consistent with the 19 goals. The goals address the following points:

- the planning process, including citizen involvement and land-use planning;
- conservation issues, including topics such as farm lands, forest lands, and natural resources;
- development issues dealing with housing, transportation, public facilities and services, and urbanization;
- coastal resources (Oregon DLCD, n.d.).

---

[3]The Land Use Act of 1973 Or. Laws ch. 80.

The Land Conservation and Development Commission (LCDC) directs the statewide planning program. This commission is composed of seven members who are appointed by the governor. The Commission has a staff of employees, the Department of Land Conservation and Development (DLCD). Aided by the staff, the commission reviews and approves local plans for consistency with the state plan goals. Once approved, the local plans are "acknowledged for compliance". If a local government plan fails to win acknowledgement, the state goals can become the basis for local development decisions. Enforcement is ensured by penalties. All the local plans of Oregon's 241 cities and 36 counties have been acknowledged. However, SB 100 also requires a periodic review process, every 4–10 years to ensure compliance. The Commission also has power to adopt administrative rules that interpret the goals. Another distinctive feature of the Oregon system is its special administrative "court", the Land Use Board of Appeals made up of three members, that hears and rules on most land-use planning matters (Liberty, 1992; Sullivan, 1993; Howe, 1993).

3.1.2. *The urbanization goal*

Goal 14 in Oregon's state plan is the urbanization goal. Its aim is as follows:

> To provide for an orderly and efficient transition from rural to urban land use (Oregon DLCD, 1995).

This goal requires that localities establish and change UGBs based on seven factors:

1. demonstrated need to accommodate long-range urban population growth requirements consistent with LCDC goals, which required demographic studies;
2. need for housing, employment opportunities, and livability, requiring economic projections;
3. orderly and economic provision for public facilities and services;
4. maximum efficiency of land uses within and on the fringe of the existing urban area;

5. environmental, energy, economic, and social consequences;
6. retention of agricultural land as defined, with Class I being the highest priority for retention and Class VI the lowest priority;
7. compatibility of the proposed urban uses with nearby agricultural activities (Oregon DLCD, 1995).

UGBs include already urbanized areas and areas where urban services are to be expanded in the future. Outside of the UGB are rural-use areas where urban densities are discouraged by their lack of urban public services and infrastructure. The UGB needs to accommodate long-range growth. This is typically interpreted as a 20-year planning period. Furthermore, since 1995, a 20-year growth boundary requirement is mandated for Portland's metropolitan areas and fast-growth jurisdictions.[4] Figure 4 provides a schematic diagram of the UGB concept.

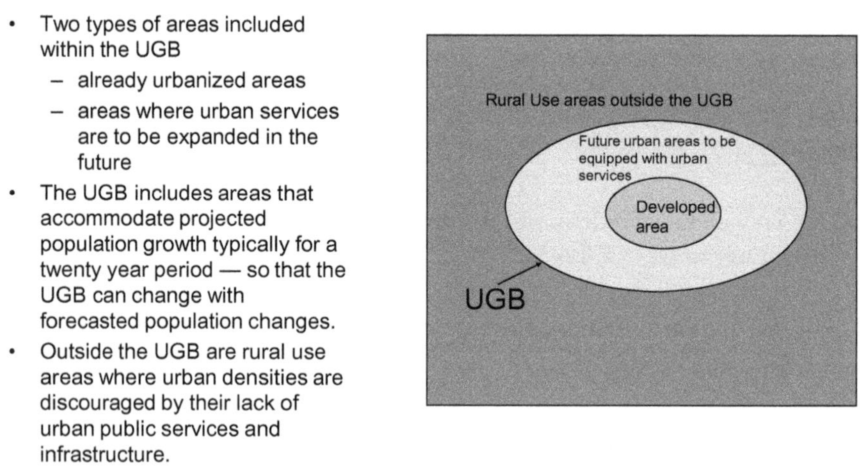

Figure 4. Urban growth boundaries.

[4]Oregon Laws: ORS 197.296. Factors to establish sufficiency of buildable lands within urban growth boundary. Retrieved on November 12, 2018 from https://www.oregonlaws.org/ors/197.296.

3.1.3. *Metro*

Portland's status in this system is special in that the state mandates Portland's Metropolitan Service District (Metro) to plan and regulate land use within its three-county jurisdiction. By 2017, Portland's metropolitan area included over 50% of the total state population.[5]

Metro is also exceptional in the country; established in 1992, it is the only directly elected regional government in the US with both service responsibilities, e.g., solid waste, regional parks, and convention center, as well as regional planning (see DeGrove and Miness, 1992, pp. 146–155). It encompasses the Portland UGB and serves more than 1.3 million residents in the Clackamas, Multnomah, and Washington counties and the 25 cities in the Portland, Oregon, metropolitan area.

Metro is governed by a council president elected regionwide and six councilors elected by district. Metro has fiscal powers, including the ability to levy property tax, sales tax, and income tax with voter approval and limited taxes without voter approval. Its primary responsibility is regional land-use planning (including transportation planning) and other issues of metropolitan concern (Portland Metro, 2018).

3.2. *Smart growth*

The term *smart growth* began to be used interchangeably with growth management in the mid-1990s (American Planning Association, 1996). Smart growth was a conscious re-packaging of growth management efforts by planning and environmental organizations, combined with insights from the New Urbanism movement, a movement that advocated more pedestrian-oriented compact development. Smart growth has had a greater emphasis on mechanisms to reduce sprawl, but continues to rely on growth management mechanisms, such as UGBs, transfer of development rights, and multi-modal transportation systems. It included incentives to discourage leapfrog development and to encourage development

[5]Total population for the State of Oregon in 2017 was 4.143 million (US Department of Commerce, Bureau of Census 2017); Portland's metropolitan area, including Vancouver, WA, was 2.453 million (US Census, American FactFinder, 2017).

in the existing urban areas. Smart growth, in particular, provided greater emphasis on public incentives, e.g., provision of infrastructure. By the mid-2000s, over 20 states had some kind of state growth management or smart growth program in place (Gray, 2007). Maryland was the first state to adopt a smart growth statute in 1997 under Governor Glendening (1997). Under the Maryland program, the state government targeted programs and funding (infrastructure and economic development funding) to support established communities and locally designated growth areas (priority funding areas) and to protect rural areas. The approach was primarily an incentive approach. The priority funding areas included municipalities, e.g., Baltimore City, areas within the Baltimore and Washington beltways, neighborhoods designated for revitalization, and county-designated growth areas. The purely incentive approach, however, has drawbacks. Since state resources for infrastructure and economic development are limited, the incentives are weak. In addition, nothing in the 1997 Act prevented sprawl from occurring, e.g., there was no Exclusive Farmland Zoning as in Oregon's program to restrict urban uses outside the UGB.

3.3. *Have urban growth management efforts been effective in the US?*

Several analyses of the effectiveness of urban growth management efforts were conducted in the 2000s. Carruthers (2002) conducted an econometric analysis of 238 metropolitan areas, with and without growth management programs. He found that most metropolitan areas with growth management systems showed no differences in terms of densities or the extent of land developed and in some cases even negative impacts. However, he found positive results in the case of Oregon's program, including greater densities. Carruthers concluded that consistency and enforcement requirements were the most important characteristics of programs that showed positive results. Anthony (2004) focused on change in urban densities in 49 states over a 15-year period, seeking to find significant differences in density among those states with urban growth management programs vs. those without. He found less of a density decline among growth-managed states than among states without growth management, but his regression analysis indicated that states with growth management programs did not have a statistically significant effect on checking sprawl. Wassmer (2006) carried out a regression analysis of metropolitan areas focused on the extent of the impact of growth management on the size of the metropolitan areas. He used a more sophisticated model that took into account the impacts of the natural evolution of cities, flight from blight effects, and the fiscalization of land-use factors. Wassmer concluded that in states with local growth controls, urban areas are 15.9% smaller, restrictive regulations are twice as effective, vertical consistency requirements are twice as effective as horizontal consistency, and the number of years that regulations are in place is also significant. Dierwechter and Carlson (2007) conducted a descriptive and spatial analysis of residential permits in Pierce Co., Washington from 1991 to 2002 and found that since mid-1990s, the percentage of development within UGA boundaries had increased. In particular, he found that results improved over time, e.g., in 1995, 60% of permits were located within urban growth areas (UGAs), and by 2002, permits within the UGAs increased to 77%. Yin and Sun (2007) conducted a regression analysis for 294 metropolitan areas in 49 states (1990, 2000) testing for significant effects of state growth management programs (SGPMs) on density. Their study concluded that metropolitan areas with SGMPs had higher percentage increases in population density. Overall, these studies provide mixed results, and a more recent study confirms such findings. Paulsen's (2013) study focused on the extent to which growth management programs affect marginal land consumption rates, testing the extent to which growth management can be effective in controlling sprawl. He concludes that in cases with strong state planning roles, there is some support for such programs to reduce sprawl, although his study also indicates that moderately regulated places actually increase sprawl!

3.4. *Challenges to growth management in the US*

Why have the US state urban growth management programs delivered such mixed results? A primary challenge to growth management in the US is the lack of metropolitan governance, or, in general the difficulty of coordinating across multiple local governments and across different levels of government. As indicated, only the Portland metropolitan area has a metropolitan government unit in charge of planning. This impedes growth management, since each local government has land-use and fiscal controls that it uses to maximize its benefits, regardless of the spillover effects on other jurisdictions. In particular, since a major source of local government revenue is the property tax, which is based on the value of property within the locality, local governments have a powerful incentive to permit development to increase their property tax base. Local governments, in addition, have incentives to turn down affordable housing developments, since these do not increase property tax revenues as much as high-priced housing or commercial/industrial properties.

The financing of urban infrastructure, another important element of urban growth management efforts, is increasingly difficult because of the tax limitation movement, which began in California in the 1970s and has since affected most states (Mullins and Wallin, 2004). The tax limitation movement first focused on property tax increases, but now often applies to most local tax revenue sources. It, in effect, was responsible for voter initiatives that have limited property tax rate increases, making it difficult for local governments to raise funds for maintaining existing infrastructure and public facilities or for constructing new facilities. Also, decreasing federal support to states and local government since the 1970s has significantly contributed to the deficit in infrastructure financing across the country. The American Society of Civil Engineers (ASCE) has been assessing the condition of the nation's infrastructure and providing a report card since 1998. It evaluates infrastructure conditions according to eight criteria: capacity, condition, funding, future need, operation and maintenance, public safety, resilience, and innovation. Its latest report card (2017) gives the overall grade of D^+ (poor, at risk) to the nation's infrastructure and identifies \$4.59 trillion needed for investment between 2016 and 2025 to bring these infrastructure systems into good condition (ASCE, 2017). Failing to close such an investment gap may imply \$3.9 trillion in losses to national GDP, \$7 trillion in lost business sales, and 2.5 million lost jobs by 2025 (ASCE, 2017). This lack of funding for infrastructure and public facilities results in ineffective smart growth programs.

Another major challenge facing growth management programs is the lack of adequate housing affordability strategies. Although many growth management programs recognize the need to address affordable housing issues, there is a lack of funding to ensure that as land development is contained to certain areas and land prices increase, affordable housing options are not lost. A line of research on growth management outcomes indicates that urban containment strategies can increase housing costs (Anthony, 2003; Downs, 2004).

Despite the proliferation of growth management programs over the past 40 years, continuing traffic congestion and air pollution in major metropolitan areas indicate that growth management has not been effective in dealing with the problems attendant to sprawl and single-occupant automobile use in most regions. Since most metropolitan areas in the US are highly dispersed and of low density, mass transit systems are expensive to construct and operate. Although the federal government and many state governments have increased their investment in transit to relieve traffic congestion in urban areas since the 1990s, transit ridership outside major metropolises, such as NYC, Chicago, and Boston, where extensive subway systems were established early in the 20th century, has remained low, averaging 5.1% across the US (US Census, 2016). The LA Metro region, for example, has made substantial investment in its transit system over the past 25 years, yet transit ridership has been declining since 2007 and has fallen significantly since 2013 (Manville *et al.*, 2018).

4. Climate Change Mitigation and Urban Form

Given the problems faced by urban growth management efforts to reduce sprawl, and their mixed results, why is this issue still a major challenge? Table 2 makes clear that urban land expansion has been accelerating, especially since 2000. The meta-analyses by Seto *et al.* (2011, 2012) and Angel *et al.* (2011), summarized in the table, conclude that if the rates of urban development, at lower densities than earlier urban densities, continue through 2030, nearly two-thirds (65%) of all urbanized land by 2030 will have been urbanized during the first three decades of this century. See the last column in the table. This table appears in the chapter on urban settlements (Chapter 12) in IPCC's 4th Climate Assessment, Working Group III-Mitigation.

Since estimates of the extent of urban land across the world in 2011 amounted to 0.2–2.4% of habitable land on the planet, this may not seem such a shocking figure. Tripling these estimates would amount to urban

Table 2. Forecasts of global urban land expansion to 2030.

Study	Scenario	Projected urban expansion to 2030 (km^2)								% of projected urban land in 2030 to be built between 2000–2030
		Urban land 2000 (km^2)	Africa	Asia	Europa	Latin America	North America	Oceania	Total (% increase from 2000)	
Seto *et al.* (2011)	SPES A1	726,943	107,551	1,354,001	296,638	407,214	73,176	16,996	2,255,576 (310)	76
	SPES A2	726,943	113,423	702,772	162,179	122,438	49,487	15,486	1,165,785 (160)	62
	SPES B1	726,943	107,551	1,238,267	232,625	230,559	86,165	18,106	1,913,273 (263)	72
	SPES B2	726,943	136,419	989,198	180,265	131,016	74,572	15,334	1,526,805 (210)	68
Seto *et al.* (2012)	>75% probability	652,825	244,475	585,475	77,575	175,075	118,175	9,700	1,210,475	65
		Urban land 2000 (km^2)	Africa	Asia	East Asia and the Pacific	Europe and Japan	Latin America and the Caribbean	Land rich developed countries	Total (% increase from 2000)	
Angel *et al.* (2011)	0% density decline	602,864	58,132	120,757	43,092	9,772	49,348	54,801	335,902 (56)	36
	1% density decline	602,864	92,002	203,949	75,674	74,290	98,554	119,868	664,337 (110)	52
	2% density decline	602,846	137,722	316,248	119,654	161,379	164,975	207,699	1,107,677 (184)	65

Sources: Angel *et al.* (2011) and Seto *et al.* (2011, 2012, 2014, p. 941).

areas occupying from 1% to 7.2% of the earth's habitable surface by 2030. However, croplands and pastures are estimated at about 40% of habitable lands and forested lands are estimated at over 31% (World Bank, 2018). Urbanization is estimated to account for the loss of 1.8–2.4% of global croplands by 2030 (d'Amour *et al.*, 2017). This estimate of the loss of croplands needs to be interpreted from the standpoint of an estimated global population increase of 13.2% by 2030 (United Nations, Department of Economic and Social Affairs, 2017). Thus, around the world, as the population increases, urbanization, which is occurring at lower densities around the world, will be significantly contributing to the loss of croplands, pastures, and forested lands. This highlights the importance of developing and implementing effective urban growth management practices.

4.1. *Congestion, air pollution, and GHG emissions*

Low-density urban regions, as found in most parts of the US, rely primarily on single-occupancy motor vehicles for work trips. For example, although the Los Angeles–Long Beach–Anaheim MSA has invested heavily in transit, 75% of trips to work are still carried out in single-occupancy autos, another 10% in carpools, and only 5.5% by transit (US Census–ACS, 2016). Motor vehicles powered by fossil fuels are sources of both air pollution and GHG emissions.[6] Since 2016, the transportation sector in the US generates the largest share of GHG emissions (US EPA, 2018). With the increased importance of this sector for reducing GHG emissions, vehicle miles or vehicle kilometers traveled (VKT) has become a major indicator of GHG emissions.

4.2. *Climate change and urban form*

"Urban areas account for between 71% and 76% of CO_2 emissions from global final energy use and between 67% and 76% of global energy use"

[6]Despite great reductions in air pollution over the past decades, the MSA still ranks #1 in the nation for ozone pollution and #4 for Particulate Matter 2.5, both of which have significant health impacts (American Lung Association, 2018).

(Seto *et al.*, 2014, p. 927). Expanding urban areas at suburban densities, especially where automobiles are the primary mode of travel, has become an important subject for climate change policy. However, research over the past 25 years has made clear that density alone is not the only indicator of urban form that can reduce single-occupancy vehicle travel and VKT. Neither does the provision of transit, by itself, guarantee significant reductions in VKT. The emerging consensus among the urban and transportation experts is that transit investments need to be accompanied by other urban form changes in the areas surrounding transit stations or corridors. Or, as Calthorpe (1993) puts it, transit investments require transit-oriented developments (TODs), which are often referred to as developments characterized by the five Ds: density, diversity (of land uses), design (of streets), destination accessibility, and distance to transit (Ewing and Cervero, 2001, 2010).

Many studies and several syntheses of the literature on the contribution of these various factors to reductions in VKT have been published (Ewing and Cervero, 2010; Stevens, 2017). The results of many of these studies are summarized in Table 3, which appears in IPCC's 4th Assessment, Working Group III — Mitigation, Chapter 12, the chapter on urban areas. The table illustrates that studies vary on aspects of the variable examined, for example, some density studies focus on population and others on dwelling units. Connectivity studies can focus on intersection density or street density. The table displays results in terms of elasticities, and the darker bars show the range of results of the studies analyzed. Thus, for example, studies focused on population density range from 0 to –0.1 elasticity. A –0.1 elasticity can be understood as an effect that upon doubling or increasing population density by 100% would produce a 10% reduction in VKT. The range of results within the studies included can be great. For example, land-use mix elasticities from the studies included vary from –0.02 to –0.28. An important point that emerges from this research is that although many of the studies indicate low elasticities for specific urban form interventions, combining several of these changes, such as density, land-use mix, and proximity to transit, can yield larger decreases in VKT (National Research Council, 2010).

Table 3. Aspects of urban form and their VKT elasticities.

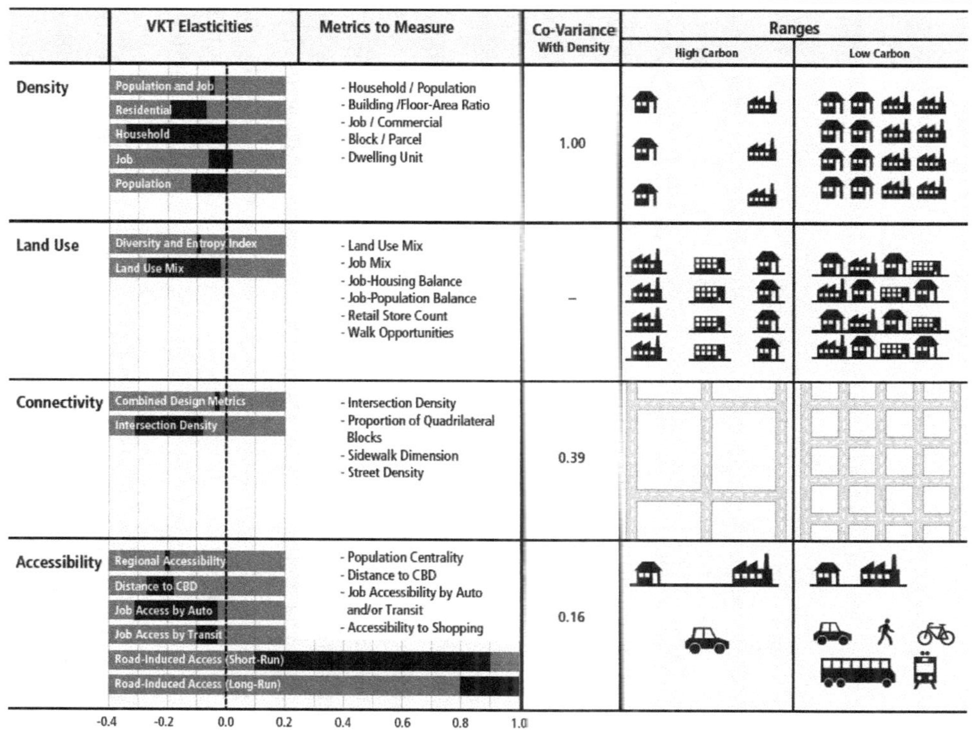

	VKT Elasticities	Metrics to Measure	Co-Variance With Density	Ranges: High Carbon	Ranges: Low Carbon
Density	Population and Job Residential Household Job Population	- Household / Population - Building /Floor-Area Ratio - Job / Commercial - Block / Parcel - Dwelling Unit	1.00		
Land Use	Diversity and Entropy Index Land Use Mix	- Land Use Mix - Job Mix - Job-Housing Balance - Job-Population Balance - Retail Store Count - Walk Opportunities	–		
Connectivity	Combined Design Metrics Intersection Density	- Intersection Density - Proportion of Quadrilateral Blocks - Sidewalk Dimension - Street Density	0.39		
Accessibility	Regional Accessibility Distance to CBD Job Access by Auto Job Access by Transit Road-Induced Access (Short-Run) Road-Induced Access (Long-Run)	- Population Centrality - Distance to CBD - Job Accessibility by Auto and/or Transit - Accessibility to Shopping	0.16		

Figure 12.14 | Four key aspects of urban form and structure (density, land use mix, connectivity, and accessibility), their Vehicle Kilometer Travelled (VKT) elasticities, commonly used metrics, and stylized graphics.

Source: Seto *et al.* (2014, p. 953).

4.3. *California's SB 375 Sustainable Communities and Climate Protection Act of 2008*

Many researchers on growth management have included California as a growth management state; however, until the passage of Senate Bill 375, the Sustainable Communities and Climate Protection Act, efforts in growth management were primarily carried out by individual cities, through residential caps, and annexation controls, and these programs were more aptly characterized as local growth controls (Landis, 2006). The results of such local growth controls in California have been mixed, effective in limiting population within the cities, but increasing housing prices, and often increasing regional congestion (Dowall, 1984; Deakin, 1989; Landis, 1992, 2006; Pallagst, 2017). SB 375 can be considered, in effect, California's statewide urban growth management program. The legislation, however, unlike the early state urban growth management programs is not directly focused on preserving agricultural or natural resource lands, but rather on urban form and on how urban form contributes to VKT and therefore to GHG emissions. The legislation mandates the 18 regional transportation agencies in the state, each of which encompass several counties, and whose primary mission has been to plan and manage state and federal funds for regional transportation improvements, to develop regional Sustainable Communities Strategies or Plans with their constituent local governments. Such plans are required to meet GHG reduction targets set every 4 years by the state's Air Resources Board (CARB), which is in charge of implementing California's overall climate change program (California Air Resources Board, 2018). CARB has designated a special board, the Regional Targets Advisory Committee, that has the power to set targets for each of the 18 regional agencies every 4 years. The board's staff reviews these plans and decides whether each of the metropolitan planning organizations (MPOs) is set to meet the 2020 and 2035 goals to reduce emissions to the levels identified in the legislation.

But California's SB 375 is, in effect, a statewide urban growth management program, in that it requires the 18 regional MPOs to reduce their GHGs with certain targets by 2020 and 2035 by linking their land use and transportation to reduce vehicle miles traveled. The program is more aligned with the second-generation state growth management and smart growth programs that focused on the character of development within urban areas. While early growth management programs sought to protect state environmental resources and second-generation programs were focused on the character of development within urban areas, this new type of statewide urban growth management program is also aimed at protecting the global environment through strategies that shape urban form at a regional urban scale, given the reality of the mega-city regional context of many local governments (Barbour and Deakin, 2012).

California's SB 375 addresses the governance problem that has plagued urban growth management efforts by using metropolitan transportation agencies that can develop metrowide plans and provide important infrastructure financial incentives for cities and counties. Through these incentives and guidelines, it leads local governments to develop land-use policies to address elements of urban form, such as density, diversity of land uses, the design of streets and buildings, and access to jobs and retail. However, the effectiveness of this approach depends on the strength of the incentives, as discussed in the next section.

4.3.1. *Urban growth management through regional agencies with state directives*

California's 18 metropolitan transportation planning agencies, covering different parts of the state, have been designated by the state as the agencies to implement SB 375. The Southern California Association of Governments (SCAG) is the metropolitan planning agency for the Los Angeles region. See Figure 5 for SCAG's planning area — note that SCAG's planning area includes all of the LA–Long Beach–CSA, and additionally, it includes Imperial County, which is an active agricultural area that is sparsely populated. SCAG is the largest MPO in the state (including six counties, 191 cities, and over 18 million residents).

The first targets that CARB set for the SCAG region called for an 8% reduction in GHG emissions per capita by 2020 and a 13% reduction by 2035. GHG emissions were calculated based on reductions of VMT using advanced travel-demand models to more effectively capture the effects of

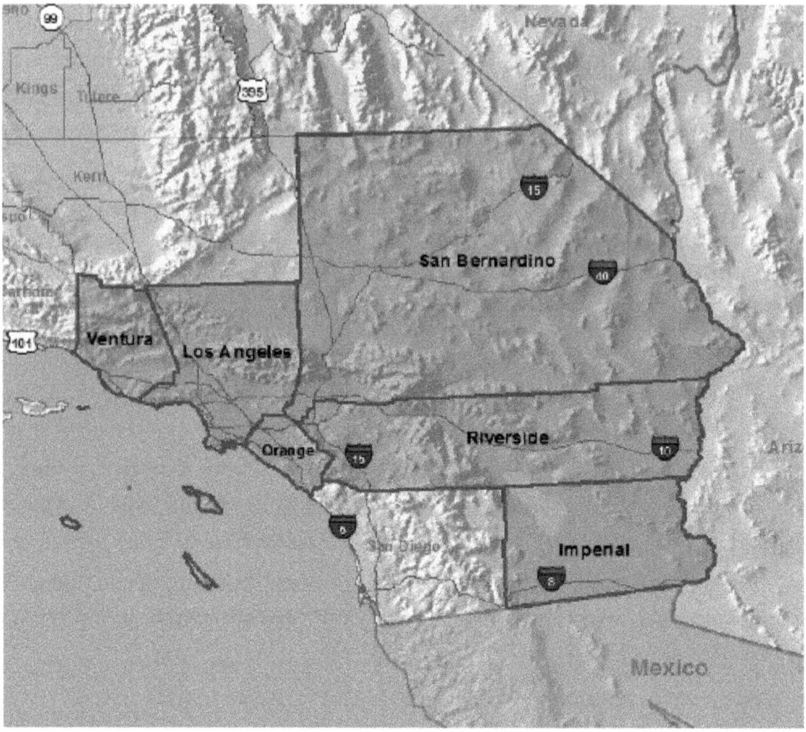

Figure 5. The SCAG planning region.

Source: California Environmental Protection Agency (2013).

land-use changes. In its first Sustainable Communities Plan, SCAG set the following goals for the region:

- two-thirds of new housing to be multi-family by 2035, compared to less than one-third in 2012;
- half of all new development on 3% of the region's land area;
- increasing the percentage of housing within high-quality transit areas (served by express bus, light rail, or subway) from 40% to 51% (California Environmental Protection Agency, 2013).

The objectives of SCAG's first plan were ambitious. In addition to its investment in transit, the objectives of more compact development and of having cities shift from zoning and permitting for single-family residential to apartment buildings required major shifts in zoning in many suburban municipalities within its region. SCAG's 2012–2035 plan was approved by CARB in mid-2012 (California Environmental Protection Agency, Air Resources Board, 2013). However, a major impediment to the implementation of this plan is the lack of sufficient funding. Although SCAG does provide financial incentives to local governments, according to local officials interviewed at the time, the amount of funding is not sufficient to affect changes at the local level (Barbour and Deakin, 2012; Barbour, 2016).

5. Future Drivers of Urban Form and Performance

The first part of the chapter focused on trends in metro-regions in the US, with a focus on the Los Angeles metropolitan area — which has been the proverbial auto-dominated and congested metropolis — and on the efforts to reduce urban expansion into agricultural and natural resource lands and to reduce sprawl. It linked these developments to a recent trend in climate change mitigation policy that recognizes the connection between different aspects of urban form, VKT, and GHG emissions. It concludes that California's climate change mitigation policy focusing on metropolitan transportation performance is, in effect, an evolved type of statewide urban growth management system (Barbour and Deakin, 2012). The second part of the chapter will focus on two major future drivers of urban form and performance, technological changes in the form of IT and automation as well as on climate change drivers, in particular, sea-level rise and extreme climate events magnified by climate change.

5.1. *Technological trends and their potential impacts in metropolitan areas*

Technological changes can impact major land uses in metropolitan areas, the location of work, urban form, and VMT. This section illustrates this with two examples. First, it discusses the impact of e-commerce on retail, especially on shopping malls, and the opportunities that some failing malls provide for more compact, mixed-use development. This section then raises the issue of how the increasing automation of industrial processes will affect industrial land demand and commuting patterns.

5.1.1. *E-commerce impact on retail land uses*

Information technology, which has enabled e-commerce, is already having an impact on brick-and-mortar retail. In the US, the estimate is that e-commerce has grown from less than 1% in 2000 to over 9% by 2018 (Credit Suisse, 2018), whereas foot traffic in brick-and-mortar stores has been decreasing at an annual rate of 5–10% per year, and recently, sales have begun to decline (Cushman and Wakefield, 2018). Many anchor stores, such as Macy's or Sears, and, in 2017, over 400 department stores located in shopping malls were expected to close (Credit Suisse, 2018). Since department stores typically occupy about half of the US mall space, such closings threaten the viability of their shopping malls. As a result, many shopping malls around the country are failing. Industry experts warn that although the best-quality malls will survive, many others will fail (Credit Suisse, 2018; Cushman and Wakefield, 2018).

In the US, shopping malls have large footprints in the urban fabric, from 40 to 120 acres. As shopping malls fail, they provide opportunities for urban redevelopment, especially opportunities for mixed-use centers and higher density housing (Blanco, 2018). The increasing use of Internet shopping reduces household shopping trips, which should reduce overall trips and VMT in a metropolitan area.

At the same time, e-commerce, for example, Amazon, requires vast amounts of logistical space. In the LA Metro area, Amazon already occupies 10 million square feet in suburban areas, with many facilities occupying more than a million square feet and some even spanning 50 acres in size. This raises the following research question: How will trips for shopping and for delivering goods bought through the Internet change metropolitan commute patterns both from the customer side as well as from the e-commerce logistics side?

5.1.2. *Automation's impact on metropolitan areas*

Automation is another trend that has received much attention recently. There is some preliminary research on the impact of automation on different size cities, concluding that larger cities, with larger percentages of their workforce with specialized skills, are likely to experience less job loss due to automation than smaller cities, with less specialized labor forces, which are more subject to automation (Frank *et al.*, 2018). But so far, there is a lack of current research focusing on the potential impact of automation on urban form, trip generation, and VMT. The following could be some of the research questions: Does automation of industrial products require a smaller or larger industrial site (of course, this could vary by type of product)? Will automation of services reduce the demand for other types of commercial land uses, e.g., banking, and not just retail, and/or reduce trips to and from services? Will automation that requires a smaller workforce have a discernible impact on the commute to work and on VMT? We already have data that 5% of the working population in the US works from home. The following question remains to be answered: To what extent will automation increase the population working from home over the next 20 years?

5.2. *Climate change*

The first part of this chapter focused on mega-city regions in the US and their efforts to reduce sprawl and to shape urban regions in order to reduce VMT and drew the strong connection of these efforts to policies aimed at climate change mitigation. The current technological drivers briefly discussed above focus on components of mega-city regions which have been relatively stable for the past half century. This section will focus on several potential impacts of climate change on cities, sea-level rise, increasing temperatures, and extreme events. While the impact of automation on urban regions is still under-researched, there is substantial research on the potential impacts of climate change on many metropolitan regions. This section highlights research in California that documents the potential impacts of sea-level rise and extreme events on metropolitan development. It ends with a reflection on how higher temperatures and extreme events in the wildland–urban interface (WUI) amplify the importance of urban growth management as a vital climate adaptation strategy.

5.2.1. *Sea-level rise*

California is at the forefront of climate change policy in the US and has been conducting periodic climate assessments, which include original research and projections of the impacts of climate change on sea-level rise, increasing temperatures, and frequent fires and flooding. The state released its 4th Climate Assessment during the summer of 2018, and among the studies included is a set of updated sea-level rise projections. Their new model projects that

> "...under mid to high sea-level scenarios, 31 to 67 percent of Southern California beaches may completely erode by 2100 without large-scale human interventions. Statewide damages could reach nearly $17.9 billion from inundation of residential and commercial buildings under 50 cm (~20 in) of sea-level rise, which is close to the 95th percentile of potential sea-level rise by the middle of this century. A 100-year coastal flood, on top of this level of sea-level rise, would almost double the costs" (Bedsworth *et al.*, 2018, p. 9).

In addition to the state's periodic climate assessments, which provide state-of-the art modeling and projections for the different regions within the state, another important asset that local governments in California have to begin to plan for climate change impacts is Cal-Adapt. Cal-Adapt is a website providing access to curated datasets and information from the scientific community, which is funded and supervised by the California Energy Commission. It includes datasets and visualization tools at various scales and from multiple models that are updated on an ongoing basis (https://cal-adapt.org/about/). See Figure 6 for a screenshot of a sea-level rise scenario for the San Francisco Bay Area.

Although researchers and state agencies in California have been conducting scientific studies on the impacts of climate change on the state and the state is an active global leader in climate change policy and action, adaptation to climate change has lagged in local communities. Part of this lack of action at the local level is due to the fiscal constraints on local government's taxation powers, due to the lingering effects of Proposition 13, as discussed in a previous section, which reduced the power of local governments to raise taxes, as well as the connection of property tax to land use. In effect, in California, as well as in other states in the country, the major method by which local governments can raise local revenue is through new development that brings in new tax revenues. Despite this, a number of coastal localities in California have been armoring their

where 85 people lost their lives, around 14,000 residences and close to 5,000 other buildings were destroyed, and over 153,000 acres were burnt (Cal Fire, 2018a).

Another important impact of increasing temperatures is their effect on the snowpack in the Sierra Nevada, which is a major supply of water, especially for Southern California and for the agricultural areas in the state. By 2050, the state projects that the snowpack will hold less than two-thirds of its historic median, and by 2100, less than half to one-third (Bedsworth *et al.*, 2018, p. 27).

California already experiences the highest variability in precipitation every year across the US, experiencing multi-year wet or dry periods. However, the most recent drought occurring during 2012–2017 was a mega-drought, the worst since the 1800s, that called for state action imposing mandatory cutbacks in water use (California Office of the Governor, 2015). Climate change will likely increase the incidence of such events. The state also experiences extreme precipitation events, historic floods, with attendant mudslides. The combination of wildfires, flooding, and mudslides is already evident. The Thomas Fire which was the largest fire in the state's history at the time (Cal Fire, 2018b), burned large parts of Santa Barbara and Ventura counties in December of 2017 and prompted large-scale evacuations. Within a month, in January 2018 rains precipitated mudslides in the hillsides stripped by the wildfires, which caused 21 deaths in the area and considerable property and infrastructure losses.

In addition to sea-level rise impacts, extreme climate impacts, such as wildfires, flooding, and resultant mudslides, are directly related to the location of urban settlements. This differs from the urban form characteristics, such as density or proximity to transit, relevant to climate change mitigation efforts discussed earlier. Climate change impacts are likely to influence both the location of new urban development and, in the case of sea-level rise impacts in the latter half of this century, the relocation of existing urban development. These efforts will involve some form of urban growth management focused on the location of urban development to reduce the climate change impacts of sea-level rise, storm surges, flooding, and wildfires. While the early versions of urban growth management were focused on protecting agriculture and wild lands from urban disruptions, the upcoming versions of urban growth management are likely to focus on protecting urban areas and residents from extreme climate impacts. It is likely that this motivation may be more effective in compelling action than earlier environmental motivations.

6. Conclusion

This chapter reviews the characteristics of the Los Angeles mega-city region, the second largest urban region in the US (after the New York City mega-region), which is characterized by relatively low-density development throughout much of its extent and plagued with some of the worst urban traffic congestion in the world. It describes efforts since the 1970s in the US to manage urban growth and discusses research findings on such efforts. It then addresses the renewed interest in urban form from the perspective of climate change mitigation. A description of California's climate change mitigation legislation and program follows and concludes that this program is, in effect, a statewide urban growth management program focused on internal urban form features.

While the first part of this chapter focuses on past and current efforts to manage urban form in mega-city regions with a focus on Los Angeles, the second part focuses on the future impacts on mega-city regions of both technological and climate changes. The section on technological change raises issues of how an increasing number of US shopping malls are closing, to an extent due to the impact of e-commerce, and the opportunities this raises to change large patches of the urban fabric. It also raises the issue of increasing automation and what this may mean for industrial land demand, commute patterns, and urban traffic congestion. It then takes up the issue of climate change adaptation, referring to recent studies developed for California's 4th Climate Assessment. Focusing on sea-level rise and extreme events, such as wildfires and flooding, it suggests that such extreme impacts call for new urban growth management efforts focused on locating and relocating urban development to reduce vulnerability to such events.

References

Abbot, C., D. Howe and S. Adler (eds.) (1994). *Planning the Oregon Way: A Twenty Year Evaluation*. Corvallis, OR: Oregon State University Press.

American Lung Association (2018). *State of the Air 2018*. Retrieved on September 12, 2018 from http://www.lung.org/assets/documents/healthy-air/state-of-the-air/sota-2018-full.pdf.

American Planning Association (1996). *Modernizing State Planning Statutes: The Growing Smart^{sm}*, Working Papers. Planning Advisory Service Report 462/463. Chicago, IL: American Planning Association.

American Society of Civil Engineers (2017). Infrastructure Report Card. Retrieved on November 28, 2018 from https://www.infrastructurereportcard.org/.

Angel, S., J. Parent, D. L. Civco, A. Blei and D. Potere (2011). "The Dimensions of Global Urban Expansion: Estimates and Projections for All Countries, 2000–2050." *Progress in Planning* 75: 53–107, doi: 10.1016/j.progress.2011.04.001, ISSN: 0305-9006.

Anthony, J. (2003). "The Effects of Florida's Growth Management Act on Housing Affordability." *Journal of the American Planning Association* 69(3): 282–295, https://doi.org/10.1080/01944360308978020.

Anthony, J. (2004). "Do State Growth Management Regulations Reduce Sprawl?" *Urban Affairs Review* 39(3): 376–397, https://doi.org/10.1177/1078087403257798.

Barbour, E. (2016). "Evaluating Sustainability Planning Under California's Senate Bill 375." *Transportation Research Record: Journal of the Transportation Research Board* 2568 (January): 17–25. https://doi.org/10.3141/2568-04.

Barbour, E. and E. A. Deakin (2012). "Smart Growth Planning for Climate Protection: Evaluating California's Senate Bill 375." *Journal of the American Planning Association* 78(1): 70–86.

Bedsworth, L., D. Cayan, G. Franco, L. Fisher and S. Ziaja (California Governor's Office of Planning and Research, Scripps Institution of Oceanography, California Energy Commission, California Public Utilities Commission) (2018). Statewide Summary Report. California's Fourth Climate Change Assessment. Publication number: SUM-CCCA4-2018-013. Retrieved on September 16, 2018 from http://www.climateassessment.ca.gov/state/index.html.

Blanco, H. (2018). *TOD Opportunities among Failing Malls*. White Paper, National Center for Sustainable Transportation and METRANS Center.

Bosselman, F. and D. Callies (1971). *The Quiet Revolution in Land Use Control*. Washington, D.C.: US Council on Environmental Quality.

Bren d'Amour, C., F. Reitsma, G. Baiocchi, S. Barthel, B. Güneralp, K.-H. Erb, H. Haberl, F. Creutzig and K. C. Seto (2017). "Future Urban Land Expansion and Implications for Global Croplands." *Proceedings of the National Academy of Sciences* 114(34): 8939–8944.

Cal-Adapt. Exploring California's Climate Change Research. Retrieved on October 12, 2018 from http://cal-adapt.org/.

Cal Fire (2018a). Incident Information. Camp Fire. Last modified November 25, 2018. Retrieved on November 26, 2018 from https://www.fire.ca.gov/current_incidents/incidentdetails/Index/2277.

Cal Fire (2018b). Top 20 Largest California Wildfires. Retrieved on November 26, 2018 from http://www.fire.ca.gov/communications/downloads/fact_sheets/Top20_Acres.pdf.

California Air Resources Board (2018). Sustainable Communities and Climate Protection Program. Retrieved on November 12, 1928 from https://ww2.arb.ca.gov/our-work/programs/sustainable-communities-and-climate-protection-program.

California Department of Finance (2018). E-1 Population Estimates for Cities, Counties and the State — January 1, 2017 and 2018. Retrieved on September 18, 2018 from http://www.dof.ca.gov/Forecasting/Demographics/Estimates/E-1/.

California Environmental Protection Agency, Air Resources Board (2013). Facts about California's Sustainable Community Plans. *Southern California Association of Governments (SCAG)*. Retrieved on October 14, 2018 from https://ww2.arb.ca.gov/our-work/programs/sustainable-communities-and-climate-protection-program.

California Office of the Governor (2015). Executive Order B-29-15. Saving Water and Ordering a Reduction in Potable Water Use. April 1, 2015. Retrieved on November 12, 2018 from https://www.gov.ca.gov/wp-content/uploads/2017/09/4.1.15_Executive_Order.pdf.

Calthorpe, P. (1993). *The Next American Metropolis: Ecology, Community, and the American Dream*. Princeton Architectural Press, New York, New York.

Carruthers, J. I. (2002). "The Impacts of State Growth Management Programmes: A Comparative Analysis." *Urban Studies* 39(11): 1959–1982.

Credit Suisse (2018). CMBS Retail Outlook: Transformation accelerating. January 4, 2018. Retrieved on July 20, 2018 from https://research-doc.credit-suisse.com/docView?language=ENG&format=PDF&sourceid=csplusresearchcp&document_id=1080091741&serialid=pXHSk4mvE%2FPg%2BYlsoOUnVyVpX6htl%2By2jlDMyUDG0rI%3D.

Cushman and Wakefield. (2018). Marketbeat. US Shopping Center Q1, 2018. Retrieved on July 10, 2018 from http://www.cushmanwakefield.com/en/research-and-insight/2018/us-q1-2018-marketbeat.

Deakin, E. (1989). "Land Use and Transportation Planning in Response to Congestion Problems: A Review and Critique." *Transportation Research Record* 1237: 77–86.

DeGrove, J. M. (1984). *Land Growth and Politics*. Chicago: Planners Press.

DeGrove, J. and D. Miness (1992). *The New Frontier for Land Policy: Planning and Growth Management in the States*. Cambridge: Lincoln Institute of Land Policy.

Dierwechter, Y. and T. Carlson (2007). "Effects of Urban Growth Boundaries on Residential Development in Pierce County, Washington." *The Professional Geographer* 59(2): 209–220.

Dowall, D. E. (1984). *The Suburban Squeeze: Land Conversion and Regulation in the San Francisco Bay Area*, Vol. 3. University of California Press, Berkeley, California.

Downs, A. (2004). *Growth Management and Affordable Housing: Do They Conflict?* Brookings Institution Press.

Ewing, R. and R. Cervero (2001). "Travel and the Built Environment: A Synthesis." *Transportation Research Record: Journal of the Transportation Research Board*, 1780: 87–114.

Ewing, R. and R. Cervero (2010). "Travel and the Built Environment: A Meta-Analysis." *Journal of the American Planning Association* 76(3): 265–294.

Florida, R., T. Gulden and C. Mellander (2007). "The Rise of the Mega-Region." *Cambridge Journal of Regions. Economy and Society* 1(3): 459–476.

Frank, M. R., L. Sun, M. Cebrian, H. Youn, and I. Rahwan (2018). "Small Cities Face Greater Impact from Automation." *Journal of The Royal Society Interface* 15(139): 20170946, https://doi.org/10.1098/rsif.2017.0946.

Georg, I., T. Blaschke and H. Taubenböck (2016). "New Spatial Dimensions of Global Cityscapes: From Reviewing Existing Concepts to a Conceptual Spatial Approach." *Journal of Geographical Sciences* 26(3): 355–380.

Glendening, P. (1997). "A New Smart Growth Culture." *Spectrum: The Journal of State Government*. 70: 30–32.

Gottman, J. (1957). "Megalopolis or the Urbanization of the Northeastern Seaboard." *Economic Geography*, 189–200.

Gottman, J. (1961). *Megalopolis: The Urbanized Northeastern Seaboard of the United States*. New York: The Twentieth Century Fund.

Gray, R. C. (2007). "Ten Years of Smart Growth: A Nod to Policies Past and a Prospective Glimpse Into the Future." *Cityscape* 9(1): 109–130.

Hall, P. and K. Pain (2006). From Metropolis to Polyopolis. In: P. Hall and K. Pain (eds.), *The Polycentric Metropolis: Learning from Mega-city Regions in Europe*. London & Sterling, VA: Earthscan, pp. 3–16.

Howe, D. (1993). Growth Management in Oregon. In: *Growth Management: The Planning Challenge of the 1990s*, edited by J. M. Stein. Newbury Park, CA: Sage.

Knapp, G. and A. C. Nelson (1992). *The Regulated Landscape: Lessons on State Land Use Planning from Oregon.* Cambridge: Lincoln Institute of Land Policy.

Kuang, W., W. Chi, D. Lu and Y. Dou (2014). "A Comparative Analysis of Megacity Expansions in China and the US: Patterns, Rates and Driving Forces." *Landscape and Urban Planning* 132: 121–135.

Landis, J. D. (1992). "Do Growth Controls Work?: A New Assessment." *Journal of the American Planning Association* 58(4): 489–508.

Landis, J. D. (2006). "Growth Management Revisited: Efficacy, Price Effects, and Displacement." *Journal of the American Planning Association* 72(4): 411–430.

Lang, R. E. and D. Dhavale (2005). *Beyond Megalopolis: Exploring America's New "Megapolitan" Geography*. Alexandria, VA: Metropolitan Institute, Virginia Technical University.

Liberty, R. L. (1992). "Oregon's Comprehensive Growth Management Program: An Implementation Review and Lessons for Other States." *Environmental Law Reporter* 22(6): 10368–10391.

Litman, T. (2015). Analysis of Public Policies That Unintentionally Encourage and Subsidize Urban Sprawl. Retrieved on August 2, 2018 from http://static.newclimateeconomy.report/wp-content/uploads/2015/03/public-policies-encourage-sprawl-nce-report.pdf.

Manville, M., B. D. Taylor and E. Blumenberg (2018). Falling Transit Ridership: California and Southern California. *UCLA ITS and SCAG*. Retrieved on October 13, 2018 from https://www.scag.ca.gov/Documents/ITS_SCAG_Transit_Ridership.pdf.

Mullins, D. R. and B. A. Wallin (2004). "Tax and Expenditure Limitations: Introduction and Overview." *Public Budgeting & Finance* 24(4): 2–15.

National Research Council (2010). *Driving and the Built Environment: The Effects of Compact Development on Motorized Travel, Energy Use, and* CO_2 *Emissions — Special Report 298*. National Academies Press.

Oregon Department of Land Conservation and Development (DLCD) (n.d.). Retrieved on August 12, 2018 from https://www.oregon.gov/LCD/Pages/goals.aspx.

Oregon Department of Land Conservation and Development (DLCD) (1995). *Oregon's Statewide Planning Goals & Guidelines* (1995 Edition) Salem, OR: Department of Land Conservation and Development.

Oregon Secretary of State. Oregon Land Use Records. Retrieved on September 18, 2018 from https://sos.oregon.gov/archives/Pages/records/land-use-law.aspx.

Pallagst, K. (2017). *Growth Management in the US: Between Theory and Practice*. Routledge.

Paulsen, K. (2013). "The Effects of Growth Management on the Spatial Extent of Urban Development, Revisited." *Land Economics* 89(2): 193–210, https://doi.org/10.3368/le.89.2.193.

Porter, D. (ed.) (1986). *Growth Management: Keeping on Target?* Washington, D.C.: ULI-The Urban Land Institute, with the Lincoln Institute of Land Policy.

Portland Metro (2018). Metropedia. Retrieved October 20, 2018 from https://www.oregonmetro.gov/.

Radeloff, V. C., D. P. Helmers, H. Anu Kramer, M. H. Mockrin, P. M. Alexandre, A. Bar-Massada, V. Butsic, T. J. Hawbaker, S. Martinuzzi and A. D. Syphard (2018). "Rapid Growth of the US Wildland Urban Interface Raises Wildfire Risk." *Proceedings of the National Academy of Sciences* 115(13): 3314–3319.

Seltzer, E. (2013). *Land Use Planning in Oregon: The Quilt and Struggle for Scale*. Lincoln Inst. of Land Policy. White Paper. Retrieved on September 18, 2018 from https://www.pdx.edu/usp/sites/www.pdx.edu.usp/files/Seltzer%20Lincoln%20Working%20Paper%20Land%20Use%20Planning%20in%20Oregon%20March%2020%202013%20%282%29.pdf.

Seto, K. C., B. Güneralp and L. R. Hutyra (2012). "Global Forecasts of Urban Expansion to 2030 and Direct Impacts on Biodiversity and Carbon Pools." *Proceedings of the National Academy of Sciences*, September 2012, https://doi.org/10.1073/pnas.1211658109.

Seto, K. C., M. Fragkias, B. Güneralp and M. K. Reilly (2011). "A Meta-Analysis of Global Urban Land Expansion." *PLOS ONE* 6(8)23777, https://doi.org/10.1371/journal.pone.0023777.

Seto, K. C., S. Dhakal, A. Bigio, H. Blanco, G. C. Delgado, D. Dewar, L. Huang, A. Inaba, A. Kansal, S. Lwasa, J. E. McMahon, D. B. Muller, J. Murakami, H. Nagendra and A. Ramaswami (2014). Human Settlements, Infrastructure and Spatial Planning. In: *Climate Change 2014: Mitigation of Climate Change. Contribution of Working Group III to the Fifth Assessment Report of the Intergovernmental Panel on Climate Change*, edited by O. Edenhofer, R. Pichs Madruga, Y. Sokona, E. Farahani, S. Kadner, K. Seyboth, A. Adler, I. Baum, S. Brunner, P. Eickemeier, B. Kriemann, J. Savolainen, S. Schlomer, C. von Stechow, T. Zwickel and J. C. Minx. Cambridge, United Kingdom and New York, NY, USA: Cambridge University Press.

Sievanen, L., J. Phillips, C. Colgan, G. Griggs, J. Finze Hart, E. Hartge, T. Hill, R. Kudela, N. Mantua, K. Nielsen and L. Whiteman (2018). California's Coast and Ocean Summary Report. California's Fourth Climate Assessment. SUMCCC4A-2018-011.

Stevens, M. (2017). "Does Compact Development Make People Drive Less?" *Journal of the American Planning Association* 83(1): 7–18.

Sullivan, E. J. (1993). Oregon Blazes a Trail. In: *State and Regional Comprehensive Planning: Implementing New Methods for Growth Management*, edited by P. Buchsbaum and L. J. Smith. Chicago: American Bar Association.

United Nations, Department of Economic and Social Affairs, Population Division (2015). *World Urbanization Prospects. The 2014 Revision (ST/ESA/SER.A/366).*

United Nations, Department of Economic and Social Affairs, Population Division (2017). World Population Prospects: The 2017 Revision, Key Findings and Advance Tables. Working Paper No. ESA/P/WP. Retrieved on November 12, 2018 from https://esa.un.org/unpd/wpp/publications/files/wpp2017_keyfindings.pdf.

US Census (2010). American FactFinder. Population, Housing Units, Area and Density: 2010-US — County by State, and for Puerto Rico. Retrieved September 18, 2018 from https://factfinder.census.gov/faces/tableservices/jsf/pages/productview.xhtml?src=bkmk.

US Census (2012). Los Angeles-Long Beach, CA. 2012. Combined Statistical Area. Retrieved from: https://www2.census.gov/geo/maps/econ/ec2012/csa/EC2012_330M200US348M.pdf

US Census (2018). Annual Estimates of the Resident Population: April 1, 2010 to July 1, 2017 — United States — Metropolitan Statistical Area; and for Puerto Rico. 2017 Population Estimates. Retrieved on September 18, 2018 from https://factfinder.census.gov/faces/tableservices/jsf/pages/productview.xhtml?src=bkmk.

US Census, American FactFinder. State of Oregon Population estimate 2017. Retrieved September 20, 2018 from https://factfinder.census.gov/faces/nav/jsf/pages/community_facts.xhtml.

US EPA (2018). Inventory of U.S. Greenhouse Gas Emissions and Sinks. Retrieved on October 28, 2018 from https://www.epa.gov/sites/production/files/2018-01/documents/2018_complete_report.pdf.

US Department of Commerce (2012). Los Angeles-Long Beach Combined Statistical Area. Retrieved September 18, 2018 from https://www2.census.gov/geo/maps/econ/ec2012/csa/EC2012_330M200US348M.pdf.

US Department of Commerce (2013). Combined Statistical Areas of the United States and Puerto Rico. Retrieved on September 18, 2018 from https://www2.census.gov/geo/maps/metroarea/us_wall/Feb2013/csa_us_0213.pdf.

US Census (2016). Means of Transportation to Work by Selected Characteristics. 2012–2016. *American Community Survey 5-Year Estimates*. Retrieved on September 21, 2018 from https://factfinder.census.gov/faces/tableservices/jsf/pages/productview.xhtml?pid=ACS_16_5YR_S0802&prodType=table.

Wassmer, R. W. (2006). "The Influence of Local Urban Containment Policies and Statewide Growth Management on the Size of United States Urban Areas." *Journal of Regional Science* 46(1): 25–65.

World Bank (2018). Agricultural Lands and Forest Areas Database. Retrieved on November 12, 2018 from https://data.worldbank.org/indicator/AG.LND.AGRI.ZS.

Ye, L. (2014). "State-Led Metropolitan Governance in China: Making Integrated City Regions." *Cities* 41: 200–208.

Yin, M. and J. Sun. (2007). The impacts of state-growth management programs on urban sprawl in the 1990s. *Journal of Urban Affairs* 29(2): 149–179.

Chapter 8

Linking the European SUMP Method to Strasbourg and Paris Metropolitan Circle Scenarios

Cristiana Mazzoni

UMR AUSser (UMR CNRS-MC 3329), France
Ecole Nationale Superieure d'Architecture Paris-Belleville, France
cristianamazzoni@gmail.com

Andreea Grigorovschi

Ecole Nationale Supérieure d'Architecture de Strasbourg, France
andreea.grigorovschi@strasbourg.archi.fr

1. Introduction — European SUMP and Poly-SUMP Methods for Planning Mobility Systems

Currently, one of Europe's main objectives is to overcome the negative externalities of the 20th century urban mobility, especially in metropolitan areas and to move toward sustainable policies for a democratic mobility transition focused on integrated strategies and efficient connectivity.[1]

[1] Since 1992, the European Commission has published three White Papers (1992, 2001, 2011) one Green Paper (2007), multiple guidelines, action plans, and several communications to the European Parliament on transport and mobility leading to several European Parliament important resolutions (see References).

To achieve this goal, the European Commission has attempted "to draw together the maximum of the available information and intelligence": according to the "study to support an impact assessment of the urban mobility package" (October 2013, EC DG MOVE), the benchmark on sustainable urban mobility concluded on a lack of general coordination and undefined targeted policy actions. The European Commission has therefore actively promoted the "SUMP concept": guidelines were established, which provide local authorities with a clear framework for the development and implementation of a general planning method (EC, 2013a). Through the ongoing Horizon 2020 research-actions programs (H2020) member states are driven to adopt those methods and practices at the national level and to ensure the right legislative and support conditions for their local authorities.

What is SUMP exactly? SUMP stands for the Sustainable Urban Mobility Plan, derived from the 7th European Commission research and research-actions programs. It was defined in the 2000s and adopted by several local authorities as an experimental method for drawing together information and intelligence, organizing cooperation across different policy areas and sectors, across different levels of government and administration and in cooperation with citizens and other stakeholders. The aim was to develop a plan derived from a common vision for the future of the metropolitan territory, with people and mobility systems as the main focus (EC, 2013a).

More recently poly-SUMP (polycentric Sustainable Urban Mobility Plan) has been adopted as new acronym for a planning concept adapted to the polycentric regions and the "diffuse city." Planning urban mobility is a complex task for any city, but it is even more complex when urban functions, people, and mobility are spread in different urban cores such in the polycentric regions of the new metropolitan circles. In these regions, the "diffuse city" concept is related to the pattern of concentration vs. distribution of the population, facilities, and jobs, who generate daily mobility flows in disparate sectors (Sessa, ISIS, *Poly-SUMP methodology*).

Planning daily mobility in the new metropolitan circles characterized by alternating dense and sprawling urbanity requires the coordination of policies and the services of many actors — transport and urban planners, local and regional policymakers, urban and inter-urban public transport providers — within and across different administrative boundaries. Without any such common strategies and planning, people are almost obliged to adopt the "do it yourself" solution of individual car use for any daily mobility purpose. This is increasingly problematic for large portions of the population living in these polycentric metropolitan circles.

Exploiting the "diffuse city" concept, the European Commission launched the poly-SUMP/-Intelligent Energy Europe project on April 15, 2012, which ran until October 15, 2014. Coordinated by Regione Marche (Italy), the project was implemented by a consortium of regional authorities and experienced consultants and research institutes in urban transport planning across Europe — Marche (IT), Central Alentejo (PT), Central Macedonia (GR), Rhine Alp (AT), Heart of Slovenia (SI), and Parkstad Limburg (NL). The aim of this poly-SUMP project was to develop a polycentric sustainable mobility planning methodology, testing concrete planning processes based on the Future Search Workshop, organized in the six participating regions of Europe, and checking the transferability of the approach to other metropolitan regions. The expected outcome of the project were detailed guidelines to develop and implement mobility planning experience in the polycentric European regions. A particular focus was given to public transports as a central issue for a sustainable metropolitan development and for a balanced correlation between metropolitan cores and circles.

2. Future Search Workshops and Exploratory Scenarios: State-of-the-Art and Methodology

Since the 1990s, American studies have highlighted that a reduction in urban density (i.e., sprawl) corresponds to an increase in private car trips and less efficiency in the public transport network. The Transit-Oriented Development (TOD) paradigm was developed as a logical consequence in an attempt to define an ideal urban and metropolitan pattern (Calthorpe, 1993). The creation of compact, pedestrian-oriented, mixed-use communities is mostly centered on high-quality regional train systems and stations. This makes it possible to live a lower-stress life without complete dependence on cars for mobility and survival.

The concept of TOD is rarely used in Europe, although many European cities have historically been built around transit systems, earlier with routes for horse and pedestrian traffic, then including train systems and at last streets and highways for automobiles (Dupuy, 1995). Since the 1990s, European cities such Copenhagen in Denmark, Hamburg in Germany, or Rotterdam in Holland, stress the idea of integrated mobility solutions and focus their mobility policies on bottom-up frameworks defining qualitative metropolitan markers as new solutions to the serious and growing problems of "diffuse city" (Indovina, 1991) and of "in-between" territories in metropolitan circles (Sieverts, 2004).

Based on these experiences and linked to both "high technology" and "soft" solutions, the European SUMP method highlights not only the smart but also the human factors (quality of life, multi-actor governance, transversal policies) in the relation between urban density, integrated public transports, and metropolitan development, by creating denser communities linked to regional and high-speed trains systems (Figure 1). This is why, for its first step — the "preparing well step" — the SUMP method is inspired by both the German *Zukunftswerkstatt* (Workshop of the Future) defined at the beginning of the 1980s, and the North-American Future Search Conference, developed at the beginning of the 1990s. If the second one sought to accompany organizations in the search for common ground, the German *Zukunftswerkstatt* (Workshop of the Future) was created and engineered with this objective: to allow ordinary citizens to participate in urban planning in order to achieve a "democratization from below" through such metropolitan processes.

Thus, the Future Search Workshop is a three-day meeting involving 60–100 people who share a common purpose. It is a learning laboratory for bringing everyone together to improve whole systems. It rests on the following four main conditions for success (Missions Publiques):

- Get the "whole system" in a room: this means that all parties having a stake in the outcome should be invited and motivated enough to come so that the working group represents a significant cross-section of the stakeholders;

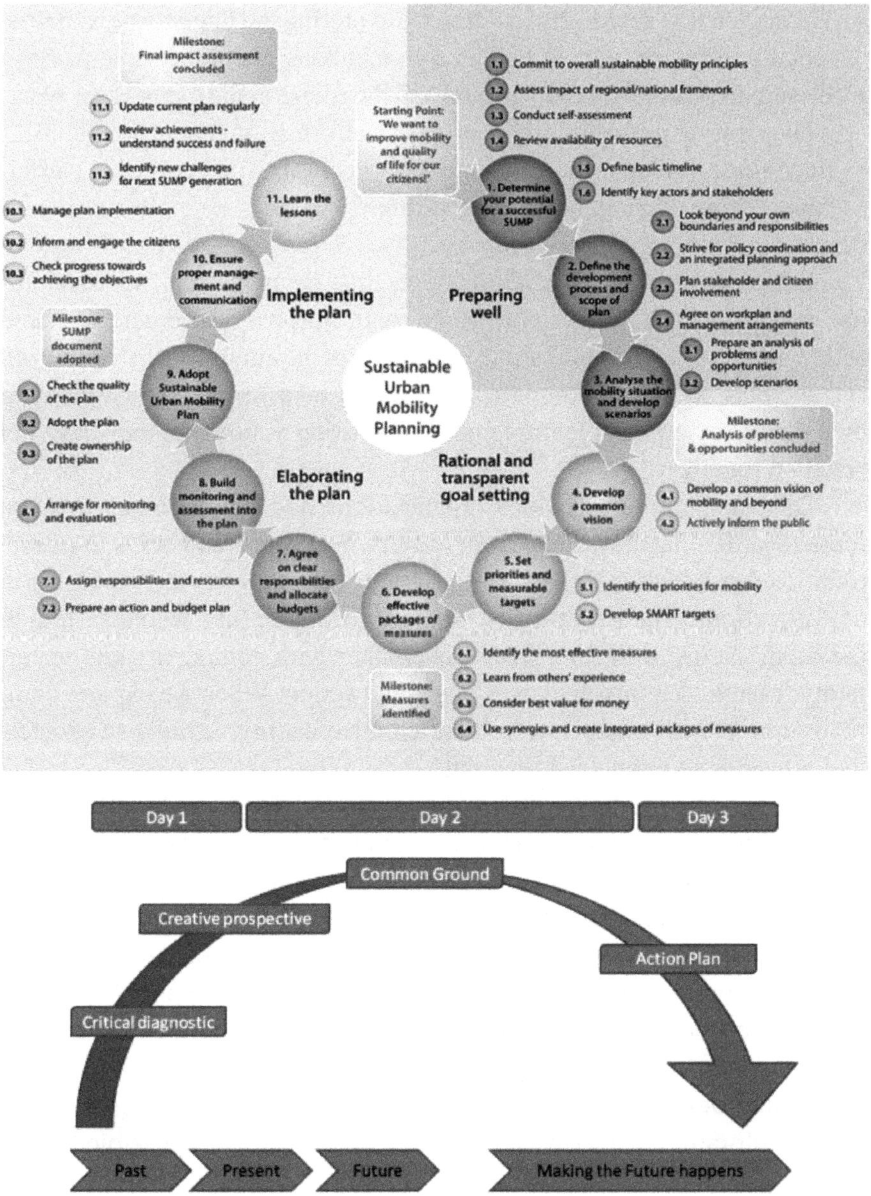

Figure 1. The SUMP method and the three-days workshop of the future related to the "preparing well phase."

- Think globally, act locally: starting by exploring the larger context before seeking to fix any part and get everyone talking about the same world;
- Be sure to put the common ground and the future in the focus of the work, while treating problems and conflicts as information, not action items;
- Encourage self-management and responsibility for action by participants before, during, and after the future search.

Therefore, the SUMP method adopts this "future search" approach for its "preparing well" phase with three main purposes: to create a shared action plan for an organization, network, or community; to enable all stakeholders to act on common ground and take responsibility for their own plans; to help people implement an existing vision that they have not acted on together.

This methodology enables organizations and communities to learn more together than any one person can discover alone and helps to extend traditional processes of change and organizational/policy development in new directions. The key word is "shared": bringing the "whole system in the room" helps to make a shared encounter with complexity and uncertainty feasible, leading to clarity, hope, and action. When we explore common ground with others, we release creative energy, leading to projects that all value and none can do alone.

The result of such a collaborative workshop is not only a document with actions (what stakeholders are going to do) and task forces (who from the workshop is going to do it) but also depicting a common vision shared by the actors. Related to "a utopian and perfect future," this vision is represented through several normative mobility scenarios, "stories depicting how this utopian situation was reached" (Missions Publiques), while also mobilizing the "exploratory scenario" mode of thinking (Börjeson *et al.*, 2006).

Unlike other means of scenario development (predictive or normative), exploratory scenarios support the idea that it is impossible to predict what will really happen as well as to try to define and then reach an ideal configuration. This scenario approach aims neither to explore the future by unfolding a range of possible consequences (risks, strengths, gaps, etc.) without trying to predict probable futures nor to find the most preferable one. In other words, exploratory scenarios investigate possible futures on the "what" and "why" levels — What can happen? and

Why would it be interesting/risky/damaging for it to happen? — whereas the revealed possibilities are meant to evolve and further trigger the "how" level — How could this be possible? Published in 2006 by Martin Borjeson (Swedish strategist, scenario developer, and futurist) and his colleagues within the field of Future Studies, this approach is based on different concepts of future — probable, preferable, and possible. Within our disciplinary field, regarding the question of scenarios as a tool for envisioning possible territorial futures, we refer mainly to Viganò (2012).

In this way, exploratory scenarios are conceived of as a tool to stimulate and enrich the collective reflection and debates on metropolitan development (Mazzoni and Grigorovschi, 2015). They are not to be confused with action-oriented proposals as in a range of choices for decision-making. Exploratory scenarios give the stakeholders a chance (at least during their initial development) to fly free of any ongoing political trends and directives, escape institutional constraints and administrative perimeters and set aside the question of governance.

Moreover, this should not be confused with utopian or romantic approaches, since the scenarios' baselines are always attached to territorial realities, as in geographical and landscape features, local landmarks, cultural representations, and ways of living and sharing this metropolitan space. Thus, scenario developments as experienced in a "future search" rely on quantitative and qualitative data in order to cover and explore not only explicit features, such as physical layouts and ways in which the territory functions, but also implicit ones, such as mental constructions related to the former. This implies both a spatial and a conceptual exploration of possible futures during scenario development (Grigorovschi, 2016).

3. Revealing Possible Futures for Strasbourg and Paris Metropolitan Circles through the Exploratory Scenario Approach

In a comparative analysis between several cities, an exploratory scenario can be understood as a tool to stress different planning orientations and objectives related to both the metropolitan territory and the local situation. In fact, even though the results of the SUMP's "preparing well phase" can be considered naïve or "immature," unfinished and sometimes even lacking credibility, this inductive and bottom-up method is able to point out real topics and objectives coming from the background of each situation. Raising awareness to possibilities, rising technical or political question marks in terms of governance, legal frameworks, practical implementation, the scenarios become a tool for sharing knowledge at different scales: local, metropolitan, and European ones and moving forward in seeking innovative ideas for synergic metropolitan development.

A closer look at specific case studies in Strasbourg and Paris shows different situations related to mobility strategies for sustainable metropolitan development and for balanced correlations between urban cores and metropolitan circles. Between Strasbourg and Paris, there are very different key factors that interplay in urban public transports and that are shaping the identity of metropolitan areas (cores and circles) as well as their mobility patterns. Qualitative factors besides quantitative ones are actually explaining the gap between the two realities of Paris and Strasbourg, including: the history of urban infrastructures, local settlement patterns, urban fabric structure, accessibility to public transports, implementation of policies/planning strategies, environmental policies and goals.

3.1. *Exploratory scenarios for Strasbourg*

In the French context, Strasbourg is an exemplary case study for its sustainable metropolitan development and its tension between the local and global: Strasbourg represents a "balanced metropolis," with a strongly symbolic border dimension to its regional claims. These local and regional components were developed in the long term after the polycentric "Rhineland model" of German and Swiss cities. Furthermore, geographical and cultural proximity to Germany — and its *Energiewende* — also makes the Strasbourg area an interesting case study when it comes to energy transition and its impact on the territorial development (Mazzoni and Grigorovschi, 2015).

In addition, Strasbourg has recently become a local authority with special status — the Eurométropole[2] — replacing the former local author-

[2]According to the French law on cities (LOW) of January 27, 2014.

ity, the Communauté Urbaine de Strasbourg-CUS. Supposed to "enhance metropolitan economic functions, transport networks and academic resources, research and innovation, in a spirit of regional and interregional cooperation and with a desire for balanced development of its territory" (LOW 2014-58), the newly created Eurométropole is thus a key actor for the future metropolitan development. This is a major challenge, especially in the particular context of Strasbourg, where the concept of metropolitan development territory includes the metropolitan system of the Upper Rhine along with the idea of innovative governance of the projects, shared between several institutional actors referring to multiple scales and diversified skills. In this perspective, one of the best ways for Strasbourg to prepare itself for the development of the Eurométropole is to combine the city and university to form a cluster of excellence between actors working on the new meaning of sustainable metropolitan development and governance.

The concept of Metropolitan development territory refers to the complex interdependencies between regional dynamics and worldwide challenges, in particular climate change and energy provision, which were considered as prominent issues with potential effects on spatial structures and dynamics. Even if there is a growing agreement that the challenges of the metropolitan and transnational territories are important, it is not always clear for the local stakeholders in what ways they can build and represent these structures and dynamics (Mazzoni and d'Emilio, 2014). The competences necessary to act directly — and coherently — through an integrated metropolitan and transnational perspective on spatial dynamics are to be known and reinforced.

In the field of sustainable urban planning and urban design, AMUP laboratory (Architecture, Morphology/Morphogenesis and Project) in Strasbourg explores this kind of articulation between various spheres, including that of multi-modal infrastructure planning and that of governance at the scale of the metropolis. Within this structure, the goal of the research actions is to create collaboration with the local authorities on metropolitan mobility planning. Such partnerships have been initiated through national researches between 2000 and 2015 (supported by the French Ministry of the Culture — MCC and the French Ministry of Environment and Energy — MEDDE). In 2014, the cooperation between

AMUP laboratory and Eurométropole of Strasbourg (former CUS) resulted in the creation of a new framework, the "Atelier des mobilités métropolitaines" (IMM Chair/AMUP-Eurométropole Strasbourg, 2014). Since the beginning, the Atelier focuses mainly on experimenting with new methods for the construction of common objectives and knowledge, shared between researchers and stakeholders. This framework was enlarged further in 2014 through the "Atelier Franco-Chinois des mobilités métropolitaines" (ENSAS — Tongji University in Shanghai). The aim is to study the realities of the metropolitan governance in these agglomerations, in particular regarding aspects of integrated mobility and slow-mobility systems.[3] The research activities refer to one specific form of urban mobility: the tramway. However, the idea is not to limit the research to the discussion of the pertinence and feasibility of a light-rail/rail infrastructure in Strasbourg, but rather to explore a whole set of solutions that innovatively articulate different scales (inner city/metropolitan circles/ metropolitan region) and different transportation modes in order to facilitate the development of sustainable transportation and urban planning configurations. The light-rail/rail infrastructure for which Karlsruhe has become a model is used as a starting point in order to study the relationship between transport infrastructure, decision-making processes, and the nexus between urban and transport planning. This innovative transport solution is analyzed in the context of challenges (e.g., economic, social, environmental) with which the metropolitan area of Strasbourg is confronted.

---

[3]The team has already researched these topics within several national and international projects (selection): *Tram-train, ou l'énergie des courtes distances dans Strasbourg Métropole. Acteurs, logiques et processus du projet métropolitain durable*, research program "Ignis Mutat Res. Penser l'architecture, la ville, le paysage au prisme de l'énergie", MCC/MEDDE, 2013–2015; *Strasbourg*: *la démocratie locale pour construire un récit sur la métropole durable*, research program "Plateforme d'observation des projets et stratégies urbaines" (POPSU), MEDDE, 2011–2013. Also, recent international seminars and round tables were further discussing these issues: *Urban Public transport*, round table coordination (C. Mazzoni, ZHUO Jian), 7th Forum of Sino-French Sustainable Urban Transport Systems (THNS), CAUP-Tongji, Shanghai, November 1, 2014; FabLab on Urban mobility France–China; *Nanjing and Strasbourg, new tramway projects*, seminar-workshop (coordination C. Mazzoni, ZHUO Jian), Urban Institute of Shanghai, November 30, 2014.

According to German experience, developing a "slow mobility" strategy is a process with substantial involvement of citizens and stakeholders who often have strongly divergent interests. Local authorities have to be able to moderate these diverging interests and bring them to a productive end, i.e., produce decisions that will be beneficial to the community as a whole and its long-term development. Once the mobility strategy has been formulated there will again be very controversial discussions to establish the necessary projects. And again, after the projects have been decided upon, more controversial discussions will ensue as to the projects' exact designs and refinements including the permission and building processes. In order to be able to carry out these tasks and decisions, local authorities have to be strengthened with respect to both their general expertise on the relevant issues and their capabilities to moderate the decision processes. They need help to find new strategies and processes along the whole decision-making chain.

From the territorial development viewpoint, the Karlsruhe experience in the matter became a reference. The public transport system in Karlsruhe and its surroundings were managed by the Karlsruher Verkehrsbund GmbH (KVV), which is the third largest public transport system in the Federal State of Baden-Württemberg. The KVV provides services on 931 km rails and its coach lines have a cumulated length of 2,300 km. In 2013, 177 million passengers used the transport system, and the overall revenues of the service providers were €133 million. In order to provide more attractive routes from the city to the surrounding regions without changing trains, the city of Karlsruhe has implemented a tram–train system — the so-called Karlsruhe Model. In 1992, the first two-system-tram was introduced. Nowadays, the tram–train traffic uses the railway network of the city of Karlsruhe as well as the railway network of Deutsche Bahn in the surrounding areas. The system also features flexibility in the choice of electrical concepts. The wide range of the tram–train system is remarkable and this is partly due to the fact that cities and villages of the surrounding region wished to be integrated into it and also contributed to the required investments.

For Strasbourg, the exploratory scenario approach has been chosen as a key feature, among other conceptual and methodological trends and weak signals, by the researchers and technicians' team. In this regard, for the "Atelier des mobilités métropolitaines," exploratory scenarios became one of the main tools for inventing and questioning the future metropolitan circle. The approach favors an inductive mode of thinking in search of possible futures for the "city of short distances."

3.1.1. *The integrated mobility scenario: Spatial exploration*

Initiated by AMUP laboratory's researchers, PhD students and interns, scenarios developed within the Atelier are conceived of as a way to stimulate and enrich the collective reflection and debates on the metropolitan development territory in Strasbourg.[4] The Integrated mobility scenario is one of the first created by the team. Its starting point is the idea that the essence of Strasbourg, as a metropolis of "short distances," could be a light-rail/rail infrastructure associated — on a very local scale (e.g., the neighborhood scale) — with a soft mobility network. For this scenario, preliminary preparations required a proactive scientific watch on the current mobility issues and debates within the metropolitan context of Strasbourg, micro data mining regarding railway network use, as well as "stocktaking" cross-border cartographic work.

The hypothesis is questioned and articulated on three different scales: the Upper Rhine metropolitan region, Strasbourg's metropolitan circle, and the metropolis' urban cores. Each of these frameworks was determined by geographical and urban configurations as well as human practices within the territory, and they all focus on the cross-border dimension. Also, two different timeframes are considered: the middle run, settled in 2030, and the long-term horizon of 2100. This is mainly due to the fact that some developments require restoring several abandoned rail corridors and the construction of new railway sections, for which the investments would be impossible to obtain within a short period of time. The scenario envisions a denser network of regional express train lines (RER/S-BAHN), which, on the one hand, would consolidate the north–south urban development of the Upper Rhine territory, and introduce transversal east–west, cross-border connections, on the other hand. On the scale of

[4]This section of the chapter was published in Mazzoni and Grigorovschi (2015). The article shows the different scenarios graphically represented by the team.

Strasbourg's metropolitan circle, several express lines (RER) would highlight the "30 minutes cross-border metropolis" since they are almost all diametrical (passing through the city center) and their maximum travel time between the termini would be about 1 h long. Moreover, certain lines crossing the Rhine would connect Strasbourg's hinterland to their German neighbors, without breaking bulk or change in the mode of transportation. In the same way, most of the sites of high economic, cultural, and touristic value of the metropolitan area, such as airports, airfields, leisure parks, as well as typical villages and resort towns, would be connected to this express network which makes them easily accessible from both sides of the Rhine.

Even though most of the lines would rely on the existing railway infrastructure, there would also be a few new sections to be built (as a second step) in order to increase the network coverage and improve accessibility. This would also enhance the attractiveness and thus the urban development of some areas, which for the moment are only covered by the regional bus services or only accessible by car. Finally, regarding the metropolis' urban cores, it is interesting to outline that although the railway connection between the main cities of Strasbourg and Offenbourg already exists, the fact that they would stop being termini stations (the RER lines disserving further destinations within the scenario) would in turn give a new status to the territories situated in-between. An accelerated urban development would thus be expected for this area.

At the level of the city center, a cross-border tram–train draws a city-ring-line defining a bigger center district in-between the main railway stations of Strasbourg (France) and Kehl (Germany), which offers a direct connection to the European Quarter. Passing through the harbor area (on the French side), the city ring could also be used for urban logistics, covering "last mile" delivery, particularly during the night. This line would use both rail and light-rail infrastructure (tramway); therefore, two interconnection platforms would be needed.

All these express and tram–train connections would create the conditions for increasing the urban density in the districts surrounding the stations. On this local scale, it is also interesting to imagine "soft"/"slow mobility" solutions, such as an extended cycling and pedestrian network, which would further and finely irrigate the territory around stations.

3.1.2. *The integrated mobility scenario: Conceptual exploration*

From a conceptual viewpoint, the scenario questions the mental constructions of the territory. On a large scale, the Upper Rhine metropolitan region, currently set out as two north–south parallel axes along the river, would acquire a new east–west dimension by reinforcing and increasing the cross-border connections. A new structuring image appears, that of a territorial skeleton supported by the Rhine as a backbone.

Symbolically, this image tells the story of two parallel urban systems (which used to function independently one from another) coming together and turning toward the Rhine in the process. Previously seen as their dividing line, the river emerges as a shared valuable element, keeping them together.

Furthermore, Strasbourg's metropolitan area would become coherent and recognizable throughout another territorial figure — diametrical beams. In fact, by analogy, the concept of beams recalls the human energy flow drained by the new express lines envisioned within the scenario. Their diametrical nature is really the key point for understanding this image, highlighting the fact that metropolitan cores become truly central for the entire metropolis, French and German sides jointly. The metropolis' territory comes together as a whole since the beams would pass through the cores and continue their journey toward the opposite metropolitan fringe. However, the diametrical aspect is not to be confused with a circular configuration *per se*. It is rather the symbolic interpretation behind the circle that gives more meaning to this image as it implies the idea of unity. Indeed, put together, these diametrical beams reveal and structure the wide surface of the new "30 minutes cross-border metropolis."

Last but not least, on a smaller scale, another conceptual image synthesizes the architecture of the metropolis. The Dual-Core braiding offers an alternative mental construction for the whole metropolis and especially for the territories in-between the cores. The metaphor of the Dual-Core stands for the two main central cities of Strasbourg and Offenburg connected to each other and working together. Without really merging into one single metropolitan center, the two cores would continue to co-exist, each with its own autonomy, but together they mark a central part of the new metropolis throughout this single integrated mobility network.

The braiding suggests precisely the intertwining between the rail, light-rail, cycling, and pedestrian networks irrigating the territory and structuring it on different levels, scales, and speeds. Although the image of braiding applies within the whole metropolitan area, the Dual-Core braiding narrates the development of this new metropolitan cross-border centrality.

Besides the version of the integrated mobility scenario presented earlier, other possible futures are envisioned through this exploratory approach: alternative developments regarding later timeframes or even completely different visions are thus explored. From a methodological point of view, we also question the ability of the common graphic representations (especially maps and plans) to synthesize and communicate the multiple messages and meanings developed. In this sense, our research team also explored different ways of optimizing graphical and visual communication tools, like aerial oblique viewpoints and moving maps.

To conclude, the "Crossing borders" urban design competition co-organized in 2012 by the Eurometropolis of Strasbourg (France) and the City of Kehl (Germany) was for the team of researchers and professionals the occasion to question this scenario approach within a highly complex cross-border urban situation, bringing together the German and French strategies for land use planning, financing, and operational governance. Divided between three countries (France, Germany, and Switzerland), the Upper Rhine valley appears to be a territory of complex and interactive mobility systems that have existed throughout history, regardless of administrative and political borders. In the last decades, these synergies converge toward the Rhine and tend to concentrate and intensify within specific places inside the biggest Upper Rhine metropolises (Strasbourg, France; Basel, Switzerland; Karlsruhe, and Germany). Exploratory scenarios for Strasbourg, which we have done with master students and PhD candidates and in the frame of CMYT Studio, stress the high potential and yet under-exploited harbor and Central train station areas. The planning history of Strasbourg, considered through the relation to the city harbor and train station, shows that both territories has always played a key role in defining a "sustainable" and "long-term" planning practice. Since the 19th century, Strasbourg essentially initiated a "life-cycle" based urban process. Furthermore, ever since the historic establishment of trade routes along the Rhine, the "long-term" urban planning school of thought seems to characterize not only the development of Strasbourg but also of all the cities within the Upper Rhine valley. This "long-term" urban development contributes to the development of the polycentric urban network of the valley, structured by a very dense communication system, over both short and long distances. Ports and railway stations represent the strategic nodes of this system, sustaining its proper functioning and ensuring lasting durability.

The 2012 design competition focused on such a strategic cross-border site located on both sides of the river Rhine next to Strasbourg and Kehl harbors. The site is also one of the most important sectors of the metropolitan circle of Strasbourg, unified and structured along a new cross-border tram line. The exploratory scenario we have designed explored the possibility of this trans-border new urban core by attentively observing it on several scales, questioning the dense spatial and symbolic story not only of its present relations but also of the past (Mazzoni and Grigorovschi, 2017).

3.2. *The Grand Paris metropolitan design process*

What we experienced in Strasbourg would not have been possible without the projects and the theoretical debates that took place since the 1980s in the Paris region. Indeed, it is possible to affirm that the debate on the Grand Paris of the late 2000s has definitively put into crisis the theoretical and practical approach based on urban design as asserted since the 1980s, and has opened new questions on the tools, objects, and topics of the architectural project on the metropolitan scale. A fundamental double fact emerged from the debate on the Grand Paris and above all from the outcome of the international consultation *Le grand Pari(s) de l'agglomération parisienne* (2009): on the one hand, the "urban design approach" as practiced in France since the 1980s has encountered a theoretical stagnation in the disciplinary sphere and has become, since the 1990s, a political instrument of control and pacification of conflicts according to top-down sectorial practice; on the other hand, the emergence of a "metropolitan design approach" imposed a new vision and new instruments of dialogue between the stakeholders, without which the technocratic vision would have slowed down the emergence of a real interdisciplinary debate (Secchi, 2000; Lussault, 2007; Mongin, 2008). We will explain in the following paragraphs these two questions.

3.2.1. *The Plaine St. Denis project as first example of French "urban design" project*

In the Paris region's planning, the Plaine Saint-Denis project has often been mentioned for its exemplary French urban design approach. The story of this project is linked to three municipalities in the northern metropolitan circle of Paris — Saint-Denis, Saint-Ouen, and Aubervilliers — and three communist mayors who decided, in the early 1980s, with the financial help of the Ile-de-France Region, to invent a new process for the conversion of their industrial sites: 750 hectares occupied by factories, warehouses and storage hangars for goods, and cut by a network of railway lines and local roads for the distribution of working-class patio homes. At the beginning of the project and for five years (1985–1990) a group of experts — sociologists, economists, philosophers, and anthropologists — tried to define the "identity" of this territory starting from the articulation between quantitative data and qualitative analysis. The difficulties were related to the specificity of the site: the largest French territory occupied by heavy industry, which has welcomed, since the 1930s, a large number of Spanish refugees and, since the 1970s, new immigrants from Central Africa. Following the crisis of 1973 and the closure of the factories, in the early 1980s the area was presented as a set of disused lands, surrounded by decrepit housing and with an extremely high rate of unemployment. Despite these negative factors, the analysis results from the research team revealed the social, economic, and landscape potential of the site and made it possible to launch an innovative conversion process.

In fact, the story of the Plaine Saint-Denis project is also a theoretical one, written and designed by the architects and landscapers — Pierre Riboulet, Yves Lion, and Christian Devillers — who have defined with the experts and the politicians a series of guiding principles for the theory and teaching of the "urban design approach" and have verified them in a concrete way, articulating on the site historical, geographical, political, economic, sociological, and morphological issues. They founded the Hyppodamos group and set up an Atelier located in the core of the Plaine Saint-Denis territory, animated by weekly meetings with the population.

The urban design project was published in 1993: it includes about a 100 written pages and drawings that highlight the qualities of this new urban core situated on the north of the first metropolitan circle of the Great Paris territory. Michel Corajoud describes in it the characteristics of the landscape and highlights the quality of the voids as public spaces and their relationship at different scales with the existing junctions, roads, rails, and canals.

The lesson coming from this experience is, first of all, the role of the urban design project as a tool able to organize the knowledge of the territory and the dialogue between stakeholders — technicians, politics, and citizens — and, linked to this first point, the fact that this tool was born from the meeting between both practitioners and politicians. In the case of the Plaine Saint-Denis project, elected officials launched the first ideas and gave to practitioners the main research axis for the project. Linked to the new phenomenon of decentralization and to the new role of municipalities in urban and territorial planning, the Plaine Saint-Denis project was therefore born as an alternative to traditional urban planning based on a general urban plan and a cascading implementation of plans, with top-down approaches. In fact, the French technocratic planning vision of the 1950s–1970s, based on a deterministic approach, was no longer able to propose tools and frameworks taking into account the profound changes in the social, economic, political, and morphological reality of the metropolitan territory. The urban design project needed a theoretical debate that overcomes the gap between the different fields of competence of the territory and saw architects, town planners, and landscapers involved together in the definition of theoretical-operational tools able to overcome the quantitative approach, and to impose new visions of the territory starting from contrasting and dialectical positions.

However, France excels in experimentalism but then always finds a way to bring everything back to the norm, to top-down and hypothetical-deductive approaches that have always been its strength. A seven-year pause from the design of the Hyppodamos urban design project to the implementation of the first Zone d'aménagement concerté (ZAC) allowed the creation of a new political institution — Plaine commune — with full powers to define the transition from the urban design project to its management. And this institution was not able to transform the analyses and researches that led to the preparation of the project into tools and procedures adapted to the new dimensions of the metropolitan question. The following sectorial projects were built within the framework of the rigid regulations of the ZACs, in which the famous "consultation" served to transmit to the citizen the decisions already defined previously by technicians and architects and certainly not to bring the decision-making power closer to the citizen.

Therefore, if in France, the urban design approach, as developed in the 1980s, has contributed to creating new bottom-up strategies in the first step of the project (that we could easily associate to the "preparing well" of the SUMP method), its management was intended as a top-down implementation, led by the public administration and has compromised the theoretical debate.

At the beginning of the 2000s, the questions that the metropolitan territory, with its circles and cores, proposed to the organization of the projects were new and disruptive and it was impossible to translate it into general norms. This is why the term of metropolitan design emerges in the latest 2000s: this approach should not only highlight the articulation between the first step design phase and the implementation phases but also include, in the relationship between territorial planning and urban design, a critical analysis of uncertainties and risks. It should underline, through the project, the local complexity — social, political, geographical, economic, and topographical — and its link with the global complexity of the metropolitan territory.

3.2.2. *The Greater Paris "figures" as exploratory scenarios for the metropolitan design approach*

What is interesting to note here with regard to the Paris region planning in the first 2000s is the question of the gap still existing between urban planning and urban design, due to the mutual reference to distinct objects: on the one hand, the regional and metropolitan territory, planned and managed at the level of the national public administration and its engineers, on the other the municipalities, with their neighborhood and city cores, designed according to the local practices of the ZAC. What the Italian culture of the metropolitan planning and urban design has highlighted during the 1960s and which constitutes the great difference with respect to French culture, is the need to find a valid articulation between their different levels of reflection and management and to synthetize it in a new dimension: the metropolitan design dimension. This dialectical articulation between metropolitan planning and urban design has been and continues to be in Italy the subject of debate and disciplinary reflection (Mazzoni, 2013).

As far back as 1960, the architect and urban planner Ludovico Quaroni emphasized in his conferences and papers the new dimensions of the polycentric metropolitan territory: it offers an inter-penetration of several levels and experiences; in it the space multiplies and expands, brought closer by speed. Its inhabitants are no longer just citizens of a single place, and not only from this place are they trained culturally (Indovina, 1991). The polycentric metropolitan territory, composed by its circles and cores, is a space in which people multiply, and relationships between them are enriched, development processes are accelerated and with them human exchanges. And, if in the dense city alleys, courtyards, hallways, passages, arcades, roads, articulate the path according to a system that seems so regular, spontaneous, without hardness, in the metropolitan circles the dimensions multiply and the boundaries expand to such an extent that you can no longer perceive the separation between the spaces, and a strong sense of disorientation prevails. Its characteristic is that of a unitary but not homogeneous organism, formed by several cities, juxtaposed, superimposed, distant, at times enemy to each other, and yet inseparables. This new, limitless metropolitan territory, which consists of many cores, has to be planned on two levels. The first one, that of the metropolitan planning, will serve to define the great ideas without which urban design projects, sectorial, and belonging to the second level, would not be able to find a deeper meaning and would flow into purely technical-normative projects.

On the first level, the idea of metropolitan planning as expressed by the Italians indicates, as is well known, the directions of growth, the links between economic planning and spatial planning, mobility infrastructures and lines, the location of ports, airports, major stations, motorway junctions, etc. But, at the same time, the metropolitan planning has to emerge as metropolitan *design*. It has to put forward these elements as a series of structural hypotheses and express them through the graphic formulation of a design, both in the creative sense of the term and in the sense of the transmission of a vision that it presupposes. Plans, models, and other works will be the graphic formulation of an idea, born rationally far from architecture; that architecture begins to come into being through the signs, which presuppose the new structure of the city cores.

These signs are evoked rather than represented; they are almost "ghosts of cities." The important attitude, again according to Quaroni, is to stay away from the idea of a top-down normative planning and close to the idea of a bottom-up design. It is evident that at the metropolitan scale, the plan cannot represent the form for the city, giving the word form the meaning of architectural envelope, of contour lines. However, it will be possible to design at the metropolitan scale the general form of the city, meaning by this the non-expressive figures that refer to its essence. And it is precisely this idea of "figure," which involves both the underlying idea and its representation through drawings that constitutes the core of the question. In this metropolitan design approach, the figure of the territory, born endogenously from the territory itself, allows us to grasp its essence and lay the foundations for the development of sectorial projects that have a clear and explicit link with the ideas expressed on a large scale.

In this sense, most of the plans and drawings for the Grand Paris, linked to the international consultation *Le grand Pari(s) de l'agglomération parisienne* (2009), exceed the size of the urban design project and refer above all to a vision, an idea which interprets and translates the metropolitan dimension through several figures: "linear metropolis" and "polycentric metropolis" connected by mobility networks were proposed by Antoine Grumbach, Roland Castro, and Christian de Portzamparc, and the "porous-city" by Secchi-Vigano Studio. In parallel to the architects' plans, the analysis of Michel Lussault and Michel Collot, close to the disciplines of human geography and landscape, is the theoretical background of this new metropolitan design approach. Their analysis stresses the importance of raising awareness of the landscape and its multiple dimensions and articulations, the importance of the individual perception of space, its different scales and living times. Linked to Merleau-Ponty's phenomenological theories, these drawings and theories underline the necessity of finding an overall design that links the various sectors together and allows us to perceive the dialectic between the circles and the cores, the large voids, the natural and infrastructural corridors, the wastelands, and constructed parts. An overall design based on the figurative relationship between the different parts, understood not only in a visual way but also and above all as pieces of the human city that lives, acts, and struggles. In fact, the metropolitan territory can suggest strong emotions even through an oil refinery or a heavy infrastructure: "It is precisely in the strong contrasts, which we find on the edge of industrial areas, in the ports and in certain suburbs rich in slovenly infrastructure of the nineteenth century, that we can perhaps touch the idea of the whole modern city thinking" (Quaroni, 1967). The transition zones, the fringes, and limits of the new metropolitan circles suggest the violent condition of the current city, with its energy, complexity, strong contrasts, and the needs of integration of a human scale.

To conclude, we can point out that one of the elements of great interest linked to the international consultation for the Grand Paris of 2009 was precisely the fact of having experimented with several conceptual figures for the metropolitan design project, linked to the theories of the Italian Tendenza movement. These conceptual figures did not generate homogeneous top-down models: they have been able to generate global visions of the whole metropolitan territory resulting from several fragments, which emerge from the territory, and at the same time they have been able to express its geographical, social, economic, and cultural contents, leaving the doors open to a "unexpected future." The great challenge of the urban architecture discipline, linked to the development of the contemporary condition of metropolitan circles and cores, is to be able to invent, in dialogue with other disciplines, new figures of the territory that allow an inductive vision of sustainability through representations and projections into the future that can be instruments of dialogue not only between politicians and technicians but also with individuals who practice it and live it daily (Mazzoni and Tsiomis, 2012). From these figures it is easy to articulate the large and small scales.

4. Conclusion

Given the complexities of actors, temporalities, and scales, the current metropolitan project cannot follow established models and templates. Related to German, Italian, and French theories and practices of the recent 50 years, the European Commission's SUMP method introduced correlated top-down and bottom-up approaches that are able to organize sustainable metropolitan development for balanced interconnection between urban cores and metropolitan circles, with particular focus on public transports, integrated mobility strategies, and efficient connectivity.

The examples of Strasbourg and Paris, linked to reconquering and recycling brownfields and industrial wastelands in their first metropolitan circles through new mobility patterns show that the exploratory scenario is an emerging tool related to urban and metropolitan design. It reveals a narrative of collective actions gathered and structured in coherent ways through the SUMP method. Each scenario is a "possible future" that integrates partial stories — mobility systems, local geography, topography, socio-economics inputs — into a whole. In this way, the SUMP method is able to respond to the current impossibility of integrating in the metropolitan development the multiplicity of challenges and uncertainties characterizing the contemporary condition. The SUMP scenario tool, including inductive exploratory approaches, is able to question the urban sprawl in metropolitan circles, to explore the increase of public transport ridership and transit efficiency, to imagine compact, mixed-use development in new urban cores, reducing energy consumption and emission rates from cars, stimulating local economic development and job growth, revitalizing declined urban districts, and improving quality of life as bottom-up strategies. Thus, the SUMP scenario tool based on an inductive and figurative method should give a shared vision of the new metropolitan condition with its circles and cores. It should propose a balanced articulation between the global level and the sectorial projects. It can become a reinvention of spaces starting from the different perceptions, practices, and ways of life of citizens, a narrative of the primordial geographical components of the landscape — land, water, slopes, etc., and their relation to architecture.

These are the materials on which to build a theoretical-disciplinary debate on metropolitan design. A debate that shows how the metropolitan project can highlight the reciprocity between the local dimension and the global strategic dimension, becoming an opportunity for comparison and clarification of conflicts without being reduced to a set of technical–practical rules dropped from above on the individual places and on the territory. If we believe the words of Paolo Virno expressed in his *Grammar of the Multitude* (Virno, 2001), with the hypothetical-deductive approach lowered from above, we risk suffocating the creative thrust, rich in new energies, that comes from below, from the multiple places of the territory and from the "multitude" that inhabits it and enriches it with the strength of its "impersonal and transversal" thinking, which is also "unique and unrepeatable."

References

Börjeson, L., M. Höjer, K. Dreborg, T., Ekvall and G. Finnveden (2006). "Scenario Types and Techniques: Towards a User's Guide." *Futures* 38, 723–739.

Breheny, M. J. (ed.) (1992). *Sustainable Development and Urban Form*. Louvain-la-Neuve: European Research in Regional Sciences.

Bulkeley, H. and M. Betsill (2005). "Rethinking Sustainable Cities: Multilevel Governance and the 'Urban' Politics of Climate Change." *Environmental Politics* 14(1), 42–63.

Bulkeley, H. and M. Betsill (2013). "Revisiting the Urban Politics of Climate Change." *Environmental Politics* 22(1), 136–154.

Calthorpe, P. (1993). *The Next American Metropolis: Ecology, Community, and the American Dream*. New York: Princeton Architectural Press.

Commission of the European Communities (2007). *Towards a New Culture for Urban Mobility*. Green Paper presented by the Commission, COM 551 final, Brussels.

CUS (2009). Communauté urbaine de Strasbourg. *Démarche ÉcoCités Strasbourg, métropole des Deux-Rives*.

Dupuy, G. (1995). *Les territoires de l'automobile*. Anthropos/Economica, Coll. Villes.

ESPON (2013). *Science in Support of European Territorial Development and Cohesion*, Scientific Report.

European Commission (EC) (1992). *White Paper: The Future Development of the Common Transport Policy*. Retrieved from: http://aei.pitt.edu/1116/1/future_transport_policy_wp_COM_92_494.pdf. Last access date: 2018/12/17

EC (1999). *ESDP — European Spatial Development Perspective, Towards Balanced and Sustainable Development of the Territory of the European Union*. Office for Official Publications of the European Communities, Luxemburg.

EC (2001). *White Paper: European Transport Policy for 2010: Time to Decide*. Retrieved from: https://ec.europa.eu/transport/themes/strategies/2001_white_paper_en.

EC (2006). *Keep Europe Moving-Sustainable Mobility for Our Continent: Mid-Term Review of the European Commission's 2001 Transport White Paper*. Retrieved from: https://ec.europa.eu/transport/themes/strategies/2006_keep_europe_moving_en.

European Parliament (2008). *Resolution of 9 July 2008 on 'Towards a New Culture of Urban Mobility*. Retrieved from: http://www.europarl.europa.eu/sides/getDoc.do?type=TA&language=EN&reference=P6-TA-2008-356.

EC (2009). Communication from the Commission to the European Parliament, the Council, the European Economic and Social Committee and the Committee of the Regions. *Action Plan on Urban Mobility*. Retrieved from: http://eur-lex.europa.eu/legal-content/EN/ALL/?uri=CELEX:52009DC0490.

EC (2011). *White Paper: Roadmap to a Single European Transport Area — Towards a Competitive and Resource Efficient Transport System*. Retrieved from: https://ec.europa.eu/transport/themes/strategies/2011_white_paper_en.

EC (2013a). *Guidelines. Developing and Implementing a Sustainable Urban Mobility Plan*. Rupprecht Consult-Forschung und Beratung GmbH. Retrieved from: http://www.eltis.org/sites/eltis/files/guidelines-developing-and-implementing-a-sump_final_web_jan2014b.pdf.

EC (2013b). *Urban Mobility Package*. Retrieved from: https://ec.europa.eu/transport/themes/urban/urban_mobility/ump_en.

EC (2013c). *Communication from the Commission to the European Parliament, the Council, the European Economic and Social Committee and the Committee of the Regions. Together Towards Competitive and Resource-Efficient Urban Mobility*. Retrieved from: https://ec.europa.eu/transport/sites/transport/files/themes/urban/doc/ump/com%282013%29913_en.pdf.

EC (2014). *The Poly-SUMP Methodology. How to Develop a Sustainable Urban Mobility Plan for a Polycentric Region. Guidelines*. Retrieved from: http://www.eltis.org/sites/default/files/trainingmaterials/polysump-sump-guidelines-final.pdf.

European Parliament (2015). *Sustainable Urban Mobility: European Parliament Resolution of 2 December 2015 on Sustainable Urban Mobility*. Retrieved from: http://www.europarl.europa.eu/sides/getDoc.do?pubRef=-//EP//TEXT+TA+P8-TA-2015-0423+0+DOC+XML+V0//EN.

EC (2017). *Urban Mobility Package*. Retrieved from: http://ec.europa.eu/energy/en/news/europe-move-commission-launches-new-transport-package.

European Union (2013). *Guidelines: Developing and Implementing a Sustainable Urban Mobility Plan*. Rupprecht Consult-Forschung und Beratung GmbH. Retrieved from: http://www.eltis.org/sites/default/files/guidelines-developing-and-implementing-a-sump_final_web_jan2014b.pdf.

Grigorovschi, A. (2016). *Architecture Urbaine, Cultures de Projet et Outils Conceptuels en Débats: «Figure», «Récit» et «Scénario» dans la Pensée et la Représentation de la Ville Contemporaine,* Laboratoire AMUP, PhD thesis, University of Strasbourg.

Héraud, J.-A. (2011). "Reinventing Creativity in Old Europe: A Development Scenario for Cities within the Upper Rhine Valley Cross-Border Area." *City, Culture and Society* 2, 65–73.

Indovina, F. (ed.) (1991). *La Città Diffusa*. Venezia: DAEST.

Jabareen, Y. R. (2006). "Sustainable Urban Forms: Their Typologies, Models, and Concepts." *Journal of Planning Education and Research* 28(1), 38–52.

Lussault, M. (2005). "Les territoires urbains en quête d'images." *Urbanisme* (Mai–June), 342.

Lussault, M. (2007). *L'Homme Spatial*. Paris: Le Seuil.

Mazzoni, C. (2013). *La Tendenza, Une Avant-Garde Italienne. 1950–1980.* Marseille: Parenthèses.

Mazzoni, C. and A. Grigorovschi (2015). "Strasbourg Eurométropole, a cross-border conurbation towards new sustainable mobility patterns." *Spatium* 33(June), 18–25.

Mazzoni, C. and A. Grigorovschi (2017). "Designing the 'Energy City': Future Scenarios for European and Asian Metropolises." *Urban Design Journal* 12(Mai), 42–53.

Mazzoni, C. and L. d'Emilio (eds.) (2014). *Strasbourg Métropole. Images et Récits Pour la Ville-Archipel*. Paris: La Commune.

Mazzoni, C. and Y. Tsiomis (eds.) (2012). *Paris, Métropoles en Miroir. Stratégies Urbaines en Ile-de-France*. Paris: la Découverte.

Ministers of the EU Member States (2007). *Leipzig Charter on Sustainable European Cities, Informal Ministerial Meeting on Urban Development and Territorial Cohesion, at the Invitation of the German EU Council Presidency*. Leipzig, May 24 and 25, 2007.

Missions Publiques. (2010). *Practical Guide on Running a Future Search Workshop for Polycentric Regions*. Retrieved from: www.missionspubliques.com. Last access date: 2018/12/17

Mongin, O. (ed.) (2008). "Les Chantiers du Grand Paris." *Esprit* 10(October).

Naess, P. (2001). "Urban Planning and Sustainable Development." *European Planning Studies* 9(1), 503–524.

Quaroni, L. (1967). *La torre di Babele*, Bari, Dedalo.

Riddell, R. (2008). *Sustainable Urban Planning: Tipping the Balance*. London: Wiley.

Rietveld, P. *et al.* (eds.) (2011). *Transitions towards Sustainable Mobility: New Solutions and Approaches for Sustainable Transport Systems*. Berlin Springer.

Secchi, B. (2000). *Prima Lezione di Urbanistica*. Laterza: Bari.

Sessa, C. ISIS — Institute of Studies for the Integration of Systems, *Poly-SUMP methodology*. Retrieved from: http://civitas.eu/sites/default/files/webinar_sump_in_complex_regions_polysump_sessa.pdf.

Sieverts, T. (2004). *Entre-ville, une Lecture de la Zwischenstadt*. Marseille: Parentheses.

Viganò, P. (2010). Explorer l'avenir. In: *La ville est une figure libre. Laurent Théry. Grand prix de l'urbanisme* 2010, edited by A. Masboungi. Marseille: Parenthèses.

Viganò, P. (2012). *Les Territoires de L'urbanisme. Le Projet Comme Producteur de Connaissance*. Genève: MetisPresses.

Virno, P. (2001). *Grammatica Della Moltitudine. Per Una Analisi Delle Forme di vita Contemporanee.* Soveria Mannelli: Rubbettino.

Weisbord, M. and S. Janoff (2010). *Future Search — Getting the Whole System in the Room for Vision, Commitment and Action*. Retrieved from: http://www.futuresearch.net/http://www.futuresearch.net/. Last access date: 2018/12/17

Weisbord, M. and S. Janoff (2010). *Future Search — Getting the Whole System in the Room for Vision, Commitment and Action.* San Francisco: Berrett-Koehler Publishers. Third edition.

III. Emerging Metropolitan Circles and Urbanization

Chapter 9

Two Faces of Mega-Urban Region Formation in South Korea

Yu-Min Joo

KDI School of Public Policy and Management, South Korea
yjoo@kdischool.ac.kr

1. Introduction

In today's globalized world, a few key large metropolitan areas grow and dominate as gateways to the internationally integrated economy. In addition to the mega-cities of advanced capitalist societies, such as London, New York, and Tokyo — the three key cities examined by Sassen (1991) in her seminal book *The Global City* — many other rapidly emerging countries are also showcasing the development of mega-cities (or even mega-regions) as representatives of globally connected national nodes. In particular, such mega-urban regions have most prominently taken shape in Asia (Douglass, 2000). By 2030, Asia is expected to be home to 24 mega-cities, with Europe and North America to have only three and two, respectively (UN, 2015). China alone has six mega-cities, according to 2016 data (UN, 2016), and the country now has plans to develop 19 super-regions.

To be sure, mega-cities signify competitiveness and economic growth opportunities in the new global economy. In consideration of their role as principal economic engines, governments are striving to build successful "global cities" as part of their key development strategies. However, mega-cities have not always received positive limelight in urban scholarship. In fact, it has been only recently, with the rise of the global city thesis, that large cities have begun to symbolize economic competitiveness. Previously, they had been more likely to be seen as hindrances to development associated with specifically urban problems (e.g., over-congestion, slums, informal economies, etc.) Davis (2005) notes that the perception of dominant large cities changed from that of obstacles to the national development of their host countries to that of key engines of economic growth only recently, under the framework of the global cities thesis.

Before the boom of mega-cities as the main economic drivers of the new global economy, urban scholars explained urbanization patterns and economic development as a bell-shaped relationship (Williamson, 1965; Alonso, 1980). They argued that, when a country begins to grow from a low-income status, its primacy rate (the population share of the largest city) increases, as scarce development resources and infrastructure are first poured into a single key city, or a select few of these. As economic development continues, other regions begin to develop. The theory is based on an expectation of the decentralization of development, which takes advantage of development spillovers, congestion, and over-concentration in the original city of development, and also of the fact that the country can now afford to develop other regions. It was thus hypothesized that primacy first increases with national economic development before beginning to decline.

This model, which was based on observations of trends within earlier cases of industrialization in advanced Western societies, has not been as easily observed in developing and emerging economies elsewhere. The dominance of mega-cities has persisted in developing countries, gaining ground rather than receding along with their advancing economic growth. Amid the persistent primacy of mega-cities, international agencies have encouraged developing countries to seek ways to grow alternative centers to minimize the problems caused by over-concentration rather than expecting regional convergence to occur spontaneously over time (Renaud, 1981; UN, 1993).

However, with the newly emphasized importance of big and globally connected cities in the global economy, nation states are more concerned with vying to create competitive and representative global cities of their own than with physically spreading growth to achieve balanced regional development. This shift of emphasis does not imply an elimination of the social and economic problems long associated with over-urbanization. The difficulties associated with inadequate infrastructure, pollution, and poverty persist in many developing countries' largest cities, especially as they often cannot cope with the speed and scale of migration. Yet, there is no longer a drive to search for ways to decentralize development. Acting — or aspiring to act — as key gateways to a globalized economy, these mega-cities now face less pressure to deconcentrate or disperse their development to other regions within the same country. Instead, their competitiveness and ability to tap into the global economic production system and integrate globally are the overriding considerations, and their privilege, predominance, and concentration are promoted rather than discouraged (Douglass, 2000). Hence, socio-economic polarization occurs not only within these global cities (Sassen, 1991) but also across the various regions within a nation, especially in the emerging economies of the Global South (Shatkin, 2007).

To summarize, attaining higher levels of economic development does not necessarily result in balanced regional growth in today's global economy. In fact, the likelihood of primacy now rises along with development as both the state and the private sectors concentrate their resources in the few cities with the potential to be globally successful. In neoliberal globalization, the solution to achieving global competitiveness while tackling the urban problems inherent in mega-cities may lie in creating a well-planned mega-urban cluster, with a number of secondary and smaller cities organized around the key mega-city (or even mega-cities). However, this still leaves unaddressed the challenge of the decline and shrinkage of those regions that lie outside of the global economic connection.

This chapter introduces the case of South Korea's urbanization policies and examines the patterns that have accompanied the country's industrialization and national development. South Korea is an intriguing case. Decentralized and rural in its relatively recent past, the country has rapidly emerged to host one of the biggest primacies, with half of the country's population concentrated in a single urban region. This state of affairs has come about despite the state's continuous attempts to promote a more balanced regional development — an effort that began as early as the 1970s, and the latest example of which is the new administrative capital of Sejong, to which the government began to relocate its offices from Seoul in 2012. Examining a number of key urbanization patterns, policies, and projects, this chapter examines how the country came to showcase a lopsidedly predominant capital region surrounding Seoul despite the state's continued attempts at fostering decentralization. In particular, it focuses on the "new town" projects as a fundamental tool in South Korea's urban development and management endeavors. The chapter illustrates how the conurbation of Seoul has involved both centralization and decentralization at different scales and the implications behind building this competitive economic powerhouse.

2. "The Republic of Seoul"

Seoul — the capital city of South Korea — is one of Asia's key global cities today, ranking 12th in the A.T. Kearney 2018 Global Cities Index, following close behind Tokyo (4th), Hong Kong (5th), Singapore (7th), and Beijing (9th) (Hales *et al.*, 2018). Domestically, the city manifests astonishing predominance within South Korea as the center of the country's political, cultural, educational, and economic activities. Due to its asymmetrical concentration and predominance, South Korea's capital has sometimes been described as "the Republic of Seoul," indicating its unrivaled dominance.

Seoul covers an area of only 605 km^2 — smaller than that of Singapore or Hong Kong, and comprising only about 0.6% of South Korea's total land area. However, the city acts as a metropolitan area, extending its economic and social influence far beyond its official boundaries. Seoul, together with the sizeable surrounding Gyeonggi Province (which contains 28 cities) and the city of Incheon nearby (where Seoul's international airport is located), is referred to as the Seoul Metropolitan Area (SMA) or "the capital region.[1]" The capital region, comprising less than 12% of South Korea's land area, is home to around half of the nation's people. With a population of more than 25 million, it is the fourth-largest

[1] In this book, the two terms will be used interchangeably.

metropolitan area globally after Tokyo (Japan), Shanghai (China), and Jakarta (Indonesia). The primacy of the SMA becomes even more evident when considering that South Korea has a total of eight metropolitan cities and nine provinces.[2]

In addition to being home to the lion's share of the country's population, the SMA also surpasses the rest of South Korea in its role as a major economic hub. It accounts for 46% of national GDP and 50% of national employment, and houses 47% of the firms operating in South Korea (OECD, 2018). More importantly, the majority of the South Korean chaebols[3] (e.g., Samsung, LG, Hyundai, SK, and Lotte) are headquartered in Seoul (Kim and Han, 2012). Of the top 100 companies in South Korea, 80 are located in the SMA, as are 87.7% of the Korea Composite Stock Price Index (KOSPI) companies (Pyun, 2014). In terms of research and development (R&D), over 67% of R&D investments are made in the capital region. The region also houses the headquarters of all the major media and newspaper companies and, representing the hub of education, is home to 16 of the top 20 South Korean universities (Pyun, 2014). Its prestige and the concentration of key activities and job opportunities have made the SMA into a peerless magnet for people and investment.

The unparalleled concentration of the SMA has its origins in South Korea's industrialization. Before economic development took off, South Korea was a highly rural and predominantly agricultural economy with very limited capital, recovering from the hardships of Japanese colonization (1910–1945) and the destructive Korean War (1950–1953). The country was far from manifesting primacy, with 72% of its population living in rural areas and with Seoul housing less than 10% of the national population in 1960. The capital region, then home to 21% of the nation's

---

[2]To be more precise, South Korea has one special city (Seoul), one autonomous metropolitan city (the new administrative capital city of Sejong), six metropolitan cities, eight provinces, and one autonomous province (Jeju Island).

[3]Chaebols are family-owned conglomerates in South Korea. They have been and continue to be the key engines of the country's economic development. Under the guidance of the developmental state, the chaebols expanded and diversified themselves, acquiring other firms in various sectors throughout the 1970s. In 1972, the 10 largest chaebols held an average of 7.5 firms. By 1979, this number had increased to 25.4 (Koo and Kim, 1992).

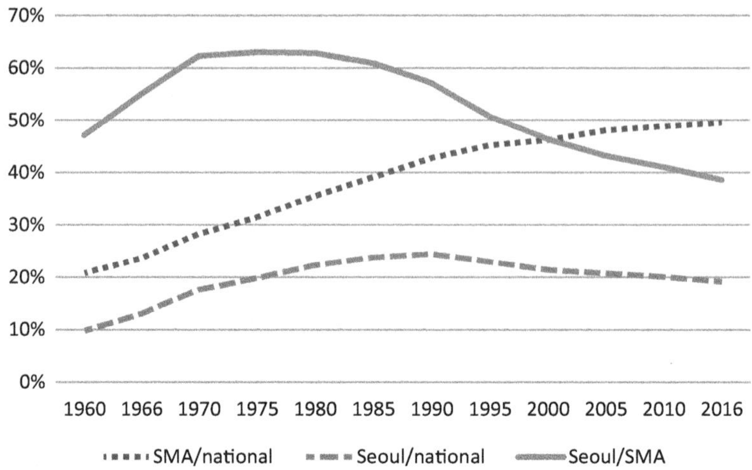

Figure 1: Seoul and SMA population percentage changes 1960–2016.
Source: Korean Statistical Information Service: kosis.kr.

total population, was far from representing primacy, especially considering that the area comprised almost 12% of the country's land area. This percentage, however, rose rapidly from 1960 onward and today stands at 50% (see Figure 1).

Figure 2 illustrates how Seoul's population grew rapidly from less than 2.5 million in 1960 to 10 million in 1988. Since then, its population has remained more or less the same, at 10 million, whereas the population of the SMA has continued to grow. In fact, it is the rapid growth of the surrounding regions that accounts for the capital region's unabated growth. As illustrated by Figure 1, in the late 1980s, the percentage of Seoul's population within SMA began to drop significantly (from over 60% to less than 40%), indicating the rapid growth of the other cities in the capital region surrounding Seoul. This implies significant expansion and growth of the SMA.

One might at first assume that South Korea's industrialization has occurred in Seoul, leading to its rapid expansion and gradual growth into a metropolitan area over time. Indeed, the initial light industrialization that depended heavily on South Korea's low-cost labor first took off in the capital city. In 1964, the very first export industrial estate was built in

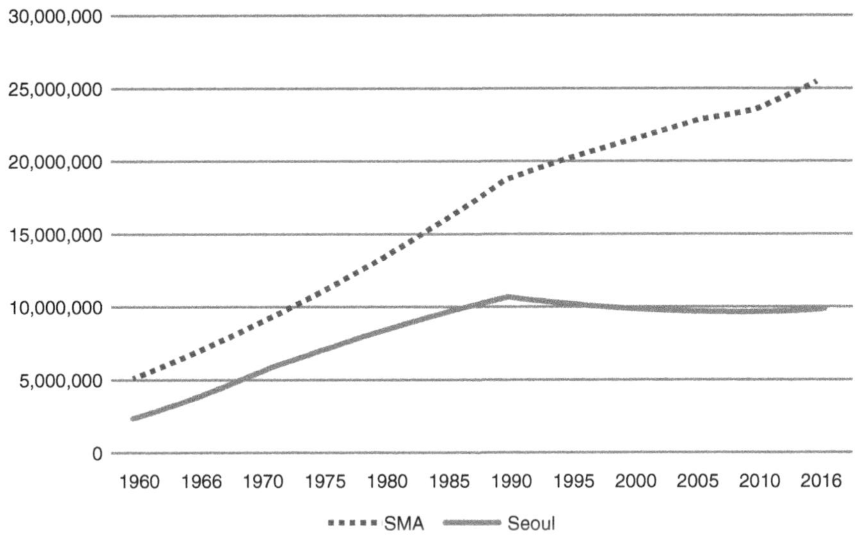

Figure 2: Population changes of Seoul and SMA 1960–2016.

Source: Korean Statistical Information Service: kosis.kr.

Guro in Seoul. However, in the 1970s, South Korea began to push for capital-intensive industries, and this wave of industrialization was focused outside of the capital region. Furthermore, Seoul has long been surrounded by its greenbelt, which attempts to curtail the city's development. The puzzling continuation of the growth of Seoul and its development into a metropolitan area require a closer understanding of the state-led industrialization and accompanying urbanization that have set the stage for South Korea's contemporary development.

3. Decentralization and Centralization During State-Led Industrialization

South Korea's economic development took advantage of the new international division of labor that began in the latter half of the 20th century. At the time, there emerged a new opportunity for selected countries in Asia to advance their industrialization and nation building. Under the developmental state thesis, the literature has examined how the Asian Tigers (i.e., South Korea, Hong Kong, Taiwan, and Singapore) rapidly climbed the ladder of economic development under the guidance of the state (e.g., Amsden, 1989; Castells, 1992). The underlying explanation has been that the developmental state set industrialization as the state's highest priority and achieved its economic goals by intervening in the economy with its plan-rationale approaches (Johnson, 1982; Amsden, 1989).

In South Korea, the developmental state established itself following the 1961 *coup d'état* led by Park Chung-hee. Through the state's developmental intervention, the South Korean economy underwent impressive export-oriented industrialization (EOI) and, only 30 years later, had become the world's 10th largest exporter, with 92% of exports from the manufacturing sector (Kim, 1997). This economic achievement was accompanied by a distinctive spatial development under state planning, where urbanization produced selective cities along the coastline instead of spreading them evenly across South Korean territory. Under the large technocratic planning bureaucracies that characterized the developmental state, spatial planning was very much a technical process, as were state-planned industrialization and the state's macro-economic policies.

One of the key concepts applied by the state was that of growth poles. Although the concept was originally developed in abstract economic — rather than geographical — space (Hirschman, 1958), it soon came to be seen as the mechanism for spatially concentrating industries in peripheral regions, away from the core cities. As South Korea lacked adequate physical infrastructure for industrialization, the idea of focused investment in a few select areas to concentrate infrastructural investments made much economic sense.

When the developmental state launched its ambitious heavy-chemical industrialization (HCI),[4] it also immediately put forth urbanization strategies and prioritized building new industrial towns[5] as growth poles to maximize industrial efficiencies. Against a predominantly rural background, the state undertook massive land acquisition and the development

[4] Six heavy-chemical industries were selected for promotion: iron and steel, non-ferrous metals, machinery, shipbuilding, electrical appliances and electronics, and petrochemicals.

[5] These state-built industrial new towns quickly grew to become South Korea's major industrial cities.

of new port and other infrastructure appropriate for heavy-chemical industries and residential and basic urban facilities for industrial workers, in the form of building new industrial towns. With markets not in Seoul but in foreign countries under EOI, having such cities located near ports for the export of bulky products and import of materials was critical (Mills and Song, 1979). While locating the new industrial towns along the southeastern coast, the developmental state also designated each new such industrial town to specialize in one (or a few) of the heavy-chemical industries it was promoting in order to better cater to the industries' specific infrastructural needs (Yu and Ji, 1998). It strategized about the industrial locations and directly designated them, as the military would strategize about its war plans on a map, and the southeastern region (comprising Korea's second-largest city, Busan) emerged as Korea's industrial core. Located far from Seoul, this new industrial core formed a second magnet, pulling industry and population to the southeast shore. Indeed, Seoul's share of manufacturing employment declined from 34% in 1970 (during the proliferation of light industries) to 22% in 1980 (after Park's successful launch of HCI) (Park, 1986; Lee, 1988).

Beginning in the 1970s, while the planned poles were inducing population growth and urbanization away from Seoul, the developmental state was initiating and directing a number of strong policy measures to mitigate and control Seoul's growth. Before HCI, Seoul had rapidly grown with booming labor-intensive light industries, and between 1960 and 1970, its population had jumped from 2.45 million to 5.53 million, more than doubling in just one decade (Figure 1). Alarmed at its rapid growth, the developmental state had launched a number of disciplinary measures to control and manage the growth of the city.

To begin with, Park Chung-hee borrowed the concept of the greenbelt in order to contain Seoul's urban development. A greenbelt refers to an area surrounding a metropolitan city designed to prohibit development — its purpose is to act as a barrier to urban expansion and sprawl (Bengston and Youn, 2006). Although the greenbelt policy was enforced throughout the country in 13 cities in South Korea, it was most extensively enforced around the SMA (Kim, 1990). Under the authoritarian regime, the designation of greenbelt, which compromised private property rights, was carried out swiftly. Formalized under the City Planning Law of 1971, the policy designated an area of 1,567 km^2 within the SMA (comprising 13.3% of its total land area) as greenbelt between 1971 and 1976 (Bengston and Youn, 2006). The greenbelt in South Korea has been preserved for more or less 30 years, and the country has been one of the few cases — aside from the UK, where the idea originated — where the greenbelt policy has succeeded (Park, 2001).

Secondly, as the state set the physical boundary around Seoul with the greenbelt, it also worked to develop and modernize the city within. In 1963, Seoul's official boundary was drastically increased to more than double its land area (Lim and Kim, 2015). This new physical boundary provided an opportunity for significant physical growth of the city. The change incorporated new tracts of land lying to the south of the Han River. With the new boundary, Seoul became bisected by the Han River, leaving two distinct areas: Gangbuk (translated as "north of the river") and Gangnam ("south of the river"). The old city of Seoul was located in Gangbuk, while, even in the 1970s, most of Gangnam remained open field and farmland. Hence, in 1970, the state launched the Plan for south of the Han River, which led to the development of Gangnam, with numerous massive-scale new residential towns in its vast open fields. To promote the residential developments, the state relocated the city's prestigious secondary schools, as well as other amenities and public institutions, into the Gangnam area (Gelézeau, 2007). These new developments thus filled Gangnam throughout the 1970 and the 1980s. Furthermore, Seoul underwent extensive urban development during the 1980s in preparation for the 1988 Summer Olympics. In addition to building new roads and stadiums, more massive-scale residential developments took place throughout Seoul, with slums quickly being replaced and the old inner-city centers of Gangbuk being refurbished. (See Joo *et al.* (2017) for details of the urban development projects carried out in preparation for the mega-event.) The 1988 Olympic Games was considered an important national event, providing South Korea with a platform to showcase its achievements to the world (Joo *et al.*, 2017). With intensive urban development throughout the previous two decades, Seoul emerged as a modernized mega-city of 10 million people.

Finally, a number of regulations were imposed to regulate the growth of Seoul. While the city focused on developing and providing adequate modernized housing for its already-booming population, the state sought to restrict the further flow of industry and population to the capital city. For instance, the 1970 Local Industrial Promotion Act provided subsidies and tax exemptions for industries that relocated out of the three metropolitan cities into designated areas (Kwon, 1985). In 1973, the Local Industry Tax Regulation was implemented to prevent the construction of new factories within Seoul. Companies in breach of this regulation were subjected to penalty taxes (Kim and Donaldson, 1979, p. 665). In 1977, more powerful coercive measures were implemented. Under the newly formalized Industrial Location Act, the government gained legislative powers to enforce relocation orders to specific polluting industries (Lee, 1985). Banwol, a new industrial town situated 35 km from Seoul, was designated to host the industries being relocated out of Seoul (Kwon, 1985). From the perspective of the firms, though, the relocation was economically inefficient. According to a survey, more than 86% of relocated firms felt that "relocation resulted in some extra time and overhead expenditures" (Choe and Song, 1984, p. 100). Almost all of the surveyed firms commented that operating expenditures had increased by as much as 40% (Choe and Song, 1984, p. 101).

In addition, under the National Plan for Population Redistribution from Seoul Metropolitan Region, launched in 1977, several functions of urban centers, such as government administration, were to be dispersed around secondary cities. The Plan also suggested that the population should be dispersed to new cities with populations in the range of around 50,000 people and that there would be "modern" services such as healthcare, transport, and public utilities within these cities (Rondinelli, 1984, p. 432). The most notable example would be a new administrative town called Gwacheon (in Gyeonggi Province), which, by 1983, housed four main government offices that had been relocated from Seoul (Kwon, 1985). The core idea of decentralization continued under the Capital Region Rearrangement Act of 1983 (and the Capital Region Rearrangement Plan of 1984), under which there were deliberate attempts to restrict particular developments, such as new factories and population-attracting universities[6] (see Kim and Gallent (1998) for details).

[6] In 1994, the law was revised, relaxing its restrictions. Today, the SMA is largely divided into the "overconcentration restriction zone," "growth management zone," and "preservation zone" (Kim and Gallent, 1998).

Overall, strong decentralization efforts co-existed with centralizing urban development during South Korea's industrialization under the developmental state. While key industrialization took place in the new industrial cities developed along the southeastern coast, Seoul's growth was controlled and restricted with greenbelt and other regulations in an attempt to curtail the further expansion of the city. In its urban management efforts, the state favored decentralization of the economic activities and population to the surrounding secondary cities. At the same time, within its official boundary, Seoul underwent significant modernization and urban development as a capital city.

These spatial development strategies ended up producing a national urban network that effectively separated Seoul from the rest of South Korea. While South Korea's manufacturing activities grew along its southeastern coast, producing an industrial core, the strong hand of the state in the process of industrialization resulted in the chaebol headquarters concentrating in Seoul, where the national state agencies were also located. This concentration of chaebol headquarters, national state agencies, and collaborating banks entailed a slanted concentration of white-collar workers in the capital city. In fact, the city's share of the new middle class (defined as white-collar workers, often with professional skills) reached 48.4% in 1975 and 60% in 1980 (Lim, 2005), creating a new hierarchical spatial division of labor (Joo, 2019). The concentrated urban investments, along with carefully controlled urban growth and the dominance of Seoul as the center of decision-making functions throughout South Korea's industrialization, set the stage for the city's dominance in the new global economy.

4. The Demise of the National Urban Network and the Making of a Global Mega-urban Region

4.1. *An overview*

From the mid-1980s onward, South Korea underwent major political and institutional transformations, which led to changes in its spatial development planning. Democratization, which took place in 1987, triggered an explosion of labor movements throughout the country. The National

Labor Law was amended to allow the formation of labor unions, resulting in substantial increases in wages and rising labor costs (Suh, 2009). South Korea's industrialization, which had relied on the competitive advantage of its cheap labor, was rapidly losing its competitive edge. Together with Japan and other Asian Tiger countries, South Korea began to relocate its factories offshore to other countries, mostly in Southeast Asia and China (Douglass, 2009).

Together with democratization, South Korea underwent decentralization reforms throughout the 1990s. The democratization declaration included promises of local autonomy, which was to progress gradually. Local assemblies were re-established in 1991, and from 1995, mayors and governors (who used to be appointed by the central government) began to be popularly elected. Attempts to increase local autonomy might at first have appeared to have a positive impact on more balanced regional development, but under the nascent local democracy and limited local capabilities, it suggested more difficulties ahead for localities and the possibility of further exacerbating regional inequalities. In fact, under the developmental state, "regional policy encourage[d] balanced growth, and place[d] limits on economic competition among localities[,] largely to sustain state legitimacy in the face of regional frictions caused by the functional primacy of the political capital city" (Hill *et al.*, 2012, p. 21). Democratization and decentralization weakened the developmental state, which had had a keen interest in producing a balanced national urban network, albeit using authoritarian measures. With local democracy, localities now had the legitimacy to pursue their own growth, and — especially with the onset of neoliberalization — they were unleashed into competition to find their own ways to attract capital in the neoliberal global economy.

Indeed, throughout these changes, a number of industrial cities began to suffer in South Korea when their key economic base — manufacturing production activities — either relocated to foreign countries or weakened in the face of steep competition, particularly from China. As these cities had been mostly acting as manufacturing production platforms, remotely controlled by headquarters located in Seoul, they lacked opportunities to build and nurture local embeddedness (Park and Markusen, 1995). As a result, when faced with challenges in manufacturing, these industrial cities struggled to find a new route to economic prosperity.

Furthermore, after the 1997 Asian financial crisis, extensive neoliberalization took place in South Korea. The country received bailout loans from the International Monetary Fund (IMF) to recover from the crisis and, as a loan condition, had to abide by a number of liberalization policies. The financial crisis thus acted as a further catalyst to transfer the opportunities, as well as the burdens, of international competition down to the local levels, instead of the centrally guided spatial development. At the same time, priority was placed on developing its core city region — the SMA — as a competitive global city, with further opening up of its economy to attract global investment. Due to the state's decentralization of heavy industries in the previous decades, Seoul was favorably positioned to take advantage of post-industrial developments and made a ready transition to hosting service economies and global functions. The overall outcome has been the increasing polarization and dominance of the SMA, and the decline of the national urban network.

4.2. *From capital city to mega-urban region: New towns as a key development strategy*

In Seoul's growth as a mega-urban region, as well as South Korea's overall urbanization, new towns have been an essential developmental strategy. New town (or more accurately, new city,[7] in terms of scale) developments have been critical to the growth of South Korea, which was a largely rural and agricultural country before its industrialization. In 1960, the country had an urbanization rate of only 28%, but this rose sharply to 75% in 1990 and to 82% today. The rapid urbanization accompanying industrialization often took the form of new town developments in rural areas. In fact, the development of numerous new industrial cities on the southeastern coast was also part of this drive to build new towns in rural areas. Within the SMA, new towns played a critical role in developing Seoul as a mega-urban region.

The development of the SMA can be considered as a series of planned physical expansions. Throughout the 1970s, Seoul expanded into its

[7] In fact, South Koreans refer to them as "*shin-doshi*," which literally translates into "new city."

Gangnam area, as explained earlier. However, since the late 1980s, Gangnam has also been filled with developments, leaving little open land available for massive residential developments. Despite the relentless and massive-scale apartment complex developments since the 1970s, the housing shortage in Seoul posed a longstanding problem, which came to a head during the 1980s (Joo, 2013; STFSAP, 2007). Therefore, the new democratic government of President Roh Tae-woo announced the ambitious Two Million Housing Construction Plan in 1988, promising to build two million residential units within his five-year incumbency. This goal required doubling the number of housing units constructed annually, which, at the time, numbered around 200,000 units per year (Lim, 2005). Of the two million units, almost half (900,000) were to be built in the capital region, and the plan included the development of five new towns (i.e., Bundang, Ilsan, Joongdong, Pyeongchon, and Sanbon) on the outskirts of Seoul, in Gyeonggi Province. (Please refer to Joo (2013) for more details of the political and economic rationale and the development processes behind the new towns.) While Joongdong, Pyeongchon, and Sanbon were new residential towns developed adjacent to existing cities in Gyeonggi Province, Bundang and Ilsan were planned as independent, standalone new towns. In fact, they were ambitious new city-building projects, with planned populations of 390,000 in Bundang and 276,000 in Ilsan.

Located 25 km from the city center, outside the greenbelt, Bundang and Ilsan's significance lie in the fact that they expand Seoul's functional boundary into Gyeonggi Province. Although these two new towns hastily adopted Ebenezer Howard's concept of the Garden City, and placed some emphasis on self-sustainability and open spaces, they were actually massive-scale new residential towns (bed-towns, to be precise) for Seoul's urban middle class, allowing them to become new homeowners while commuting to Seoul (Joo, 2013). Both Bundang and Ilsan were directly linked to Seoul's subway network. Public express buses also serviced new-town residents, connecting Ilsan to Seoul's city center in Gangbuk and Bundang to Gangnam. In light of these transportation connections, the two new towns were a commutable living choice outside of Seoul. In fact, in a survey conducted in the early 1990s, the majority of residents of the new towns — 73% in Bundang and 68% in Ilsan (KRIHS, 1993) — were found to be from Seoul. A later study also showed that the new towns have continued to depend on Seoul in terms of commuting and employment patterns, but have managed to obtain self-sufficiency in terms of retail and other commercial activities (Lee and Ahn, 2005). In short, the new towns were a successful residential project, providing high-quality living environments for the middle class working in Seoul.

As such, the new towns had strong appeal in the property market, and were able to quickly develop, exceeding their population targets in just 6–7 years. They relied heavily on the construction and sale of apartment complexes amid Seoul's dire housing shortage.[8] Given the strong demand in the property market, the new town developments were even self-financing through the sales of land (to private construction companies) and apartments (to homebuyers) (Joo, 2013). In fact, both national and local governments benefited tremendously from the new-town projects in terms of revenues, through various taxes and development fees (Lee, 2005), as the new towns suddenly turned idle rural land into much-coveted real estate.

In fact, the development of Bundang and Ilsan showed how rural land on the outskirts of Gyeonggi Province could be integrated into Seoul's property market, which, prior to their development, had been "confined" within its official boundary. The development of new towns as part of the ambitious national project also entailed significant extension of the existing transportation infrastructure. For example, in addition to the subway lines connecting Seoul to Bundang and Ilsan, the Seoul Ring Expressway, a 127.7 km stretch of roadway, was built around Seoul, linking all five new towns, as well as other key cities on the outskirts of Seoul. As Gyeonggi Province and its property developments were incorporated into Seoul's urban network, both new supply (i.e., keen interest from local governments as well as private developers) and demand (i.e., cheaper yet feasible residential options near Seoul) for residential developments

[8] At the time, the housing supply rate (which is the number of housing units divided by the number of households × 100) was slightly above 50% in Seoul, indicating the severity of the housing shortage at the time (Lim, 2005). The housing supply rate began to improve with the development of the new towns under the Two Million Housing Construction Plan and is today near 100% (Joo, 2013).

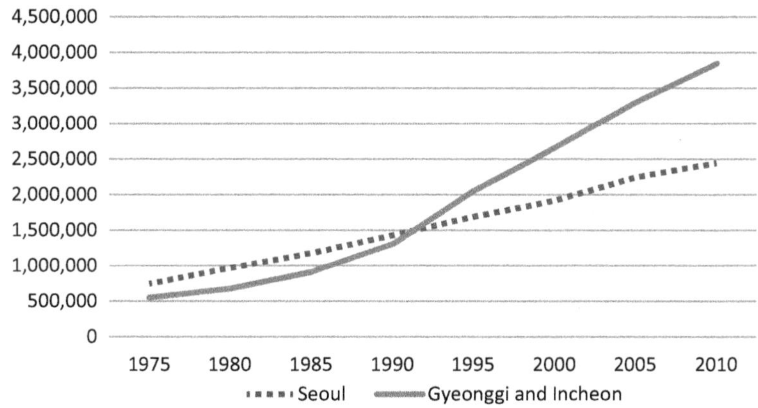

Figure 3: Number of Housing Units in Seoul and its Surrounding Area 1975–2010.
Source: Korean Statistical Information Service: kosis.kr.

outside Seoul were created. The new towns thus helped to open up the vast land areas of Gyeonggi Province to the real estate market of Seoul, but this has also led to a number of reckless (or unplanned) developments[9] in the areas surrounding Seoul. Figure 3 illustrates how, since the new-town developments in the early 1990s, the number of housing units in Gyeonggi Province and Incheon have increased rapidly, bypassing that of Seoul. This also explains the stabilization of Seoul's population since the late 1980s (Figure 2). Given Gyeonggi Province's vast areas of land, the trend continues to date. With this physical expansion outside the city limits, Seoul began to emerge as a mega-urban region.

After successful completion of the new towns in the mid-1990s, another wave — the second generation — of new-town developments began to take place in the 2000s. A total of 10 new towns, located 20–50 km from Seoul's city center, are currently under construction. Compared to the first-generation new towns, which were swiftly built by the state within 5–7 years, the second-generation new towns include local actors as their key developers and have significantly longer development

[9]The Korean term *nan-gyebal*, which can be translated as either reckless or unplanned development, has been commonly used to describe the sprouting developments led by local governments and/or private developers throughout the 2000s in Gyeonggi Province.

periods. (See Table 1 for a comparison of the two generations of new towns.)

As the land near Seoul available for large-scale developments has dwindled, a number of these second-generation new towns were located farther away from Seoul. Those located farther out are connected to each other by the Capital Region Second Ring Expressway (currently under construction), which draws a much larger circle around the Seoul Ring Expressway. The new towns' increased distance from Seoul also indicates that self-sufficiency would be more important here than in the first-generation new towns (Lee, 2012). Moreover, Bundang and Ilsan's main criticism had been their lack of self-sustainability. Much more emphasis has thus been placed on the second-generation new towns' ability to host significant economic activities to become polycentric developments in the capital region, beyond being mere bed-towns. In particular, planners have actively pursued their economic and environmental sustainability (Lee *et al.*, 2015).

In regard to the emphasis on locating economic activities in newly developed towns, a few second-generation new towns have garnered attention for their high-tech clusters, including Pangyo Techno Valley, Dongtan Techno Valley, and Gwanggyo Techno Valley, to name a few. Among them, Pangyo Techno Valley has experienced particularly notable growth, earning itself the label of the Silicon Valley of South Korea (Lee, 2017). It is home to more than 1,300 companies operating in the IT, biotechnology, and other IT-integrated industries, employing a total of 74,738 workers. In 2016, Pangyo Techno Valley produced more than KRW 77 trillion in sales — a figure comparable to that of the entire metropolitan city of Incheon (Lee, 2017). While Pangyo Techno Valley's success can be a source of inspiration for other new towns and localities seeking to become economic hubs, it should also be noted that Pangyo has an unusually advantageous location. It is located only a 15-minute subway ride away from Gangnam, which is home to South Korea's well-known high-tech cluster of IT companies, venture capitalists, and start-ups. (See Jung (2013) for an explanation of the high-tech cluster "Teheran Valley," located in Gangnam.) It is also located right next to the already well-established Bundang new town, with its vibrant commercial

Table 1. South Korea's first and second-generation new-town developments.

New towns	Planned population	Period	Developer
The first-generation new towns			
Bundang	390,000	1989–1996	KOLAND
Ilsan	276,000	1990–1995	KOLAND
Pyungchon	168,000	1989–1995	KOLAND
Joongdong	166,000	1990–1996	KOLAND, KNHC, and Buchon City
Sanbon	168,000	1989–1995	KNHC
The second-generation new towns			
Pangyo	88,000	2003–2017	LH, Gyeonggi Province, and Seongnam City
Dongtan1	126,000	2001–2018	LH and SH Corporation
Dongtan2	286,000	2008–2021	LH and Gyeonggi Urban Innovation Corporation
Gimpo-hangang	167,000	2002–2017	LH
Paju-Unjeong	217,000	2003–2023	LH and Paju City
Gwanggyo	78,000	2005–2019	Gyeonggi Province, Suwon City, Yongin City, and Gyeonggi Urban Innovation Corporation
Yangjoo	163,000	2007–2018	LH
Wirye	110,000	2008–2020	LH
Godeock	140,000	2008–2020	LH, Gyeonggi Province, Gyeonggi Urban Innovation Corporation, and Pyeongtaek City Corporation
Geomdan	184,000	2009–2023	LH, Incheon City, and Incheon Metropolitan City Development Corporation

Note: KOLAND stands for the Korea Land Corporation and KNHC stands for the Korea Housing Corporation. In 2009, the two corporations were integrated to form the Korea Land and Housing Corporation (LH).
Source: MOLIT (2015, 2017).

activities. Except for Wirye, whose boundaries overlap with three different cities — Seoul, Seongnam, and Hanam — the Pangyo new town is closest to Seoul.

In addition to techno valleys, a number of second-generation new towns are pursuing and applying smart-city solutions (Lee *et al.*, 2015) with the hope that integrating smart-city solutions into the new-town developments would provide environmentally sustainable and high-quality living environments. This can also be interpreted as part of South Korea's push for smart cities as one of its new economic development strategies (Mullins and Shwayri, 2016). Integrating new-town developments with new smart-city building from scratch is a relatively fast, easier, and more visible way to promote smart-city solutions than retrofitting existing cities. Dongtan U-Eco City[10] is already a popular example of a South Korean smart city. Most other second-generation new towns, such as Paju-Unjeong, Gwanggyo, Yangjoo, Godeok, Geomdan, and Wirye, have also been included as part of South Korea's U-city (smart city) projects over recent years. With their smart technologies and improved connectivity, these second-generation new towns could end up further expanding the growth and advancement of the SMA.

Another key outcome may be the extension of the SMA beyond its own boundary. The new administration capital city of Sejong, which lies between South Chungcheong and North Chungcheong Provinces, is located 123 km south of Seoul. Between Seoul and Sejong lies a series of second-generation new towns spaced throughout the southern part of Gyeonggi Province: in order, Pangyo, Gwanggyo, Dongtan, and Godeok. In fact, a mere 58 km separate Godeok new town from Sejong. While Sejong was built under the rationale of decentralizing the capital region, one cannot help but wonder whether it is not instead further extending the conurbation of Seoul. While decentralization has been taking place in the capital region, extending even to its key surrounding areas, overall, at a national scale, this same decentralization is simultaneously consolidating the primacy of Seoul as a mega-urban region.

---

[10]In South Korea, the term "U-city" or "Ubiquitous-city" is more common than "smart city."

5. Conclusion

Throughout its urbanization, South Korea has relied on building new towns, which has contributed to both the decentralization and centralization of spatial development over the years. First, the industrial new towns, as growth poles, played a key role in building a national urban network, with Seoul as the command and control center of the economy and a cluster of industrial cities on or near the southeastern coast, with Busan (South Korea's second-largest city) at the center of the industrial core. While the heavy-chemical industries expanded and the new industrial cities rapidly grew, Seoul's growth was carefully controlled and managed. Within the state's constraining policies, Seoul hosted massive-scale developments under state guidance, quickly removing slums and filling in its open fields. Then, with the rise of the mega-city Seoul and the fall of the developmental state, new towns began to play a greater role in expanding Seoul into a metropolitan area. While the new towns can be considered to have decentralized Seoul, at the same time, by doing so, they were further centralizing the capital region. Seoul, with its highly restrictive land area, has maintained its population at 10 million (with this number in fact showing a slight decline over recent years). Its residents and even some of its economic activities have relocated to outside areas, but they still remain closely connected to, Seoul. Instead of the *national* urban network under the developmental state, the *Seoul Metropolitan* urban network has been establishing itself under the democratized state in today's globalized context.

Mega-cities are increasingly in the limelight as key economic engines and competitive gateways to the global economy. As such, perhaps it is futile to fight against the rising trend of mega-urban regions out of a concern for balanced regional development. In fact, if well-planned and -governed, mega-urban region formation could be an effective and feasible solution to the urban problems of overcrowding while nurturing competitiveness on the global scale. However, the other side of mega-urban region formation also demands attention. The success brought by unequal development implies more difficulties for the country's other regions, which not only struggle to find their own niche in the global economy but are also left out of the domestic urbanization trend. This issue is finding its manifestation in the alarming trend of shrinking cities, which can be found not only in Japan and South Korea but also, astonishingly, in rapidly growing and urbanizing China. Instead of, or in addition to, focusing on the development of competitive mega-urban regions, the national state should think hard about how to intercede on behalf of, and plan for, other regions that are being left out. As overall economic development can no longer be expected to spatially spread its wealth, the state's role will become increasingly important in the era of mega-urban regions.

References

Alonso, W. (1980). "Five Bell Shapes in Development." *Papers of the Regional Science Association* 25, 5–16.

Amsden, A. H. (1989). *Asia's Next Giant: South Korea and Late Industrialization*. Oxford: Oxford University Press.

Bengston, D. N. and Y. C. Youn (2006). "Urban Containment Policies and the Protection of Natural Areas: The Case of Seoul's Greenbelt." *Ecology and Society* 11(1), 1–16.

Castells, M. (1992). Four Asian Tigers with a Dragon Head: A Comparative Analysis of the State, Economy, and Society in the Asian Pacific Rim. In: *States and Development in the Asia Pacific Rim*, edited by R. Appelbaum, and J. Henderson. London: Sage, pp. 33–70.

Choe, S. C. and B. N. Song (1984). "An Evaluation of Industrial Location Policies for Urban Deconcentration in Seoul Region." *Journal of Environmental Studies* 14, 73–116.

Davis, D. (2005). "Cities in Global Context: A Brief Intellectual History." *International Journal of Urban and Regional Research* 29(1), 92–109.

Douglass, M. (2000). "Mega-Urban Regions and World City Formation: Globalisation, the Economic Crisis and Urban Policy Issues in Pacific Asia." *Urban Studies* 37(12), 2315–2335.

Douglass, M. (2009). *Transborder Intercity Networks in East Asia: Regionalizing Globalization for Economic Resilience. Anyang: Korea Research Institute for Human Settlements Monograph.*

Gelézeau, V. (2007). *The Republic of Apartments: South Korean Apartment Complexes as seen by a French Geographer.* Seoul: Humanitas.

Hales, M., A. M. Pena, E. R. Peterson and N. Dessibourg (2018). 2018 Global Cities Report. *AT Kearney*. Retrieved on July 23, 2018 from: https://www.atkearney.com/2018-global-cities-report.

Hill, R. C., B. G. Park and A. Saito (2012). Introduction: Locating Neoliberalism in East Asia. In: *Park, Locating Neoliberalism in East Asia: Neoliberalizing Spaces in Developmental States*, edited by B. G., R. C. Hill and A. Saito. Chichester: Wiley-Blackwell, pp. 1–26.

Hirschman, A. O. (1958). *The Strategy of Economic Development*. New Haven: Yale University Press.

Johnson, C. (1982). *Miti and the Japanese Miracle: The Growth of Industrial Policy: 1925–1975*. Stanford: Stanford University Press.

Joo, Y. M. (2013). New Town Developments in Korea: Then and Now. In: *Urban Megaprojects: A Worldwide View*, edited by Del-Cerro Santamaria, G. Bingley: Emerald Group Publishing Limited, pp. 3–25.

Joo, Y. M., Y. Bae and B. Kassens-Noor (2017). *Mega-Events and Mega-Ambitions: South Korea's Rise and the Strategic Use of the Big Four Events*. London: Palgrave.

Joo, Y. M. (2019). *Megacity Seoul: Urbanization and the Development of Modern South Korea*. London: Routledge.

Jung, N. (2013). "Relational Governance and the Formation of a New Economic Space: The Case of Teheran Valley, South Korea." *International Journal of Urban and Regional Research* 37, 1233–1253.

Kim, E. M. (1997). *Big Business, Strong State: Collusion and Conflict in South Korean Development, 1960–1990*. Albany: State University of New York Press.

Kim, H. M. and S. S. Han (2012). "Seoul." *Cities* 29, 142–154.

Kim, J. C. (1990). "Urban Redevelopment of Green Belt Villages: A Case Study of Seoul." *Cities* 7(4), 323–332.

Kim, S. H. and N. Gallent (1998). "Regulating Industrial Growth in the South Korean Capital Region." *Cities* 15(1), pp. 1–11.

Kim, S. U. and P. J. Donaldson (1979). "Dealing with Seoul's Population Growth: Government Plans and their Implementation." *Asian Survey* 19(7), pp. 660–673.

Koo, H. and E. M. Kim (1992). "The Developmental State and the Capital Accumulation of South Korea." In: *States and Development in the Asian Pacific Rim*, edited by R. Appelbaum, and J. Henderson. London: Sage Press, pp. 121–149.

KRIHS (Korea Research Institute for Human Settlement) (1993). *A Research on Residential Pattern Following New Town Developments in the Capital Region*. Seoul: KRIHS.

Kwon, W. Y. (1985). "Regional Development Policy in Korea with Special Reference to Population Decentralization from Seoul." *Journal of Geography* 12, pp. 79–97.

Lee, B. H. (2012). *2011 Modularization of Korea's Development Experience: Korean Version of New Town Development.* Seoul: Korea Research Institute for Human Settlements.

Lee, C. M. and K. H. Ahn (2005). "Five New Towns in the Seoul Metropolitan Area and their Attractions in Non-Working Trips: Implications on Self-Containment of New Towns." *Habitat International* 29, pp. 647–666.

Lee, G. Y. (2005). "An Analysis of Reasonable Sharing of Expenses for Public Facilities in Public Land Development." *Journal of the Korean Urban Management Association* 18(2), 151–170.

Lee, J. S. (1988). "Regional Development Policies in Korea: Retrospect and Prospects." *The Korea Spatial Planning Review* X, 79–99.

Lee, K. S. (1985). "Decentralisation Trends of Employment Location and Spatial Policies in LDC Cities." *Urban Studies* 22, 151–162.

Lee, M. H. (2017). South Korea's Answer to Silicon Valley Sees Rapid Growth. *KoreaBizWire*, 9 August. Retrieved in July 25, 2018 from: http://koreabiz-wire.com/pangyo-techno-valley-growing-rapidly/90905.

Lee, S. K., H. Y. You and H. S. Kwon (2015). Korea's pursuit for Sustainable Cities through New Town Development: Implications for LAC. *Inter-American Development Bank: Discussion Paper*, Korea Research Institute for Human Settlements, Seoul, pp. 1–44.

Lim, D. G. and J. B. Kim (2015). *The Birth of Seoul Metropolis*. Seoul: Banbi.

Lim, S. H. (2005). *A Half Century of Housing Policy*. Seoul: Gimundang.

Mills, E. S. and B. N. Song (1979). *Urbanization and Urban Problems.* Cambridge: Harvard University Press.

MOLIT (2015). Introduction to the First Generation New Towns. MOLIT. Retrieved on July 28, 2018 from: http://www.molit.go.kr/USR/policyData/m_34681/dtl?id=523.

MOLIT (2017). Introduction to the Construction of the Second-Generation Capital Region New Towns. MOLIT. Retrieved on July 28, 2018 from: http://www.molit.go.kr/USR/policyData/m_34681/dtl?id=524.

Mullins, P. D. and S. T. Shwayri (2016). "Green Cities and 'IT839': A New Paradigm for Economic Growth in South Korea." *Journal of Urban Technology* 23, 47–64.

OECD (2018). *Inclusive Growth in Seoul, Korea*. Paris: OECD Publishing.

Park, H. (2001). Environmentally Friendly Land Use Planning, Property Rights and Public Participation in South Korea: A Case Study of Greenbelt Policy Reform, Master's thesis, Virginia Polytechnic Institute and State University.

Park, S. O. (1986). "Spatial Dynamics of Industrial Structure in Korea." *Geography* 34, 67–81.

Park, S. O. and A. Markusen (1995). "Generalizing New Industrial Districts: A Theoretical Agenda and an Application from a Non-Western Economy." *Environment and Planning A*, 27(1), 81–104.

Pyun, C. H. (2014). What is Scarier Than Population Concentration Is This! *DongA Ilbo*, 29 July. Retrieved on July 25, 2018 from: http://news.donga.com/more20/3/all/20140729/65479444/1.

Renaud, B. (1981). *National Urbanization Policy in Developing Countries.* Oxford: Oxford University Press.

Rondinelli, D. A. (1984). "Land Development Policy in South Korea." *Geographical Review* 74(4), 425–440.

Sassen, S. (1991). *The Global City: New York, London, Tokyo.* Princeton: Princeton University Press.

Shatkin, G. (2007). "Global Cities of the South: Emerging Perspectives on Growth and Inequality." *Cities* 24, 1–15.

STFSAP (Special Task Force for State Affairs Press) (2007). *Forty Years of Real Estate in Korea.* Seoul: Hans Media.

Suh, D. (2009). *Political Protest and Labor Solidarity in Korea: White-collar Labor Movements after Democratization (1987–1995).* New York: Routledge.

UN (1993). *World Urbanization Prospects: The 1992 Revision.* New York: United Nations.

UN (2015). *World Urbanization Prospects: The 2014 Revision (ST/ESA/SER.A/366)*, United Nations, Department of Economic and Social Affairs, Population Division. Retrieved on July 28, 2018 from: https://esa.un.org/unpd/wup/Publications/Files/WUP2014-Report.pdf.

UN (2016). *The World's Cities in 2016 — Data Booklet (ST/ESA/SER.A/392)*, United Nations, Department of Economic and Social Affairs, Population Division. Retrieved on July 28, 2018 from: http://www.un.org/en/development/desa/population/publications/pdf/urbanization/the_worlds_cities_in_2016_data_booklet.pdf.

Williamson, J. G. (1965). "Regional Inequality and the Process of National Development: A Description of Patterns." *Economic Development and Cultural Change* 13(4), 3–84.

Yu, Y. H. and G. H. Ji (1998). *Industrial Estate of South Korea.* Anyang: Korea Research Institute for Human Settlements.

Chapter 10

The Growing Megapolis Jakarta: Urbanization, Cities-Integration, and Future Issues

Gumilar Rusliwa Somantri

Department of Sociology, Universitas Indonesia, Indonesia
gumilar.rusliwa@gmail.com

1. Introduction

After the Reformation of 1998, Indonesian society has entered a new era of free democracy, with a strong role played by civil society as well as massive integration into the global capitalist economy (Nguyen and Richter, 2003; Kuntjorojakti, 2012; Smith and Feagin, 1993). In this regard, Jakarta has been the urban center of the nation's reformation process. Hence, Jakarta as the capital city of Indonesia plays a role as a major trendsetter of socio-political and economic changes in the country while the regions enjoy wide latitude through local autonomy. In terms of economic dynamics, Jakarta has been integrated into the global economy more intensively and extensively over the last decade. The vestiges of the slow-down of the economy during the multi-dimensional crisis (1997–2009) have been totally replaced by the presence of a dynamic market and a respectable increase in purchasing power among urban dwellers. What we witness in Jakarta is an amazingly rapid urban development in the outskirts of the city and this is also energizing the cities of Bogor, Depok, Tangerang, and Bekasi, known widely by the acronym Bodetabek (see Gottdiener and Hutchison, 2011, p. 289).

Jakarta's neighboring cities are being rapidly integrated into a huge arc of interlinked cities. This phenomenon resides in the historical continuity of Jakarta's urbanization process from the colonial era to the present day (Somantri, 2007; Bhambra, 2016). The city's expansion process has taken place through the integration of the main city with these new growth areas along Jakarta's periphery. In the 21st century, Jakarta has expanded to consume the spaces between it and nearby cities and sociologically has been annexing it. It seems the expansion of Jakarta's influence will not stop with the integration of the Bodetabek area. The ongoing development of modern infrastructure, highways, Mass Rapid Transit (MRT), and the urban Light Rail Transit (LRT) system connecting within Jakarta and to its neighboring cities and new towns in the eastern, southern, and western outer areas will lead to the formation of a mega-city that surpasses anything seen before (see Detter, 2015). This naturally will present us with a set of very challenging issues that need to be addressed.

2. The Dynamics of Urbanization

The history of Jakarta's growth started at the turn of 15th century. At that time, Jakarta was a small, but strategic port city that was inhabited by only 10,000 people. At the time, the city was named Sunda Kelapa. Along with the other three port cities in northern coastal region of West Java, Sunda Kelapa was under the control of the major Sundanese Hindu Kingdom, Padjadjaran. At the beginning of 16th century, Padjadjaran power was in decline, just as the Demak Islamic Kingdom (Sultanate) located in the coastal area of Central Java was on the rise. The Demak Sultanate's power was spreading to include some important coastal kingdoms in West Java, including Cirebon and Banten. The ruler of Cirebon and Banten were actually the descendants of King Sribaduga Maharaja of Padjadjaran who had converted from Hinduism to Islam. At the beginning of the 16th century, Sunda Kelapa was conquered by the Banten Sultanate's power under the leadership of a young commander, Fatahillah. Sunda Kelapa during the Fatahillah era became involved in the war with the Portuguese's military forces in 1527. Following his seminal victory in the war, Fatahillah changed the name of Sunda Kelapa to Jayakarta (1527–1619) which means glorious victory (Surjomihardjo, 1973; Nas, 1986).

In 1602, the Dutch arrived in Jayakarta and brought a trading mission. The diplomatic tactics of the Dutch armed trading company (VOC) under the leadership of van Leur led to Fatahillah giving permission to the Dutch to build a fortress with storage facilities for goods, especially exotic spices like pepper, nutmeg, and clove before their shipment to Amsterdam. From year to year, the Dutch expanded the fortress by buying surrounding land from local people. Batavia in 1619 occupied only a small area in the northern part of the bay of Jayakarta. By 1621 the territory of the fortress did not exceed 6.1 hectares. By 1770, the Dutch fully controlled Jayakarta and changed the name of the city to Batavia, after the land of the ancient Batavians or Batavia (part of the modern Netherlands). In 1799, with the VOC operations facing bankruptcy, the Dutch government took control of the company's activities across the entire Indonesian archipelago. This marked the formal colonization of all parts of the Indonesian islands by the Dutch. The new system of control was headed by a governor general who represented the Dutch central government. The colonial government expanded Batavia to the south (Weltevreeden) (see Surjomihardjo, 1973; Abeyasekere, 1989; Somantri, 2007).

Accordingly, some city appendages like Meester Cornelis (the present day Jatinegara area), Senen, a newly-created upper class compound of Menteng, and Tanah Abang were integrated into Batavia–Weltevreeden. In 1936, the colonial government developed an ambitious plan to build a satellite city called Kebayoran Baru about 8 km to the south from the center of Batavia–Weltevreeden. The realization of the plan was interrupted by the invasion of the Japanese during World War II. The Japanese control of Jakarta was short-lived and ended with Indonesian independence in 1945. The Indonesians who took charge changed the name Batavia–Weltevreeden into Jakarta. The Dutch gained control of Jakarta again in 1946 and pushed out the newly proclaimed local government to Jogjakarta. The power of the Dutch in Jakarta ended in 1949 following the acknowledgement of Indonesia sovereignty by the Dutch Queen. During those four years of occupation, the Dutch realized the postponed plan to build satellite city of Kebayoran Baru. The satellite city was set up by the Dutch during this occupation period in order to deal with Jakarta's population of about 500,000 (see Abeyasekere, 1989).

Jakarta in 1949 was suggested again to be the capital city of Indonesia. During the administration of President Soekarno, Jakarta had experienced relatively rapid development. Soekarno built some important main streets that connected the primary center with many newly emerging secondary centers. At that time, the government built Thamrin street, Gatot Subroto street, General Sudirman street, and Rasuna Said street, all funded by war compensation from Japan. President Soekarno also built a national sports stadium with the support of the Soviet Union. During the Soekarno era, the government also built some important city landmarks such as the Monas National Monument, Hotel Indonesia, and a shopping precinct called Sarinah, all of which survive to this day. Jakarta in this era developed into a dominant city in terms of political, socio-cultural, and economic importance (see Murray, 1991; Somantri, 2007).

Politically, Jakarta was the center of political dynamics in Indonesia and was trying to find its forms and values. Culturally, Jakarta played a significant role as the very heart of the cultural process in building the Indonesian character and identity as a new state. Economically, Jakarta was important as the main center of financial and domestic trading amid the country's limited contacts with international transactions. At the end of President Soekarno's time in power in 1965, the population of the city had reached two million. The growth was fueled by a massive migratory rural–urban influx during the Darul Islam (DI) rebellions in rural areas of Java in 1958–1963. Rural–urban migration to Jakarta was even bigger in 1965–1966 following the political instability that plagued many areas after the bloody 1965 power struggle involving the Army and a radical political party (see Purbo, 1979; Bresnan, 1993; Jellinek, 1991).

The position of Jakarta as the major city of Indonesia continued and was even stronger during period of Soeharto's centralized administration. Jakarta was very central in the process of economic liberalization of the country. This was in contrast to the political system that developed in a more "conservative" form. Politically, Indonesia practiced what it called "Pancasila Democracy." This was touted as the "third-way" or an "alternative system" to Western political models such as liberalism or socio-democracy (see Liddle, 1996; Alatas, 1997). Pancasila Democracy opened the space for civil society to play a role although in a comparatively limited way.

In concomitance with the massive process of the integration process, Jakarta was promoted as the locus of the "quasi" industrialization in the country (see Mahutga, 2014). Foreign investment capital flooded into Jakarta. At that time, we find huge industrial complexes were built in the Eastern and Western outskirts of Jakarta. Jakarta's urban center expanded tremendously in a process of annexation of the bordering rural areas of West Java province. As a result, the area of Jakarta increased from less than 400 km^2 in 1970 to more than 650 km^2 in 1990. Jakarta's population expanded three-fold in three decades during Soeharto's administration, from 3 million in 1970 to about 10 million in 1998 (Evers and Korff, 2000).

In line with urban growth, Jakarta proceeded with rapid development of infrastructure and facilities including skyscrapers, cloverleaf intersections, toll-roads, and the like. However, both migrants and local Jakartans (Betawi) were largely a low-income population group in the city. They resided in low-income neighborhoods called *kampung*. These shaped Jakarta into an urban paradox that has been marked by the presence of dual structures of highly modern as well as traditional ones (Jellinek, 1991; Evers and Korff, 2000; Somantri, 2007).

3. Cities-Integration and the Rise of a Megapolis

Jakarta in the last two decades has been developing even faster than during the era of the New Order government. This is thanks to the reformation that Indonesia started in the 1998, which lead Jakarta into massive involvement in the liberal world economy (see Kuntjorojakti, 2012). As a result, the Jakarta of the 21st century has seen its population swell to 15 million and its footprint as a political–administrative area grow to nearly 700 km^2. One of the very obvious feature of the city today is the existence of many international business icons. We observe many global companies have been established their offices in the golden-triangle area of Jakarta especially along Thamrin, Sudirman, Gatot Subroto, and Rasuna Said streets. We witness also that many up-market shopping precincts as well as luxury apartment complexes have been developed in the primary as well as secondary centers of Jakarta. In this regard, Jakarta has been transformed into an important modern global megalopolis or megapolis for short (see Detter, 2015; Yamada and Kawakami, 2016).

It is a fact that this new globalized Jakarta has created a huge number of job opportunities for the people in both the formal and shadow sectors of the economy (see Bruff and Hartmann, 2014). The distinction between these is mirrored in the places that the employees live in — high-end apartments and town house complexes vs. run down urban *kampungs*. However, there is also a sizable number of people working in Jakarta who commute from the peripheral cities on a daily basis.

These circular migrants commute every day from Bogor, Depok, Tangerang, and Bekasi, the Bodetabek Area, to Jakarta. They go by electric-train, bus, cars, and also by motor-bike. During the rush hour in the morning and in the afternoon, commuters flood the trains and the streets of Jakarta. Heavy traffic takes over and pollution increases during the rush hour. The effect of this commuter group is that Jakarta's population shrinks by night.

The central as well as the municipal government understand that the cost of developing and upgrading the infrastructure in the city as well as transport options to nearby cities is trivial in the face of the positive impact it has on the socio-economic productivity of Jakarta. Many signs of this are evident under the government of President of Joko Widodo and the obvious success of this is a rebuke on the decades of lost time under previous administrations.

For instance, talk about building an MRT started in 1980. However, the process of coming up with a concrete plan and putting this into action was so slow. The success of the present development of MRT/LRT, inner-city and outer-city highways, and finishing the new modern international airports and ports all across the country shows what can actually be done if there is a will. The government has also taken on the delicate issue of the improvement of the quality of the Trans-Jakarta bus system. In the meantime, the upgrading of the Semanggi cloverleaf interchange is held by the municipal government, in line with it is the heavier traffic in the area from time to time. The government has also widened the arterial roads that connect Jakarta to nearby cities.

Thus, the highly dynamic urbanization process of Jakarta has been echoed over the Bodetabek area during the last three decades (see Nam and Kim, 2017). For instance, Depok city in 1990 had only 200,000 people. The city's population increased 10 years later to almost 1 million people. The population of the city has now reached the figure of about 1.8 million. The case of Bekasi city tells a similar story. In this connection, the population of Bekasi and Tangerang cities almost tripled between 1990 and 2018. The population of Bogor city also increased significantly in that period of time although less dramatically than Depok, Bekasi, and Tangerang cities. This is partly due to the fact that Bogor city is situated a comparatively long distance from Jakarta, about 50 km.

Beside demographic dynamics, we also can observe the expansion the urban territory of the Bodetabek area. This has increased along with the unstoppable development of new-towns and real estate complexes in the area. This is followed by the development of modern public facilities (Pawe and Saikia, 2018). This includes of the establishment of hospitals, supermarkets, four to five stars hotels, private universities, and schools. We can conclude that the cities of the Bodetabek area have been transformed into satellite cities of the core city of Jakarta. Interestingly also is that the Bodetabek area has been integrated socially as well as physically. We see almost no difference between Jakartans and the citizens of Bodetabek in term of lifestyle, language variety, cultural orientation, and the like. However, the center, Jakarta, remains dominant in regard to the hierarchical structures of economic, socio-economic, and political importance where their quality and scale are noticeable (see Korff, 1996; Detter, 2015).

Accordingly, the peripheral cities' integration into Jakarta has been characterized by the incorporation of the urban sprawl across that huge area. Two decades ago, the major arterial roads and highways that connect Jakarta and the surrounding cities passed through green and dry-agricultural land. But economics and demand have changed that and those green, agricultural spaces have been used to build economically high value structures such as hospitals, business offices, shopping precincts, industrial complexes, as well as vast new property islands. In short, the greater area of Jakarta altogether with the Bodetabek area have morphed into an immense single modern urban sprawl — a megapolis (see Gottdiener and Hutchison, 2011).

We are witnessing the emergence of a rapidly growing megapolis that is Jakarta. Jakarta is dominant, and megapolis Jakarta has become a single entity with the satellite cities of Bodetabek. The megapolis is one, but the politics and administration of Jakarta and the nearby cities are not be managed under the same roof. The Jakarta municipal administration currently is overseen by one governor and has five mayoralty units (West, South, East, and Central Jakarta as well as the island chain Pulau Seribu). Meanwhile, Bogor, Depok, and Bekasi belong to the West Java provincial region. Tangerang city is also part of the other authority structure, namely Banten Province. This means that megapolis Jakarta will have problems in managing area-wide issues such as floods, poverty, pollution, public transportation, housing, trash management, urban justice and well-being, ethnic segregation, conflict, and others (Speier *et al.*, 2018). However, there is a better picture with the issues of defense and security. The related problems to the issues are responded by the same command of the military as well as police regional organization that includes Jakarta and the nearby cities.

4. Future Issues for Megapolis Jakarta

The future issues affecting megapolis Jakarta relate firstly to its politico-administrative structure. It seems the future megapolis Jakarta has to be managed by a single authority at the level of a government ministry. Hence, the head of the authority would be a minister who is directly responsible to the head of government and state. That minister will coordinate through two governors who would be supported by at least 10 mayors. The first governor will coordinate five mayors in Jakarta. The second governor will manage the mayoralty offices of the nearby cities. This structure makes sense since megapolis Jakarta is the home for more than 20 million urban dwellers.

The second future issue concerns the complex function of Jakarta as the capital of Indonesia, as a trade city, as an education city, and so on. It seems megapolis Jakarta in the future can still hold its symbolic status as the capital of the state. Further, megapolis Jakarta will focus on facilitating trade and business. Meanwhile, the center of governmental affairs must be to move out of the city to some other place. One option would be to move the center of governmental activities to Bogor city. The second option would be to establish a new center of governmental affairs in the area close to Cipali toll road as well as the newly developed international airport in Majalengka regency. These two options are less likely to face resistance from stakeholders such as the business community. The proposed move of government as well as state center to a far-off area or island, such as Kalimantan, would negatively impact business, land-prices, and so on. Hence, both of the possibilities mentioned earlier have the least negative impacts to the stakeholders.

The third future issue is the need to establish close collaboration between the megapolis government with universities in dealing with solving the existing problems using interdisciplinary approaches (Arjomand, 2017). This would guide the government into a new strong position of research-based policies and programs for building urban centers, and also improving the well-being of citizens. This collaboration has to be facilitated by encouraging active participation by people and communities as well as the business sector.

The fourth future issue is how the mega-city Jakarta will deal with its present socio-economic and cultural gulfs, in particular socio-economic class and regional ethnicity. This humanistic issue must be managed in order to reduce the potential of conflict due to Indonesia's significant diversity (see Bryson, 2005). In this regard, the megapolis government has to anticipate a growing disparity among the urban population through strengthening trans-cultural communication, increasing programs for empowering small and medium businesses, and paying better attention to urban justice issues (see Gottdiener and Hutchison, 2011).

Last but not least, the fifth future issue of megapolis Jakarta is the importance of strengthening civil society as a balance for urban governmental power. It is necessary to build a strong civil society to hold people in power to account, to oversee the process of sustainable urbanization, especially taking action against growing undesirable phenomena in the megapolis dynamic such as pollution, the uneven distribution of wealth and quality of life, and the reduction of green public spaces (Speier *et al.*, 2018). Hence, the presence of a functional and constructive civil society will support the government's work in order to build humanistic urban islands in Jakarta and elsewhere in the country (see Rueland, 1996).

5. Concluding Remarks

The journey across the long-duration of Jakarta's historical urbanization process leads us to the fact that the development of the city has been driven by the center of socio-economic power in the wider arena, namely capitalism. During the colonial era, Batavia's encounter with capitalism was facilitated by the monopolistic and kleptocratic agenda of the Dutch. After independence, Jakarta was the country's only window to the international world. The massive drive of integration into the world-capitalist economy started at the beginning of the 1970s during the Suharto era (Robison, 1986). Jakarta has gone on to play a significant role in bringing Indonesia into full engagement with the world economy. Hence, Jakarta has in the process been transformed into a major metropolis close to the features of a dominant primary city (see Heris, 2017).

Jakarta after the reformation of 1998 has entered a new phase of urban development. The rapid urbanization process has directed Jakarta into a new gigantic structure that we can call a megalopolis or megapolis for short by integrating its satellite cities into one single urban entity. This offers proof that urban development in Jakarta has tended to follow the same pattern of integration from the colonial era until today (Somantri, 2007).

Speaking about the future urbanization in Jakarta, it seems that the megapolis of Jakarta will face a number of tough challenges over the next 20 years. The first issue is population. This mega-city will be the home for about 30 million inhabitants. This mega-city will also experience a comparatively complex set of urban functions. Another issue is environmental and sustainability issues. The city is vulnerable to flooding and to the sinking of land as a result of artesian well exploitation. Recent research states that north Jakarta is sinking at 25 cm per year and will be under water by 2050. This, climate change and sea-level rise pose existential threats that require an effective inter-disciplinary solution (see Arjomand, 2017). Therefore, many challenges have to be responded accurately by a set of structural as well as socio-cultural adjustments including putting Jakarta's control under a higher authority, revitalizing productive civil society, as well as developing strong bridge to the global academic communities. In this regard, the megapolis Jakarta of the future will have a chance to stand as a city shaped by humanistic principles, and a place where urban life is the envy of people elsewhere around the world.

References

Abeyasekere, S. (1989). *Jakarta: A History*. Singapore: Oxford University Press.

Alatas, S. F. (1997). *Democracy and Authoritarianism in Indonesia and Malaysia*. Chicago: Maaroufa Press Inc.

Arjomand, S. A. (2017). "The Rise of Interdisciplinary Studies in Social Sciences and Humanities and the Challenge of Comparative Sociology." *European Journal of Social Theory* 20(2), 292–306.

Bhambra, G. K. (2016). "Comparative Historical Sociology and the State: Problems of Methods." *Cultural Sociology* 10(3), 335–351.

Bresnan, J. (1993). *Managing Indonesia: The Modern Political Economy*. New York, NY: Columbia University Press.

Bruff, I. and E. Hartmann (2014). "Sociology and the Conceptual Foundations of the Comparative Capitalism Literature." *Capital and Class* 38(1), 73–85.

Bryson, B. (2005). *Making Multiculturalism: Boundaries and Meaning in U.S.* English Departments. Stanford, CAL: Stanford University Press.

Detter, H. (2015). "Satisfying Transportation Needs in Fast-Growing Metropolitan Areas: Mobility Solutions for Mega-City in Developing Countries." *OPEC Energy Review* 39(4), 418–444.

Evers, H.-D. and R. Korff (2000). Southeast Asian Urbanism. Muenster & London: Lit Verlaag.

Gottdiener, M. and R. Hutchison (2011). *The New Urban Sociology*. Central Avenue, Boulder: Westview Press.

Heris, M. P. (2017). "Evaluating Metropolitan Spatial Development: A Method for Identifying Settlement Types and Depicting Growth Patterns." Regional Studies, *Regional Science* 4(1), 7–25.

Jellinek, L. (1991). *The Wheel of Fortune*. London: Allen and Unwin.

Korff, R. (1996). Global and Local Spheres: The Diversity of Southeast Asian Urbanism. *Journal of Social Issues in Southeast Asia* 11, 288–313.

Kuntjorojakti, D. (2012). *Meneropong Indonesia Masa Datang*. Jakarta: Universitas Indonesia Press.

Liddle, W. R. (1996). *Leadership and Culture in Indonesian Politics*. Sydney: Allen & Unwin.

Mahutga, M. C. (2014). "Global Production Networks and International Inequality: Making a Case for a Meso-Level Turn in Macro-Comparative Sociology." *Journal of World System Research* 20(1), 11–37.

Nguyen, T. D. and F.J. Richter (2003). *Indonesia Matters*. Singapore: Time Editions.

Nam, K. and B. H. S. Kim (2017). "The Effect of Spatial Structure and Dynamic Externalities on Local Growth in Seoul Metropolitan Area." *Urban Policy and Research* 35(2), 165–179.

Nas, P. (1986). *The Indonesian City: Studies in Urban Development and Planning*. Dordrecht: Foris.

Murray, A. J. (1991). *No Money, No Honey: A Study of Street Traders and Prostitutes in Jakarta*. Singapore: Oxford University Press.

Pawe, C. K. and A. Saikia (2018). "Unplanned Urban Growth: Land Use/Land Cover Change in the Guwahati Metropolitan Area, India. *Geografisk Tidsskrift-Danish Journal of Geography* 118(1), 88–100.

Purbo, H. (1979). "Mass-Housing in Indonesia and Job Opportunities in Informal Sector." *Prisma* 12, 3–13.

Robison, R. (1986). *Indonesia*: The Rise of Capital. Sydney: Allen & Unwin.

Rueland, J. (1996). *The Dynamic of Metropolitan Management in Southeast Asia*. Singapore: ISEAS.

Smith, M. P. and J. R. Feagin (eds.) (1993). *The Capitalist City*. Oxford, UK: Blackwell Publishers.

Somantri, G. R. (2007). *Migration within Cities: A Study of Socio-Economic Processes, Intra-City Migration, and Grass-Roots Politics in Jakarta*. Jakarta, IDN: LP FE-UI Press.

Speier, C. J., M. M. Mondal and D. Weichgrebe (2018). "Evaluation of Compositional Characteristics of Organic Waste Shares in Municipal Solid Waste in Fast-Growing Metropolitan Cities of India." *Journal of Material Cycles and Waste Management* 20(4), 2150–2162, doi: https://doi.org/10.1007/s10163-018-0757-y.

Surjomihardjo. (1973). *Perkembangan kota Jakarta*. Jakarta: Dinas Musium.

Yamada, E. and T. Kawakami (2016). "Distribution of Industrial Growth in Nagoya Metropolitan Area, Japan: An Exploratory Analysis Using Geographical and Technological Proximities." *Regional Studies* 51(11), 1876–1888.

Chapter 11

Mexico: Metropolitan Circles Development, Interactive Cities, and Future of Urbanization

Clemente Ruiz Durán

School of Economy,
Universidad Nacional Autónoma de México, Mexico
ruizdc@unam.mx

1. Introduction

Population projections indicate that the tendency to concentrate in urban areas will increase throughout the world, especially in countries where there is a greater margin for it. Mexico will continue to be ranked number eight in 2050, with 134 million people residing in these types of settlements (with an expected total population of 151 millions), however, nations with higher volumes will change in some cases: China, India, and the United States will have the first three places (without changes of position), Nigeria (with an impressive jump), Indonesia (same placement), Brazil (two fewer places), and Pakistan with a considerable increase will follow (United Nations, 2017). When comparing these projections with those of the total population, Mexico occupied in 2015 the 10th place among the most populated countries in the world, with 126 million (United Nations, 2017). In 2015, the 74 Metropolitan Zones (MZs) concentrated 75.1 million inhabitants, equivalent to 62.8% of the total population of the country. The 2015 delimitation reiterates the consolidation of the country as a metropolitan country, the 74 metropolitan areas comprise 417 municipalities in the 32 states, with a population concentration that slightly exceeds 6 out of 10 Mexicans. The evolution since 1960 indicates that the number of metropolitan areas has increased six fold, its population has multiplied by eight, the amount of territorial demarcations and municipalities has increased more than six times and its participation in the national population has grown little more than double.

2. Metropolitan Areas Growth

A study by the Ministry of Social Development (SEDESOL, 2011) identifies that the greatest increase in the urban surface occurred between 1980 and 2000. In the Valley of Mexico, while the population grew 1.42% in the period 1980–2010, the surface did it 3.57 times; in Guadalajara was 1.98 and 3.82 times, respectively, and in Monterrey 1.98 and 4.95. In the group of cities with more than 450,000 inhabitants there were huge increases in the area of Villahermosa MZ (30.13), MZ de Toluca (26.28), MZ of Cancun (25.79), MZ of Pachuca (21.14) and MZ of Tuxtla Gutiérrez (16.95). Of the 93 cities to which it refers in only one MZ the population growth was higher than the surface: La Paz (2.35 vs. 2.07). The largest increase occurred in Cabo San Lucas (76.38 times).

The incorporation of urban land is associated with the construction of new developments, not only in the peripheries of many cities but also in more distant places and disconnected from the central area, which it is where employment is usually concentrated. This has increased labor mobility, and given that it is often done without planning, derives in the consequent increase of vehicular traffic, of the times of transfer, and of pollution, in summary, in the loss of quality of life for MZ population. It has also influenced this expansion pattern the construction of other urban elements such as shopping centers, roads, industrial parks, etc., that have consumed new areas, as never happened before (Table 1).

To support metropolitan areas coordination a Fund was created at Federal level to promote infrastructure development among the counties in the Metropolitan Zones. "The Metropolitan Fund will have the purpose of granting resources to infrastructure programs and projects; which demonstrate to be viable and sustainable, oriented to promote the adequate planning of the regional, urban development, the public transport and the non-motorized mobility and of the ordering of the territory to impel the economic competitiveness, the sustainability and the productive capacities of the metropolitan zones, contribute to its viability and to mitigate its vulnerability or risks to natural disasters, environmental phenomena and those fostered by the demographic and economic dynamics, as well as urban consolidation and the optimal use of the competitive advantages of

Table 1. Metropolitan zones growth: 1960–2015.

Indicator	1960	1980	1990	2000	2005	2010	2015
Metropolitan zones	12	26	37	55	56	59	74
Demarcation and metropolitan localities	64	131	155	309	345	367	417
Federal states with MIZ	14	20	26	29	29	29	32
Population (millions)	9.0	26.1	31.5	51.5	57.9	63.8	75.1
% of national population	25.6	39.1	38.8	52.8	56.0	56.8	62.8

Source: CONAPO.

regional, urban and economic functioning of the territorial space of metropolitan areas."[1] The budget is quite limited $175 million, that gives little space for restructuring.

One of the main problems is that there has not been a proposal for Metropolitan governments. Federal Government has defined the Metropolitan areas with a commission of different Ministries of Central Government. The working group has included multiple counties and in some cases are in different Federal States, so coordination among them becomes quite complex as they might be of different parties, as is the case of the Valley of Mexico Metropolitan Area with governments of different parties (PRI and Morena). A second step beyond the definition of MA will be the design of governance mechanisms that allow them a better coordination.

3. Location of Metropolitan Areas

Metropolitan areas are spread in the territory as Figure 1 shows; though they have evolved in different stages, in the first place the Valley of Mexico that has historical roots kept the pace of expansion well into the 21st Century, transforming it from a bureaucratic–industrial conglomerate into a service and financial spot. Guadalajara and Monterrey kept their industrial profile but expanded their service structure by bringing in the digital divide and a financial network; what has been more interesting is how growth of other metropolitan areas has been pushed by the development of transnational corporation expansion under the North American Free Trade Agreement, that is the case of northern Mexico wherein bond electronics and auto industry reshaped the area, or the building of an auto export platform in Central Mexico. However, the other areas that had emerged in the south as MA, do not have a clear-cut scheme of forces driving metropolitanization.

Expansion was not homogenous through all the period; traditional MA has mixed with a process of emerging intermediate MA, and also incorporated more localities into the already existing ones in the period 2005–2010. The growth in the period 2010–2015 was marked

[1] http://dof.gob.mx/nota_detalle.php?codigo=5511862&fecha=31/01/2018.

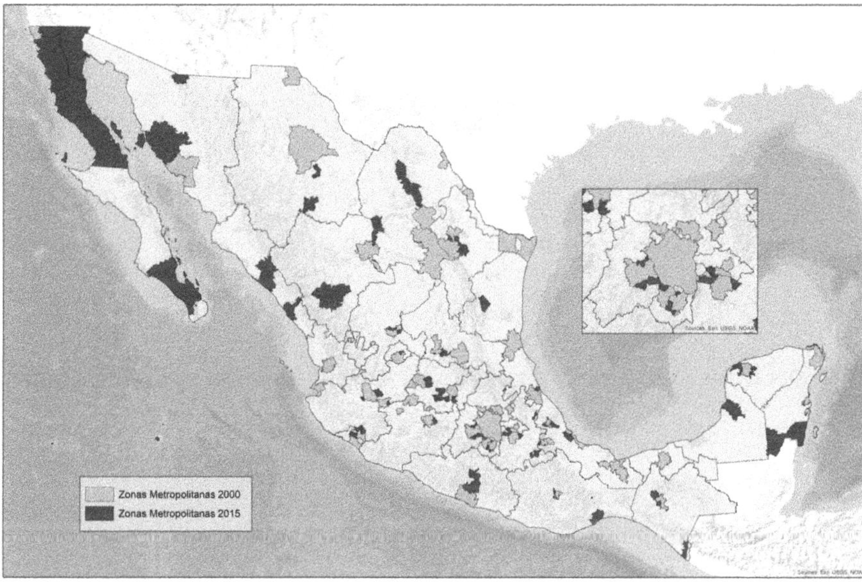

Figure 1. Mexico: Expansion of the metropolitan areas, 2000–2015.
Source: INEGI.

by the emergence of new areas driven by the emergence of new industries (Figure 2).

4. Growth Forces that Pushed MA Expansion

Metropolitan circle development has been linked to different forces, of which one of them has been manufacturing restructuring led by different forces: on the macro level the stimulus came through the cost mechanism of low-wage paradox and with the improvement of education level that was stronger in large cities thereby promoting technical and university degrees.

What is interesting is that the promotion of investment did not came from a sophisticated central office but rather by a mix of federal and state level promotions. Debt crisis pushed federal government to promote state and local government support for the promotion of industrial clusters. This process became official with the creation of a Board of State

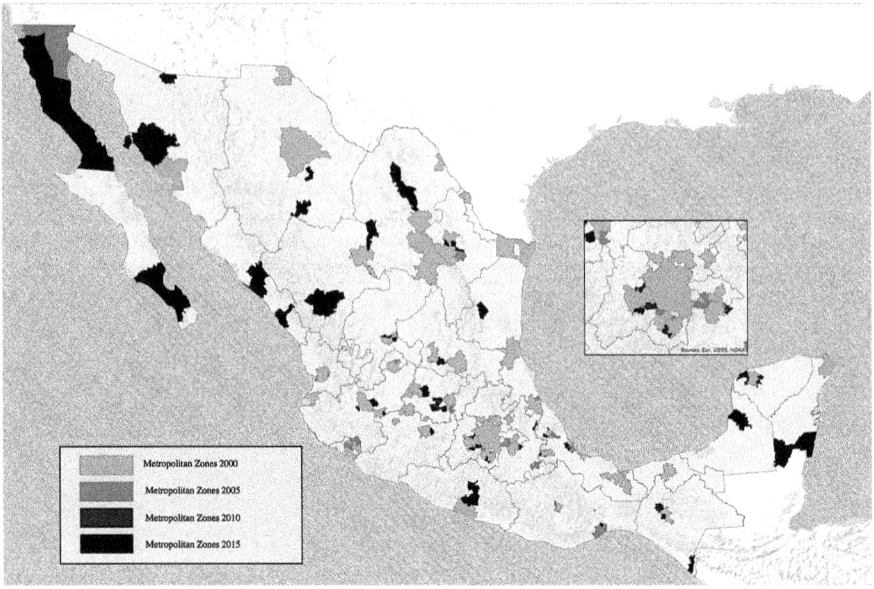

Figure 2. Metropolitan areas delimitation by 2000, 2005, 2010, and 2015.
Source: INEGI.

Governors Conference (CONAGO) in 2002, that led to the emergence of planning process at state level. Governors became active agents for promoting and planning, and were also responsible for developing business environment and attracting foreign investors into their territory; in some cases they were supported by a long-term planning. Institutional development led to a broad policy of promotion to attract foreign investors through a policy of land use, supported by infrastructure development in industrial parks; businessmen created the Association of Industrial Parks that today hosts more than 538 parks in the country, enabling financial tools to promote new urban settlements, as the case of the trust funds for industrial real-estate denominated FIBRAS, and special funds managed by state governments (Table 2).

This policy mix led to an uneven process of promotion in the regions, where federal, state, and local governments became involved, along with the participation of local businessmen to promote foreign investors into their territories. This sort of policy was successful in attracting investments in transport equipment, computers and electronics devices, chemical and pharmaceuticals, among others. The whole process was developed by stages and by regions.

- In the first phase, the northern border states took advantage of the Tijuana/San Diego border crossing point for electronics and electro domestic goods. Next was the auto industry in Sonora and Chihuahua (Ford Corporation), where Chrysler took advantage of Nuevo León and developed the Coahuila network, that latter combined the Daimler–Benz operation and GM; this was at the last decades of the 20th century. Border states led exports with 50% of the total.
- Second wave of investment developed in the Western Central area, where the aim was to push new industries. Guadalajara became the pioneer in the digital-electronic industries, led by IBM and Hewlett Packard, promoting digital businesses that led to creative industries, and also embedded software developments linked to the auto industry. This attracted the Japanese to set up a Honda plant for exports, and in the neighboring state of Aguascalientes led by Nissan one of the largest networks was developed in different stages. Guanajuato vicinity attracted Toyota, Mazda, and Volkswagen. Economies of scope led to develop auto parts industries also in Querétaro and San Luis Potosí, where not only auto industries were developed but also the Canadian Bombardier set up an assembling plant. BMW is building a very large facility for the new series 3 cars. Domestic complex was built there with national business that later attracted Samsung to the region. All the process led to a prosperity area, growing at 5% a year, well above national growth.
- Third area of clustering was the traditional industries platform in the vicinity of Mexico City and the neighboring states (Figure 3). The first auto industries were installed here. Though some of them moved to the north, some others refurnished their facilities, e.g., Ford corporation transformed its Cuautitlan plant from traditional fuels operation to the new generation of electric cars; Nissan in Cuernavaca is assembling the New York City taxis; Volkswagen and Audi had developed new facilities in Puebla. Mexico City has also attracted large pharmaceutical and medical device corporations, combined with research development linked to universities research.

Table 2. Industrial parks as a source of MA expansion.

	State name	1986	2018
1	Baja California	6	92
2	Nuevo León	8	64
3	Jalisco	6	47
4	Chihuahua	11	39
5	Coahuila de Zaragoza	7	38
6	Edo. México	11	34
7	Sonora	15	33
8	Guanajuato	4	23
9	Tamaulipas	8	23
10	Puebla	4	19
11	Querétaro	6	13
12	Sinaloa	2	12
13	Hidalgo	5	11
14	San Luis Potosí	1	10
15	Aguascalientes	3	9
16	Tlaxcala	1	9
17	Veracruz de Ignacio de la Liave	3	9
18	Yucatán	4	8
19	Ciudad de México	0	7
20	Michoacán de Ocampo	2	7
21	Campeche	3	5
22	Durango	2	5
23	Morelos	2	3
24	Oaxaca	1	3
25	Tabasco	1	3
26	Zacatecas	2	3
27	Chiapas	1	2
28	Guerrero	1	2
29	Quintana Roo	2	2
30	Baja California Sur	2	1
31	Colima	2	1
32	Nayarit	2	1
Total		128	538

Source: Gustavo Garza (1992) impacto regional de los parques y ciudades industries, Estudios Demograficos y Urbanos; AMPIP (Mexican Association of Industrial Parks) (2018) Parques industrials.

- Industrial development was *export oriented* and led to the growth of localities linked to the process, mainly border cities in the north with the US. The main metropolitan areas that had become binational are: Tijuana/San Diego, Ciudad Juárez/El Paso, Reynosa/Mc Allen, Matamoros/Brownsville, Mexicali/Calexico, Nuevo Laredo/Laredo, Nogales/Nogales, Piedras Negras-Nava/Eagle Pass, San Luis Rio Colorado/Yuma, Ciudad Acuña/Del Río, Agua Prieta Naco/Sierra Vista, Ojinaga/Presidio, and south of Tapachula.
- Migration was an additional factor of the growth of population in binational Metropolitan Areas population and land use. Flows were not only from inside Mexico but also from Central America; therefore growth of MA in this case has multiple factors, such as trade, migration and population growth and connection to other local areas.
- Foreign trade also affected the growth of Metropolis in the coastal areas. Most of ports became metropolitan areas, and there was a combination of ports focused on merchandize trade (Guaymas, Topolobambo, Mazatlán, Manzanillo, Lazaro Cardenas, Puerto Chiapas, Tampico, Veracruz, and Progreso) and others on oil trade (Altamira, Coatzacoalcos, Dos Bocas, and Salina Cruz) (see Figure 4).
- An additional factor of growth of MA in the coastal areas was tourism in the Pacific Ensenada, Los Cabos, Mazatlán, Puerto Vallarta,

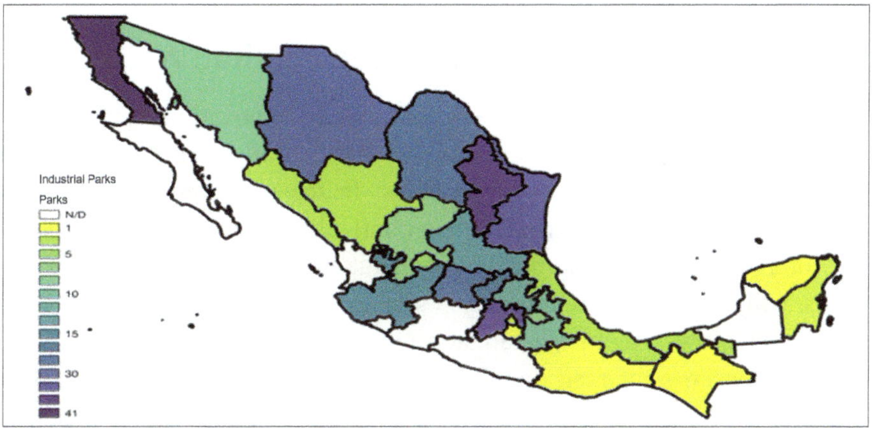

Figure 3. Mexico: Concentration of industrial parks.

Source: Own elaboration based on AMPIP.

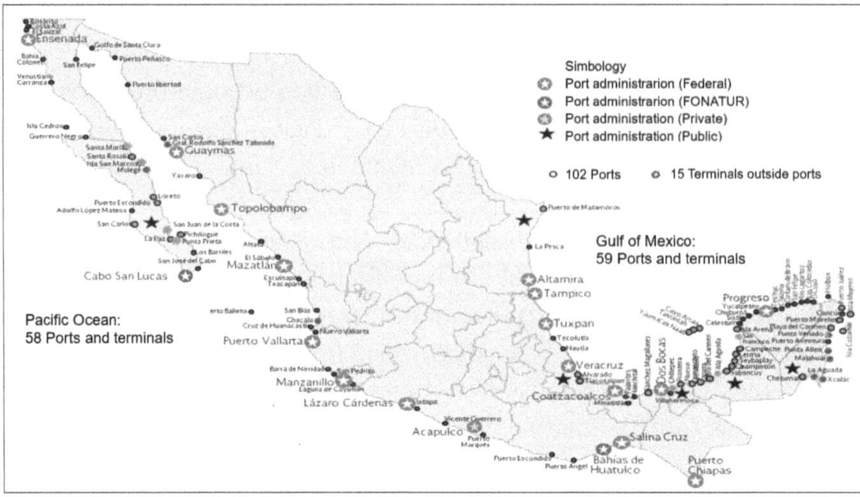

Figure 4. Mexican port system.

Source: Ministry of communications and transport.

Manzanillo, Ixtapa-Zihuatanejo, Acapulco, and Huatulco, in the Gulf and the Caribbean, Veracruz, Progreso, and the region of Cancun/Cozumel. Mexico has become one of the main cruise ships destinations with 6 million voyagers in 2017.

5. Emergence of Interactive Metropolitan Areas

Clustering led to a density process that pushed innovations and interactions among regional suppliers, and all these brought in economies of scope at different levels and modalities. In the western-central area of Mexico, interactions increased among relatively medium-size cities, pushing for a new sort of economic development and giving birth to interactive cities, which instead of increasing in size took advantage of economies of scope that allowed them specialization in different segments of the industry. What seems interesting is that clustering went beyond traditional agglomeration and brought in the new geography of cities and its interaction with other cities.

To measure interactions, we used the methodology transport annual survey of Sánchez (2016) to find out interactions among cities. Figure 5 shows the matrix of interactions derived from this analysis. Most of the interactions have developed following Global Value Chains interconnections, as explained in the input–output matrix, where it was possible to identify that auto industry, electronics and electric industries, pharmaceutical and medical devices observed the largest supply/demand interactions, through backward and forward linkages. Spatial relations developed around them as producers take advantage of economies of scope due to producers' agreement to share the same factors of production (i.e., auto manufacturers have taken advantage of Delphi plants in different cities in Mexico to supply them with harnesses for their auto production). Introducing location of the plants is possible to measure the degree of interaction, that has allowed suppliers to provide harness from the same suppliers. This sort of interaction reduces expansion in metropolitan areas as complementary practices are developed.

6. Future of Metropolitan Areas in Mexico

Main problem of analyzing the future of metropolitan areas in Mexico is the lack of planning. A first step in this direction has been the effort for updating the Metropolitan Areas Structure by CONAPO, INEGI, and the Secretary of Territorial Development, but there is a lack of coordination of how to address the problem of metropolitan areas. New government elects proposal to decentralize federal government bureaucracy, but no specific program has been published as to what are the expected effects.

Up-to-date growth of the cities has been given to the market, with some guidelines from government, so the system of cities in Mexico has developed unevenly and concentrated within the framework of the economic models adopted. The guidelines have been the programs for industrialization. In the mid-20th century, the import substitution model (ISM) favored a hierarchical model of cities with urban centers that accumulated capital, concentrated infrastructure and services, or specialized in some manufacturing, extractive, or tourist activities.

At the turn of the century the model of export promotion and the North America Trade Agreement opened up options for the emergence of networks of cities that have taken advantage of exports, which grew with the maquiladora, manufacturing and services industry connected to global circuits, although with low economic growth and weak integration of

Metropolitan Zone	State	Trade in million of pesos (constant Mexican pesos of 2003)
MZ of Aguascalientes	Aguascalientes	$50
MZ of Tijuana	Baja California	$225
MZ of Mexicali	Baja California	$130
MZ of La Laguna	Coahuila-Durango	$894
MZ of Saltillo	Coahuila	$420
MZ of Monclova-Frontera	Coahuila	$138
MZ of Piedras Negras	Coahuila	$66
MZ of Colima-Villa of Álvarez	Colima	$88
MZ of Tecomán	Colima	$34
MZ of Tuxtla Gutiérrez	Chiapas	$66
MZ of Juárez	Chihuahua	$260
MZ of Chihuahua	Chihuahua	$187
MZ del Valle of México	Mexico_City-México-Hidalgo	$11,291
MZ of León	Guanajuato	$340
MZ of San Francisco del Rincón	Guanajuato	$12
MZ of Pachuca	Hidalgo	$102
MZ of Tulancingo	Hidalgo	$27
MZ of Tula	Hidalgo	$155
MZ of Guadalajara	Jalisco	$1,902
MZ of Puerto Vallarta	Jalisco-Nayarit	$112
MZ of Ocotlán	Jalisco	$63
MZ of Toluca	México	$463
MZ of Morelia	Michoacán	$25
MZ of Zamora-Jacona	Michoacán	$8
MZ of La Piedad-Pénjamo	Michoacán-Guanajuato	$11
MZ of Cuernavaca	Morelos	$117
MZ of Cuautla	Morelos	$45
MZ of Tepic	Nayarit	$8
MZ of Monterrey	Nuevo León	$3,083
MZ of Oaxaca	Oaxaca	$30
MZ of Tehuantepec	Oaxaca	$37
MZ of Puebla-Tlaxcala	Puebla-Tlaxcala	$619
MZ of Tehuacán	Puebla	$68
MZ of Querétaro	Queretaro	$1,692
MZ of Cancún	Quintana Roo	$117
MZ of San Luis Potosí-Soledad-GS	San Luis Potosí	$277
MZ of Rioverde-Ciudad Fernández	San Luis Potosí	$19
MZ of Guaymas	Sonora	$27
MZ of Villahermosa	Tabasco	$88
MZ of Tampico	Tamaulipas-Veracruz	$1,465
MZ of Reynosa-Río Bravo	Tamaulipas	$767
MZ of Matamoros	Tamaulipas	$540
MZ of Nuevo Laredo	Tamaulipas	$509
MZ of Tlaxcala-Apizaco	Tlaxcala	$14
MZ of Veracruz	Veracruz	$340
MZ of Xalapa	Veracruz	$127
MZ of Poza Rica	Veracruz	$87
MZ of Orizaba	Veracruz	$90
MZ of Minatitlán	Veracruz	$117
MZ of Coatzacoalcos	Veracruz	$172
MZ of Córdoba	Veracruz	$82
MZ of Acayucan	Veracruz	$23
MZ of Mérida	Yucatán	$34
MZ of Zacatecas-Guadalupe	Zacatecas	$17

Figure 5. Commercial trade between Metropolitan Zones of Mexico.

Source: Adolfo Sánchez Almanza, "The City System and Urban Networks in Mexican Economic Models", en Problemas del Desarrollo, No. 184, Vol. 47, First Quarter, 2016, pp. 7–34. ISSN: 0301-7036.

regional production chains. Some cities and states, especially in the center and north of the national territory, have advanced in the cluster, with economies of agglomeration and positive externalities.

However, several challenges remain. It has to be understood that a planning process for urban development is required and macro-policies should focus in fostering growth, with special attention to the industry, but that requires that federal government resources increase through a rise in taxes and a budget to provide resources for urban planning, specifically metropolitan areas.

In the territorial sphere, the socio-economic inequality in the structure and dynamics of the national urban system has been deepened. It is important to avoid widening the development gap between north, center, and south. Among the measures to be implemented, it is important to promote regional development with several measures, such as greater cross-connectivity with corridors that facilitate the attraction of investments, the integration of productive chains and the movement of people, goods and services within the Mexican regions, and favor a greater socio-spatial balance. There are three connections to strengthen: the one on the northern border that connects the cities of Tijuana, Mexicali, Nogales, Ciudad Juarez, Piedras Negras, Nuevo Laredo, Reynosa, and Matamoros; that of Mazatlán-Matamoros, from Sinaloa to Tamaulipas; and that of the Isthmus of Tehuantepec that could support a better integration in the south.

Finally, the national urban system has been transformed from a hierarchical primitive model with high concentration toward the formation of networks of cities, taking advantages of the interactions that had developed at some regions through economies of scope. The challenge is to promote a model of territorial convergence by taking advantage of the positive factors of openness, but with an urban-regional planning that allows achieving the central objective of development, which is to improve the level of well-being of the population anywhere in the country.

References

OECD. *Functional Areas in OECD Countries: Mexico*. Retrieved from: http://www.oecd.org/cfe/regional-policy/functional-urban-areas-all-mexico.pdf. January, 2019.

Sánchez, A. A. (2016). "Sistema de ciudades y redes urbanas en los modelos económicos de México Revista." *Problemas del Desarrollo* 184(47): 7–34. Retrieved from: http://probdes.iiec.unam.mx.

SEDESOL (Secretaría de Desarrollo Social) (2011). *La expansión urbana de las ciudades 1980–2010*, México.

United Nations, Department of Economic and Social Affairs, Population Division (2017). *World Population Prospects: The 2017 Revision*, DVD Edition.

Chapter 12

Urbanization in Africa: Commonalities and Departures

Humphrey P. B. Moshi

Centre for Chinese Studies (CCS),
University of Dar es Salaam, Tanzania
hpmoshi@gmail.com/hpmoshi@icloud.com

1. Introduction

Today Africa is dubbed as one of the most rapidly urbanizing regions in the world, followed by Asia. It is expected that by 2050, about 50% of the African population will be urban (UNDESA, 2014).

However, the rate of urbanization differs across countries and regions. Whereas countries with an urbanization level of less than 30% experience an average of 4.68% growth in urbanization, most of the urbanized economies grew at an average rate of about 2.23%.

Also, there are regional variations in the pace and level of urbanization in Africa with North African countries having the highest level of urbanization, while East African countries display a low level, but a rapid rate of urbanization.

The objective of this chapter is three fold. Firstly, to review the literature on the role of cities in the context of agglomeration economies as hubs for economic development and structural change. Secondly, to analyze the nature of urbanization in Africa with a view to identify the communities and departures, when compared to other regions of the globe.

Thirdly, discuss the challenges posed due to the high rate of urbanization, while analyzing the coping mechanisms by policymakers and planners that are either in place or have to be embarked on to address the challenges.

Ultimately, a set of recommendations to address the challenges is inevitable. These range from rural-employment coordination, poverty, unemployment, infrastructure provision to environmental resilience. In sum, these demand effective planning and management of cities. However, this can only happen if issues of urbanization were mainstreamed in a country's socio-economic and environmental development visions and plans.

2. Conceptual and Theoretical Framework

Urbanization is a process through which rural population become urban. It mainly features migration of people from rural areas into cities, development of secondary and tertiary urban industries, more and larger cities, and changing urban landscapes, including changes in consumption patterns. In this regard, urbanization is a social development phenomenon that emerged in the industrial era. And since then, it has undergone four waves. According to Jianwen (2015), whereas the first wave was led and associated with the UK's industrial revolution during the 19th century and lasted more than 200 years, the second wave was led by the USA in the mid-to-late 19th century, and lasted for nearly 100 years.

The third wave was dominated by two sets of countries, those from Latin America (Brazil and Mexico) on the one hand, and Asian countries (Japan and Republic of South Korea on the other. The urbanization in these regions began after the World War II (WWII). The fourth wave, which began around the 21st century swept across certain developing countries in Asia and Africa, notably China and India, being the leaders.

It is important to bear in mind that the four phases of urbanization were driven by a number of factors. Whereas the drivers of the first three waves were industrialization, colonial expansion, development of service industries, and technological changes, the fourth wave, which is ongoing, has been propelled by economic globalization, free trade, and trans-border capital flows. Accordingly, this current phase is expected to reach maturity in 2050 (UN, 2010).

The theoretical framework of urbanization is underpinned by economies of agglomeration which underscores the benefits of "sharing," "matching," and "learning" (Harvey, 2009; AfDB, OECD and UNDP, 2016). Sharing occurs when firms and urban inhabitants share indivisible facilities and achieve joint economies of scale in local infrastructure, service, risks, and the production of specialized inputs and final goods. Matching arises from larger pools of employees, firms, buyers, and suppliers, who helps each firm or individual find specific attributes demanded. Learning is promoted by cities as density of economic actors facilitates the diffusion of knowledge and technology (Duranton, 2009).

There are many ways to describe and categorize the benefit arising from agglomeration economies. Usually, a distinction is made between urbanization economics, that is, benefits from clustering of diverse economic activities, and localization of economies, those from clustering firms in some sectors. These mechanisms of agglomeration economies usher in three outcomes: they generate increasing returns to scale that arise from geographical concentration and co-location (clustering of firms and workers is central) via cumulative causation. People and firms are attracted to places where there is already a concentration of activities, thus reinforcing and propelling existing agglomerations, and path-dependency: a single firm or producer will not find it profitable to move from an existing cluster (Overman and Venables, 2005).

Further, agglomeration economies deliver a productive advantage to firms and spur innovation. In this regard, large and diverse cities in particular, facilitate the sharing of knowledge entrepreneurship and competition, thus playing a "nursery" role and enabling firms to incubate; while some firms succeed and grow, the less productive firms close, allowing for capital and labor to be reallocated to more productive activities. Consequently, creative destruction and the churning process of firms and factors of production under the role of cities as engine of growth and development of countries (Duranton, 2009).

Apart from the economic benefit of urbanization, cities offer many social benefits in terms of enhancing human development through improved access to education, health, water, and sanitation. Empirical studies show that access to these services is typically high in urban than rural areas, and such provisions are less costly to provide in an urban setting because of economies of scale (UN-Habitat, 2010b; UNDP, 2015).

Environmentally, urbanization does offer benefits by reducing travel distances and preserving land. However, urban agglomerations and industrial concentration in cities generate environmental costs and negative externalities. According to Khan (2006), at low levels of development or per capita income, cities lack the resources to invest in environmental amenities. Therefore, households and firms only begin demanding high environmental quality when they have reached a specific threshold of per capita income, high enough to afford paying for environmental amenities. Indeed, fast economic growth, as observed in Chinese cities can harm the environment. However, these impacts can be mitigated or even prevented if urbanization is well managed and planned.

Furthermore, both theoretical and empirical analysis, identify four drivers of urbanization: rural–urban migration, international migration, national population growth (reflecting mortality and fertility rates), and reclassification of rural towns to urban areas. The existence of these drivers in turn creates strong linkages between rural and urban in terms of the need to improve agricultural productivity, not only as a means for boosting productivity and competitiveness of urban sectors but also as a strategy of triggering structural transformation of a country's economy. In other words, structural transformation or industrialization is associated with a faster rise in agricultural productivity and a faster decline in the share of agricultural output and labor force within the economy, leading to a more developed, higher productivity, and more urban economy (Timmer and Akkus, 2008).

3. Urbanization in Africa: Trends, Patterns, and Drivers

Today Africa is dubbed as one of the most rapidly urbanizing regions in the world, followed by Asia. It is expected that by 2050, above 56% of the African population will be in urban areas. Indeed, urbanization was rapid in the post-independence period, slowed in the 1990s, and picked up again in 2000s (UN-Habitat, 2010). Urbanization in Africa, excluding North Africa, rose from 15% in 1960 — around the same time as Europe in the 17th century – to 38% today which in higher than South Asia. The number of urban residents in Africa nearly doubled between 1995 and 2015 and is projected to double again by 2035 (Barofsky *et al.*, 2016).

African subregions and countries are urbanizing at different speeds, as displayed in Figures 1 and 2. For example, East Africa is the least urbanized and urbanizing fastest, while Southern Africa is the most urbanized and moving more slowly. Eight countries are largely rural with less than one quarter of their populations living in urban areas. However, the least urbanized countries are forecast to double their urbanization in 35 years (UNDESA, 2014). In contrast, a few countries are experiencing slow and even negative urbanization. These include Mauritius, Swaziland, and Zimbabwe.

Figure 2 illustrates that countries with low level of urbanization are urbanizing faster than those with higher levels of urbanization. It was observed that countries with an urbanization level of less than 40%,

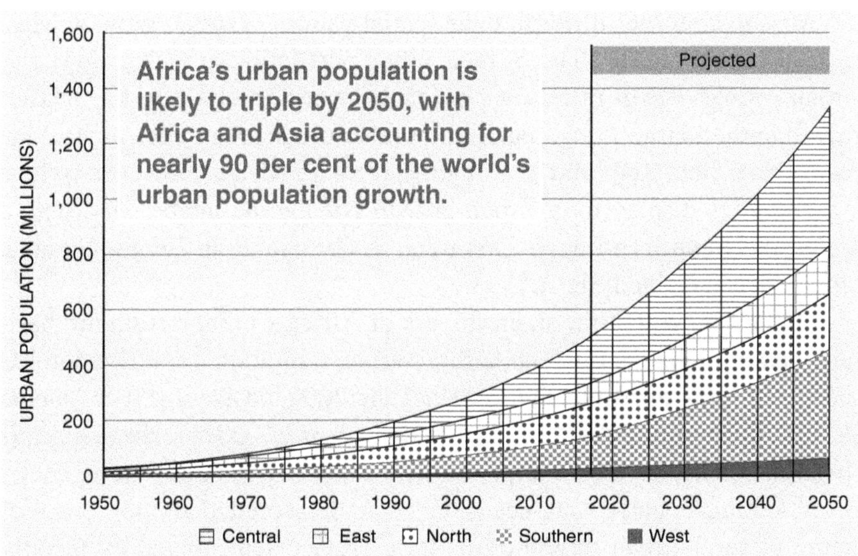

Figure 1. Urban population in African subregion, 1950–2050.

Source: UNECA (2017).

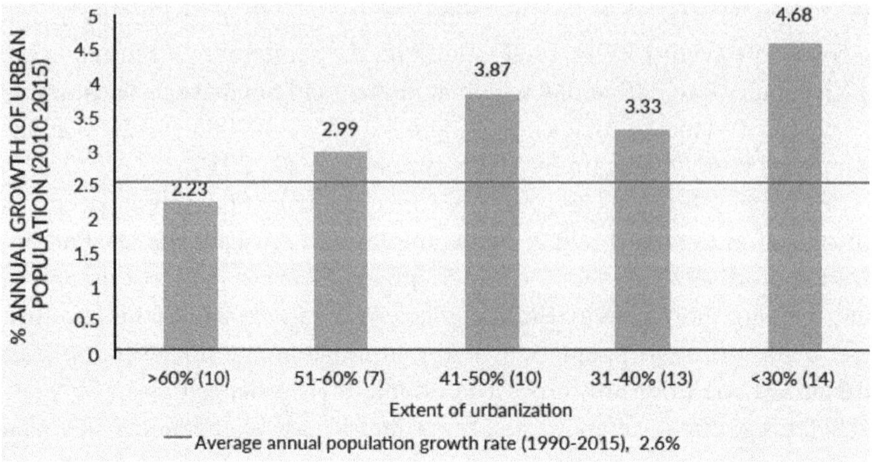

Figure 2. The pace of urbanization and the extent of urbanization.
Source: UNDESA (2015b).

experience an average of 46.8% growth, while the most urbanized countries grew at an average of about 2.23% (ECA, 2018).

African countries differ in their spatial pattern of urban growth. Most of them have a higher share of their urban population in their largest city (urban primary) than other regions of the world, and a few have faster growth in their largest city than in their other urban areas, such as Burkina Faso, Cameroon, Republic of Congo, and South Africa. However, quite a few countries display most urban growth outside the largest city, with a decreasing trend in primary. This trend is observable in Benin, Gambia, Liberia, Rwanda, and Sierra Leone.

Studies show that the main drivers of Africa's urbanization are basically demographic factors, while rural–urban migration's contribution has been decreasing overtime. During 1990 and 2000, on average it accounted for 1.07% (Dyson, 2009; Fox, 2014; Jedwab *et al.*, 2014). However, this phenomenon needs to be interpreted with caution given that heterogeneity exists among countries. It needs to be underscored that the "chaotic" nature of rural–urban migration is, to a larger extent, fueled by poverty and inequalities which happen to be higher in the rural than urban areas. Another driver of the urbanization process is reclassification.

For example, Uganda had 33 districts in 1986, but currently the number has risen to 111 districts, and each of them has an administrative and a commercial town (Awumbila *et al.*, 2014).

4. Africa's Urbanization Characteristics: The Departures

The objective of this section is to search for commonalities and differences (departures) of Africa's urbanization process with a view to show how the continent's specific characteristics have influenced the results and outcomes of urbanization.

First and foremost, the economic growth in many African countries, in the last couple of decades, and especially since the early 2000s, has had less of an impact on poverty than expected. Whereas the continent's poverty headcount ratio declined from 56.3% in 1990 to 41% in 2013, the absolute number of people in poverty is stagnating at the 2002 level, to the extent that more than 50% of the world's poor in 2013 were in Africa. This notwithstanding, in 1996–2012, poverty declined in all subregions and faster in urban than rural areas, except in Southern Africa, which witnessed a marginal decline in rural poverty, as shown in the Figure 3.

The economic growth in Africa has not been inclusive for a number of reasons; ranging from the depth of poverty, high initial inequality, mismatch between sectors of growth and employment to rapid population growth and delayed demographic transition. The implication of this phenomenon, with regard to the relationship with urbanization, is that weaker incomes, then other parts of the world, generate a narrative of "urbanization without growth" (World Bank, 2001; Fay and Opal, 2000). In this context, and in comparison with Asia, which has similar urbanization rates at higher incomes, Africa is urbanizing while poorer (Freire *et al.*, 2014).

The second characteristic is that the experience of many African countries' structural transformation has been unfavorable. Globally, the share of manufacturing in total output tends to rise with per capita income. However, in the case of Africa manufacturing and urbanization were moving side by side during the early post-colonial period of 1960–1975 but manufacturing then declined, inhibiting structural transformation. Since mid-1990s, growth has rebounded, but without strong employment growth

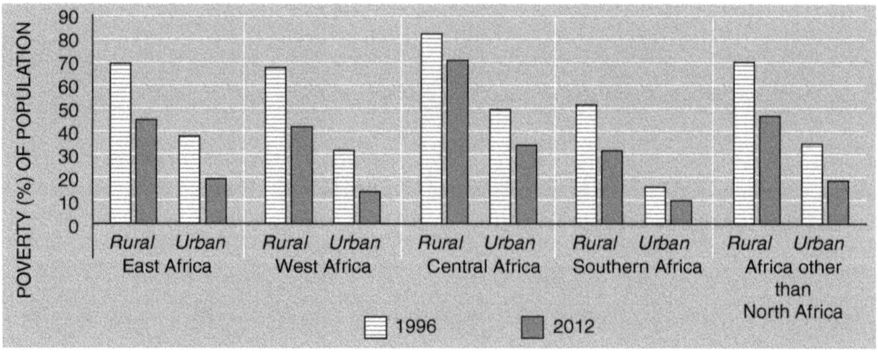

Figure 3. Poverty by subregions in Africa.
Source: World Bank (2016b).

in manufacturing (de Vries *et al.*, 2014). Ultimately, most African countries recorded a decline in their share of manufacturing value added in GDP, averaging 2.3% during 2000–2015. The unfolding deindustrialization process led to movement of labor from high sectors to low-productivity sectors, which are basically informal activities and services (McMillan and Rodrick, 2011).

The continued trend of urbanization in the face of deindustrialization has a number of implications. First, it resulted in cities with poorer population and unemployment. It needs to be recalled that 61% of men and 74% of the working population in non-agricultural sectors are informally employed to the extent that, globally the share of informal employment is the highest in Africa, excluding North Africa as shown in Figure 4. A survey of seven Francophone African cities revealed that the average income of workers in the formal enterprises is three times higher than those in informal enterprises, pointing to a wide productivity differential (ILO, 2009).

Secondly, decoupling urbanization and industrial development are problematic because industrialization is the most efficient path to sustained growth and economic convergence (AfDB, OECD and UNDP, 2016). Thirdly, given the prominence of agriculture sector in African economies, in terms of household's livelihoods and contribution to GDP, its low level of productivity, at less than 56% of global average, weakens its supply and demand value chain links to the process of urbanization, to

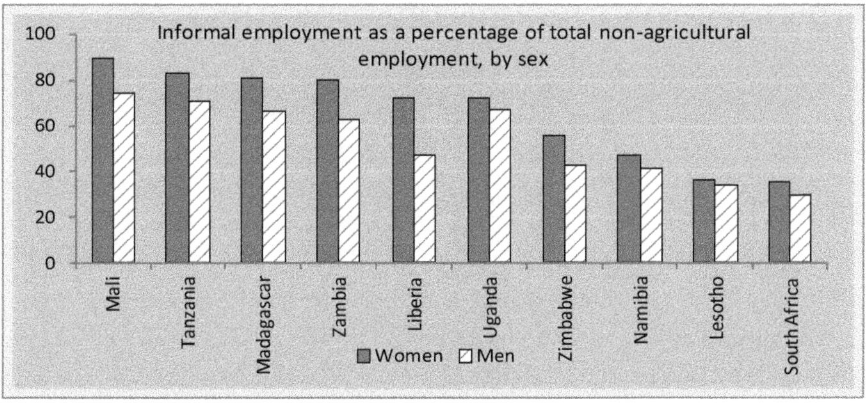

Figure 4. Informal employment is high in Africa.
Source: Sinha (2018).

the extent that the urban–rural divide is widened rather than narrowed. Hence, the link between urbanization and industrialization weakens significantly, as evidenced in Figure 5.

The third characteristic is that most of African economies are rich in natural resources and therefore these constitute the major exports. McMillan *et al.* (2011) claim that there is a very strong and negative association between a country's reliance on primary products and the rate at which structural transformation contributes to growth. Indeed, countries that specialize in primary products are at a distinct disadvantage. This is due to the Dutch disease, where low productivity labor of non-processed exports crowds out employment in higher value-added sectors. This disadvantage associated with resource endowment, coupled with colonial histories, tend to high resource rents for African countries with better economic performance at a given level of to the urbanization (AfDB, OECD and UNDP, 2016).

At the city level, natural dependency feeds in to disconnect between urbanization and structural transformation in prompting the term "consumption cities" (Jedwab, 2013a,b; Gollin *et al.*, 2014). Consumption cities are not only a product of premature urbanization but also of shifting workers from tradable to non-tradable sectors. In the absence of job-rich industrial sector, Africa has yet to generate decent jobs to address the

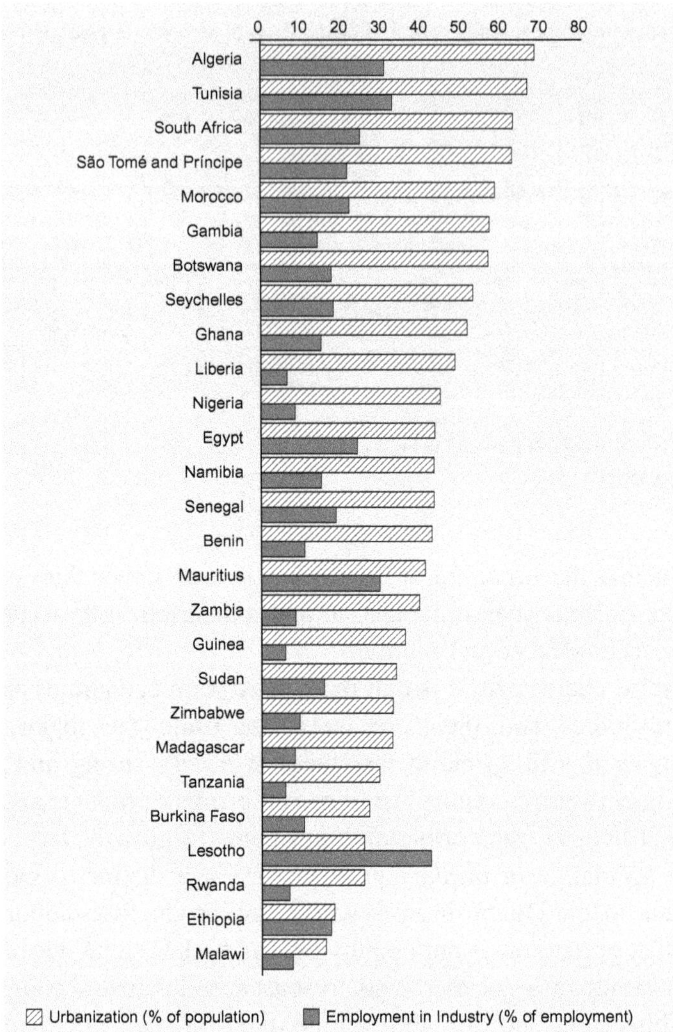

Figure 5. Urbanization and industrial employment, 2007–2015.
Source: World Development Indicators (2015).

challenge of youth unemployment. It is important to note that consumption cities are very expensive, more so than cities in countries at similar income levels by a margin of up to 31% (Nakamura *et al.*, 2006), sweeping aside any assumption that industrial development in Africa will benefit from cheap labor and land. Further, the indirect costs of poor infrastructure provision puts African firms at a competitive disadvantage, with many firms in South America and East Asia paying 50% and 70% less, respectively, for inland transport of imports and exports to and from ports, while African firms are losing up to 13% of their working hours owing to electricity outages (Iarossi, 2009).

Africa's rapid population growth is the subject of the fourth characteristic. The continent's population grew at an average of 2.6% annually in 1990–2015, more than twice the world average (UNECA and UNFPA, 2016). In the same, period Asia and Latin America and the Caribbean achieved rapid declines in annual population growth. Not only was Africa's annual growth rate the world's highest, but it has remained in the range of 2.4%–2.6% since 1990. This state of affairs is unlikely to change in the short run.

The implication of the aforementioned is that, Africa's urbanization is driven more by natural growth than migration as shown in Figure 6. Indeed, the continent's roles of migration peaked in the 1960s, and declined after that. Unlike the experience of the United Kingdom during the industrial revolution, where natural urban population growth was lower in cities due to high death rates, African cities were witness to falling mortality rates (Annez and Buckley, 2009; Fox, 2014).

Notwithstanding the seemingly demographic dividend, African countries face an enormous challenge in creating a number of decent jobs for

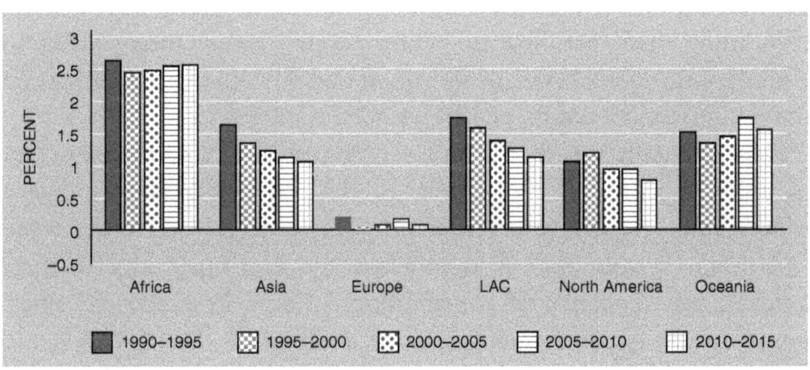

Figure 6. Average annual rate of population change, 1990–2015.

Source: UNDESA (2015b).

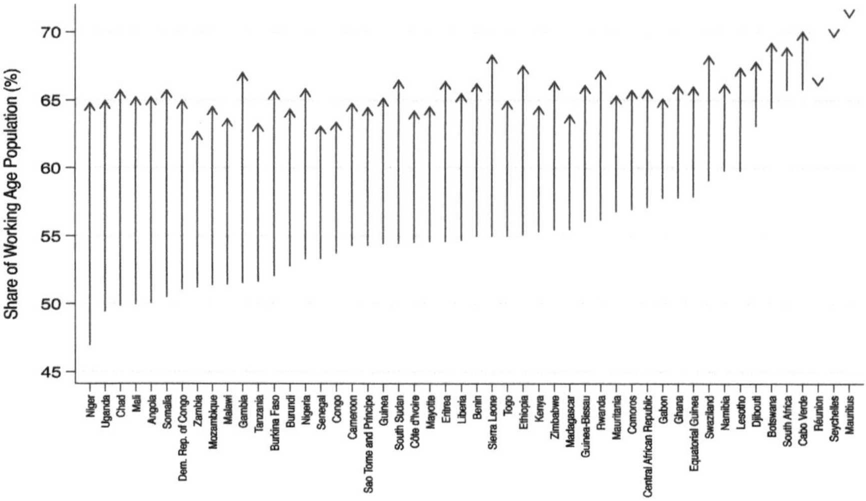

Figure 7. Current and peak share of the working-age population in Sub-Saharan Africa, 2015–2100.

Source: Bhorat (2018).

the young and expanding workforce to realize this dividend. Whereas the youth (15–24 age cohort) constituted about 35% of the working-age population in 2015, they represented three-fifths of those who were unemployed. Figure 7 shows that, in most countries, the youth unemployment is more than twice that of adults; in Nigeria, for example, the youth rate is more than five times the adult rate. In Botswana, the Congo, and South Africa, more than one-third of young people are unemployed, and the average youth unemployment rate is about 30% in North Africa, compared to the world average of 14% (UNECA, 2018).

The last characteristic of Africa's urbanization is with regard to "rank-size" rule. In many African countries, the concentration of industry is predominantly in a single urban center. This in turn leads to the creation of an urban system that is dominated by a primary city (primacy). Moreover, this tendency of concentration results in expensive cities as being relatively expensive as displayed in Figure 8. Usually, systems of cities in developed economies tend to follow the "rank-size" rule, with cities decreasing in size by a common ratio (O'Sullivan, 2007). Whereas nearly all countries globally have cities with various sizes, African

RANK IN AFRICA	CITY	GLOBAL RANK	COUNTRY GDP PER CAPITA ($)	MORE EXPENSIVE THAN...A
1	Luanda, Angola	2	4,102	Zurich, Switzerland ($80,215)
2	Kinshasa, DRC	6	456	Shanghai, China ($7,925)
3	N'Djamena, Chad	9	776	New York City, United States ($55,837)
4	Lagos, Nigeria	13	2,640	Seoul, Republic of Korea ($27,222)
5	Victoria, Seychelles	16	15,476	London, United Kingdom ($43,734)
6	Abuja, Nigeria	20	2,640	Dubai, UAE ($40,438)
7	Brazzaville, Congo, Rep.	23	1,851	Copenhagen, Denmark ($52,002)
8	Libreville, Gabon	28	8,312	Chicago, United States ($55,837)
9	Conakry, Guinea	36	531	Washington, DC, United States ($55,837)
10	Djibouti, Djibouti	40	1,813	Paris, France ($36,248)
11	Accra, Ghana	47	1,381	Milan, Italy ($29,847)
12	Yaoundé, Cameroon	50	1,251	Vienna, Austria ($43,439)
13	Abidjan, Côte d'Ivoire	56	1,399	Amsterdam, Netherlands ($44,433)
14	Douala, Cameroon	70	1,251	Doha, Qatar ($74,667)
15	Cairo, Egypt	91	3,615	San Jose, Costa Rica ($10,630)

Figure 8. Cost of living, Africa's 15 most expensive cities.
Source: Mercer (2016); World Development Indicators (2015)

countries are characterized by unbalanced systems where economic activities and administrative functions are concentrated in the capital or largest city, more than expected under the rank-size rule. This tendency is contrary to what is observed in rest of the globe. Moreover, the average share of population in the average country's largest city in Africa, excluding North Africa, is higher than the corresponding city in other regions.

One commonly cited explanation for Africa's excessive primary is centralization of power and favoritism in resource allocation, which can negatively affect the quality of life, including child mortality and education in towns and cities outside the capital (Henderson *et al.*, 2001). In such systems, small and medium-sized cities play little role in hosting rising urban populations and urban investments, unless they reach a minimum competitive size threshold or unless large cities become unlivable (Henderson *et al.*, 2001).

It needs to be underscored that the presence of primary cities, is not a problem in itself. This is because large cities are important to the urban system due to their role in spurning growth by engendering innovation and entrepreneurship, among other advantages. However, there are both benefits and costs to large cities, and both increase with size. The same forces that drive clustering of businesses and people in cities also push cities to be too large (Annez and Buckley, 2009), assuming that cities have an optimum size. A diverse national system of cities seems to be preferred, since it allows firms not only to select a large city with good urbanization economies or a smaller city with lower economies of agglomeration but also lower costs and congestion. This being the case, the optimal location will vary by type and maturity of firm. Therefore, having a functioning economic system of cities will go a long way in improving the chances of firms to maximize the matching of their location-based requirements.

5. The Way Forward

This section attempts to chart the way forward by proposing a set of policies, strategies and measures that need to be taken on board, by national development planners, with a view to unlock the growth and development potential embedded in urbanization, while addressing the observed challenges of that process.

The starting for ensuring that the urbanization is well planned and managed is to mainstream the process in national and regional development agenda. This stance is informed by the recognition that urbanization is irreversible and has immense potential for economic diversification and rural transformation. Currently, most of the African countries have visions and plans to promote industrialization as a way of achieving structural transformation of their economies, as well as addressing the challenges of poverty reduction, inequalities, and unemployment of the youth population. This being the case, urbanization becomes an indispensable vehicle for achieving such visions. However, in order to attain the goals and objectives embodied in the visions and development plans, issues of urbanization have to feature more conspicuously and compressively in the formulation of implementation strategies. These will be discussed briefly in the following paragraphs.

First, to the extent that rural–urban development is complementary, given that there are multi-faceted economic and social linkages between the two areas, it crucial to ensure that both areas are accorded their deserved attention in the allocation of resources. It needs to recall that well-functioning urban economies have benefits for rural areas too. Likewise, well performing rural economies are suppliers of agricultural products and labor to cities, while at the sometime they are markets for industrial products. This symbiotic relationship between the two areas, if adequately exploited, would definitely lead to a balanced growth. Currently, this is yet to happen given the urban-bias development model adopted by most African countries as evidenced by the low agriculture productivity and low provision of infrastructure, as well as economic and social amenities in rural areas. Indeed, the allocation of requisite resources to the rural areas will have positive spillover effects, not only in reducing rural poverty and inequalities but also in curbing unplanned migration to urban areas.

Second, in appreciation of the economic potential of cities as drivers of structural transformation in general, and industrialization in particular, African countries should place undue importance on the quality and form or urban development. However, this must be addressed early enough to avoid severe economic, social, and environmental challenges in the long run. In this regard, policies should aim at making cities, both primary and secondary, efficient and competitive, both domestically, regionally, and globally. Indeed, having such policies in place will reconnect the link between urbanization and industrialization, which is currently missing in Africa's urbanization trajectory.

Third, in analyzing issues of urbanization emphasis has been placed on a single sector or specific challenge facing cities. This form of approach tends to ignore the bigger picture, both in terms of policies and strategies, and ultimately fails to address the fundamental problem(s) facing cities, in the context of urban development. In the future, the approach to be adopted is that of a broader or holistic picture-cum-lens which is underpinned by understanding the complexity and interplay of different urban sectors, including the public and private sector's roles, as well as the economic and social aspects of the urban development. However, in order for the adopted approach to be effectively implemented, it has to be informed by a development paradigm which appreciates the critical role played by both governments and the private sector (free market) in the creation and promotion of efficient cities. Further, in order to effectively manage the complexities, putting in place a cross-sectoral coordination mechanism becomes an imperative.

6. Concluding Remarks

Globally, the role of urbanization as an engine of growth and development is highly acknowledged. Specifically, urbanization is closely linked to structural transformation, industrialization, and rural development. This chapter has attempted to analyze how Africa's urbanization has been unable to benefit from or tap the opportunities embedded in that process. In this regard, the analysis focused on identifying the main characteristics of Africa's urbanization process which have hindered or muted the realization of the continent's aspirations of economic diversification, industrialization, social development, and enhanced per capita incomes, when compared to other regions in the world. The characteristics are in fact the departures which distinguish Africa's urbanization when compared to other regions. Indeed, there are also some areas of convergence with other parts of the globe, such as the imperativeness of the process.

The findings show that Africa, to a greater extent has failed to unlock the opportunities of urbanization for a number of reasons. These range from premature urbanization, poor planning and management of the process, deindustrialization, disconnection between urban and rural development to the predominance of primary cities. These departures have not only resulted in delayed structural transformation of African economies but also in jobless economic growth, poverty-ridden and expensive cities. Moreover, and in most cases, such cities lack the basic economic and social infrastructure.

These deficiencies, notwithstanding, and due to the fact that urbanization is an unstoppable force which will continue to change Africa's landscape, putting in place an effective urbanization planning and management becomes an imperative. The framework should not only address issues of urbanization in a more holistic manner but also enhance coordination and integration of economic, social, and environmental issues in the urban development agenda.

References

AfDB, OECD (Organisation for Economic Co-operation and Development) and UNDP (United Nations Development Programme) (2016). *African Economic Outlook 2016. Sustainable Cities and Structural Transformation.* Paris: OECD Publishing. Retrieved from: http:/www.africaneconomicoutlook.org/.

Annez, P. and R. Buckley (2009). Urbanization and Growth: Setting the Context. In *Urbanization and Growth*, edited by M. Sence, P. Annez and R. Buckley. Washington, DC: Commission on Growth and Development, pp. 1–46.

Awumbila, M., G. Owusu and J. K. Teye (2014). *Can Rural Urban Migration into Slums Reduce Poverty? Evidence from Ghana.* Migrating out of Poverty RPC Working Paper 13. Migrating out of Poverty Consortium. Brighton: University of Sussex.

Barofsky, J., E. Siba and J. Grabinsky (2016). *Can Rapid Urbanization in Africa Reduce Poverty? Causes, Opportunities, and Policy Recommendations.* Washington, DC: Brookings Institute. Retrieved from: http:/www/brookings, edu/Africa-in-ocus/2016/09/07/can-rapid-urbanization-in-africa-reduce-poverty-causes.opportunities-and-policy-recommendations/.

Bhorat, H. (2018). *Economic Growth and the Pursuit of Inequality Reduction in Africa.* Addis Ababa: ECA.

Chennery, H. (1982). *Industrialization and Growth: The Experience of Large Countries.* Staff Working Paper 539. Washington, DC: World Bank.

de Vries, G., M. Timmer and K. de Vries (2014). Structural Transformation in Africa-Static Gains, Dynamic Losses. Paper prepared for the International Association for Research in Income and Wealth 33rd General Conference. Rotterdam, the Netherlands, August 24–30, 2014. Retrieved from: http/www/ org/papers/2014/deVriesPaper, pdf.

Drummond, P., V. Thakoor and S. Yu (2014). *African Department Africa Rising: Harnessing the Demographic Dividend.* Working Paper WP14/143. Washington, DC: IMF.

Duranton, G. (2015). "Growing through Cities in Developing Countries." *The World Bank Research Observer* 30(1), 39–73.

Duranton, G. and D. Puga (1999). *Diversity and Specialization in Cities: Why, Where and When Does It Matter?* Research Papers: in Environmental and Spatial Analysis 56. London: Department of Geography and Environment, London School of Economics.

Duranton, G. and D. Puga (2001). "Nursery Cities: Urban Diversity, Process Innovation, and the Life Cycle of Products." *American Economic Review* 91(5): 1454–1477.

Dyson, T. (2009). *The Role of the Demographic Transition in the Process of Urbanization*. Paper prepared for the International Workshop on the Long Term Implications of the Demographic Transition, Madrid, September 24–26, 2009. Retrieved from: http/sgfm.elcorteingles.es/SGFM/FRA/recurson/Actos/2009/Ponencias_ingles/Long_term_implications/405329092_21920099135719.pdf.

Fay, M. and C. Opal (2000). *Urbanization without Growth, A Not-So-Uncommon Phenomenon*. Policy Research Working Paper 2412. Washington, DC: World Bank.

Fox, S. (2015). "Urbanization as a Global Historical Process: Theory and Evidence from Sub-Saharan Africa." *Population and Development Review* 38(2): 285–310.

Freire, M., S. Lall and D. Leipsiger (2014). *Africa's Urbanization: Challenges and Opportunities*. Working Paper 7. Washington, DC: The Growth Dialogue. Retrieved from: http/www.danny-leipziger.com/documents/GDP_WP7.pdf.

Fukunishi, T. (2004). *International Competitiveness of Manufacturing Firms in Sub-Saharan Africa*. Chiba: JETRO.

Iarossi, G. (2009). *Benchmarking Africa's Costs and Competitiveness*. Washington, DC: World Bank.

Jedwab, R. (2013a). *Urbanization without Structural Transformation: Evidence from Consumption Cities in Africa*. Washington, DC. George Washington University.

Jedwab. R. (2013b). *Why is Africa Urbanization Different: Evidence from Resource Exports in Ghana and Ivory Coast*. Job Market Paper. Retrieved from: http://www/colorado.edu/Economics/seminars/SeminarsArchive/2012-13/jedwab.pdf.

Jedwab, R., L. Christiaenssen and M. Gindelsky (2014). *Rural Push, Urban Pull and Urban Push? New Historical Evidence from Developing Countries*. Washington, DC. George Washington University.

Jianwen, W. (2015). *Transformation and Promotion: Interpreting China's Urbanization*. Beijing: Foreign Languages Press Co.

McMillan, M. and D. Rodrik (2011). Globalization, Structural Change and Productivity Growth. In: *Making Globalization Socially Sustainable*, edited by M. Bacchetta and M. Jansen. Geneva: International Labour Organization, pp. 49–94.

McMillan, M., D. Rodrik and J. Verduzco-Gallo (2014). "Globalization, Structural Change, and Productivity Growth, with an Update on Africa." *World Development* 63(C): 11–32.

Nakamura, S., R. Harati, S. Lall, Y. Dikhanov, N. Hamadeh, W. Oliver. M. Rissamin and M. Yamanaka (2016). *Is Living in African Cities Expensive?* Washington, DC: World Bank.

Newman, C., J. Page., J. Rand, A. Shimeles, M. Soderbom and F. Tarp (2015). *Premature Deindustrialization.* Princeton, NJ: Institute for Advanced Study, School of Social Sciences.

Newman, C., J. Page., J. Rand, A. Shimeles, M. Soderbom and F. Tarp (2016). *Made in Africa Learning to Compete in Industry.* Washington, DC: Brookings: Institution Press.

O'Sullivan, O. (2007). *Urban Economics.* Singapore: McGraw-Hill.

Overman, H. and A. Venables (2005). *Cities in the Developing World.* CEP Discussion Paper 695. London: Centre for Economic Performance.

Quigley, J. (2008). *Urbanization, Agglomeration and Economic Development.* Working Paper 19. Washington, DC. Commission on Growth and Development.

Sinha, S. (2018). *Informality and Inequality in Africa.* Addis Ababa: ECA.

Timmer, L. and S. Akkus (2008). *The Structural Transformation as a Pathway out of Poverty: Analystic. Empirics and Politics.* Working Paper 150. Washington, DC: Center for Global Development.

UNDESA (United Nations Department of Economic and Social Affairs) (2014). *World Urbanization Prospects: 2004 Revision.* New York: United Nations Department of Social and Economic Affairs.

UNECA (2014). *State of African Cities 2014: Reinventing the Urban Transition.* Nairobi: UN-Habitat.

UNECA (2017). *Urbanization and Industrialization for Africa's Transformation.* Addis Ababa.

UNECA (2018). *Africa Social Development Report: Informality and Inequality in Africa.* Addis Ababa.

Vanek, J., M. Chen, F. Carre, J. Heintz and R. Hussmanns (2014). *Statistics on the Informal Economy: Definitions, Regional Estimates and Challenges.* WIEGO Working Paper 2. Cambridge, MA: Women in Informal Employment Globalizing and Organizing.

World Bank (2001). *World Development Report 2000/2001: Attacking Poverty.* Washington. DC.

Index

Lightning Source UK Ltd.
Milton Keynes UK
UKHW020752190320
360597UK00001B/34

9 789811 207075